Motivation Matters and Interest Counts

Fostering Engagement in Mathematics

James A. Middleton
Arizona State University

Amanda Jansen
University of Delaware

NATIONAL COUNCIL OF
TEACHERS OF MATHEMATICS

Copyright © 2011 by
THE NATIONAL COUNCIL OF TEACHERS OF MATHEMATICS, INC.
1906 Association Drive, Reston, VA 20191-1502
(703) 620-9840; (800) 235-7566; www.nctm.org
All rights reserved

Library of Congress Cataloging-in-Publication Data

Middleton, James A.
Motivation matters, and interest counts : fostering engagement in mathematics /
James A. Middleton, Amanda Jansen.
    p. cm.
 Includes bibliographical references and index.
 ISBN 978-0-87353-658-5 (alk. paper)
 1. Mathematics--Study and teaching (Secondary) 2. Motivation in education.
I. Jansen, Amanda. II. Title.
 QA16.M53 2011
 510.071'2--dc22
                                    2011007923

The National Council of Teachers of Mathematics is a public voice of
mathematics education, supporting teachers to ensure equitable mathematics
learning of the highest quality for all students through vision, leadership,
professional development, and research.

Printed in the United States of America

Table of Contents

Acknowledgements

We would like to express appreciation for those who read and provided feedback on early versions of chapters for this book: Michelle Cirillo, Laura Cline, Tim Fukawa-Connelly, Annette Roskam, Sarah Ryan, Corey Webel, Rob Wieman, and the participants in the mathematics education Friday Seminar group of faculty and doctoral students at the University of Delaware. At Arizona State University, the students in the Theories in Mathematics Education seminar—Kori Ambrosich, Andre Denham, Cynthia Hanks, Seonghee Kim, Younsu Kim, Melissa Laliberte, Rusen Meylani, Carla Stroud, and Eric Weber—bravely offered their stories as fodder for examining principles of motivation as well as feedback on early drafts.

Personally and professionally, we are indebted to the students and teachers that we have met and worked with throughout the years, who have helped us grow as teachers and scholars. You have inspired us.

# **Foreword**

Too often a disconnect exists between what researchers study and what teachers do. This says neither that education researchers are undedicated to teaching, nor that working teachers are uneager to enlarge their classroom experience of what works and what doesn't. Findings of research, as reported in the language of scholarly literature, simply do not usually, and certainly not promptly, find their way into practice. Teachers are too busy teaching to engage with the scholarly community, and researchers often do not engage in the questions of practice through which their work can take root. Unless the working teacher is enrolled in advanced university courses, or attending conferences or local in-service training, the interface between the scholar and the teacher has been at best indirect.

James Middleton and Amanda Jansen are determined to change that. Their book is an account of the entire body of research on motivation in mathematical education, written for teachers in the language of practice.

Jansen is a former classroom teacher who has become a researcher in order to improve opportunities for students to be successful. Middleton is a learning scientist who wants his work to affect teachers' and students' lives. The result of their collaboration is a book that makes the reader feel that he or she is peering over the shoulders of attentive, perceptive teachers into a wide variety of individual students' minds and behaviors, set against a backdrop of research findings that adds depth and meaning to every classroom incident. As is always true in the classroom teacher's world, the setting is local, and the students' needs only partly generalizable. Yet, patterns of resistance and response exist that, once the teacher learns about them—and this is the purpose of this book—will be easier for the teacher to negotiate.

Bringing these perspectives to bear on any topic in mathematics learning would have made an interesting read. But this book's treatment of them is especially timely and important because of what the authors describe as a *motivational epidemic* in this country—a motivation to avoid mathematics.

> Although the emphasis on improving mathematics achievement is growing, U.S. students' desire to achieve in mathematics and to choose mathematically sophisticated college programs and occupations is shrinking.... Compared with other countries, far fewer U.S. citizens, proportionally, choose science or engineering career paths than our foreign counterparts.... Teachers and school systems must begin to address the issue of why smart people choose to disengage from mathematical pursuits and how we can reverse this trend for the betterment of our students and the betterment of our nation (Middleton and Jansen 2011, p. 176).

Motivation, then, is the core issue: how to seed and cultivate it in a wide variety of classroom settings; how to maintain it as the mathematics becomes less obvious to the beginning learner; how to recognize and overcome task-specific resistance, and, where present, the more insidious manifestations of math anxiety. The goal for every mathematics classroom teacher, the authors state unequivocally, goes way beyond cultivating "mastery" in their students. It is to enable their students to "develop mathematics as a personal long-term interest."

The book is both text and triptych. The beginning of every chapter transports the reader to a classroom setting to interact imaginatively with individuals and groups of students. As the "teacher"—a composite of many teachers—tells their story, a bevy of researchers hovers in the foreground providing insight and guidance about what is taking place. Indeed, from my experience in the field, I would say that they're all there helping the teacher overcome students' resistance. There's Altschuler and Eccles, Bandura and Dweck, Schoenfeld and others, and, not far behind, John Dewey. Even Belenky's analysis of *connective knowing* in one instance helps the teacher make contact with a particular student. In sum, the book offers a comprehensive review of literature on mathematics motivation. But without the narratives that launch each chapter, the review would not be so compelling, nor could the classroom teacher use it as immediately.

Insights emerge, as they always do in teaching, from individual encounters. But when the body of research illuminates them, they become all the more potent. That is what the authors are trying to convey. Each author brings a different perspective to motivation as a topic. Middleton's derives from his training in psychological and cognitive science. Jansen's focus is on motivation's social nature, particularly as students' need for affiliation and connection affects their willingness to engage in mathematics. If one thinks of *interest*, to take one example, not as a *trait*, intrinsic to an individual, but instead as *situational*, then one should never understand *lack of interest* as either a label or an excuse, but as a signal yet to be turned on.

In a culture that judges children to be "good in math" or "bad in math" quite early, the thrust of this compendium on motivation is quite revolutionary: Students are all motivated, Middleton and Jansen are telling us. Teachers need to understand in what ways students are motivated, and why, if they are to make mathematics a long-term, personal interest of them all.

Sheila Tobias, February 2011

Author, *Overcoming Math Anxiety* (1978, 1993), *Succeed with Math* (1987), *They're Not Dumb, They're Different* (1990), *Breaking the Science Barrier* (1992).

References

Middleton, James A. and Amanda Jansen. *Motivation Matters and Interest Counts: Fostering Engagement in Mathematics.* Reston, Va.: National Council of Teachers of Mathematics, 2011.

Introduction

This book is an outgrowth of the recent NCTM Strategic Initiative to link research and practice. So much research is locked up in university libraries or is published in journals with small, very elite audiences—researchers talking to one another—that it is difficult to figure out exactly what information teachers receive in professional development, or in print distillations, is trustworthy. Furthermore, attempts are often made at linking research *to* practice. This implies that research should guide practice, but the equally important goal of practice guiding research gets somehow lost. Instead, NCTM rightly has placed emphasis on linking research *and* practice so that, together, we can work to improve the mathematics experiences of young people.

The authors of this book are Drs. James Middleton and Amanda Jansen, but we prefer to be called Jim and Mandy. Jim is a psychologist who, while studying students' motivation, broadly realized that mathematics was somehow special, that content mattered, and that there appeared to be no good reason for students and some teachers to hate mathematics aside from how it is taught. This spurred him to change his career to focus exclusively on improving mathematics teaching and learning. Mandy was a middle school mathematics teacher who valued getting to know her students, building positive relationships in the classroom while learning and doing mathematics, and fostering classroom experiences that reduced mathematics anxiety for her students. We are also both researchers who do *classroom* research. We have spent countless hours with teachers and students in mathematics classrooms as both teachers and researchers. The students and teachers whose stories we showcase in this volume are an amalgam of these experiences. We owe them a deep debt of gratitude.

We believe that these common experiences in research *and* practice justify the audacity of writing a book about motivation for mathematics teachers. We have tried motivating our students and failed, tried again, listened to others who have had similar experiences, and, through our research and through our practice, we have become better at both.

Research-Based Strategies

We are strongly committed to the goal that the strategies we implement in our classrooms can be research-based. What do we mean by this? When we say research-based *strategies*, we do not mean that we will offer a checklist for instruction. Rather, we will share principles about students' motivation and recommendations for teachers that these principles inspire.

The strategies we present are like the pirate's code in the film *Pirates of the Caribbean*—*guidelines* that have been successful under real conditions of practice. We do not intend to provide explicit decision rules for your practice, because there are none. We do not know your students, your school, or your community. Indeed, we think that part of motivating your own students involves getting to know them and determining which strategies introduced in this book apply to them and to what degree the strategies apply.

We do provide some guidance about how principles of motivation might inspire us or other teachers, because what teachers do clearly matters. Teachers set the agenda, inspire, cajole, select the tasks, and give the feedback that engages students and supports students' development as mathematics learners. We hope that our readers think about students' motivation in new ways, ones that affirm some of their currently productive ways of thinking about motivating students. We hope that this book will touch on teachers' motivations to create more exciting, productive mathematics classrooms inspired by research-based principles.

Navigating a Tricky Territory

This book represents our perspectives on ways to think about students' motivation, led by both our work as teachers and researchers and that of other researchers. A quick look at this book's reference lists will reveal a huge number of research studies conducted on students' motivation. We have spent time reading and thinking about other researchers' studies of students' motivations, and we've conducted our own research. The ideas and principles we discuss in this book *are not simply our own opinions*. This book's content is a careful analysis of the most useful *evidence-based* principles about students' motivation from research. When we say *research-based*, then, we appeal to an accumulated knowledge base, gathered over years by hundreds of scholars studying thousands of classrooms and teachers, involving tens of thousands of students across the grade span.

Despite this, identifying research-based principles is still tricky territory. For some potential principles, research findings have not been established at strong levels of certainty. For others, research results actually conflict, forcing us either to make a value judgment regarding the quality of the research or to step back and assess under what conditions the studies' conflicting implications might be valid. So in our effort to distill principles from the body of evidence, we exercised some level of interpretation, but we have done so cautiously. Where contradictory evidence exists, we present this fairly, but we take a stand where we believe the evidence is most compelling.

We recognize that some readers may hope for clear, definitive directions for classroom practices, despite that we may not have empirical evidence that clearly gives such directions. We share your frustration; we, too, hope for clearer direction in thinking about what teachers should do, and we believe that the principles shared in this book are a helpful step in that direction.

The Structure of the Book

This book is about motivation and how teachers can create more motivating classrooms to improve students' opportunities, experiences, and—ultimately—learning in mathematics. The principles we espouse in each chapter are the direct implications from decades of research in mathematics education and in the broader fields of educational psychology, sociology, and policy. In each chapter of part 2 of this book, we present one of these six principles of motivation with a compelling case that shows the focal principle in context. But rather than attempt to isolate these principles as if they could be clearly conveyed in a sterile, decontextualized, but deceptively easy textbook, we have chosen to provide examples taken from real classrooms. These examples emphasize human learners as complex, sometimes contradictory, but intensely *interesting* subjects. Grace is but our first encounter.

In each chapter of part 3, we will examine one of five categories of instructional strategies drawn from the research that can potentially affect students' motivation and learning positively. Although we do not hesitate to point out effective strategies that teachers in our stories attempt, nor do we shrink from suggesting some compelling opportunities you might try in your classroom, we reserve this section for explicit discussion of research-based strategies—how to begin implementing them, and what each strategy's likely outcome could be. In particular, we will discuss the following categories of instructional strategies.

1. **Judicious use of contexts (chapter 8)**—their tie to cognitive benefits, the utility of mathematics in solving problems, and the development of a value for mathematics in any context

2. **Providing challenge (chapter 9)**—optimizing the inherent trade-offs between challenge and control for students with diverse interests and abilities

3. **Limiting the use of rewards and other reinforcers (chapter 10)**—understanding the hidden cost of rewards and their relation to the development of performance goals versus mastery goals, and explicitly promoting a wider range of opportunities to demonstrate competence in mathematics

4. **Exploiting interests (chapter 11)**—building the individual curiosity, persistence, and personal relevance of one's students into the design of learning tasks

5. **Building relationships (chapter 12)**—enhancing the connected learning between teacher and student, between student and student, and between student and mathematics as a field of study

We conclude the book in part 4 (chapter 13) by drawing implications across all the cases presented, showing them not as a set of individual situations, but as two compelling arguments—that all students are motivated, and that by coming to understand our students' individual and collective characteristics, we can do something to affect their lives positively. After all, that is why we are engaged in education—because together we can make the world a better place by investing our time and energy in the nurturance of young people, such that they themselves can effect change on the world, perhaps using some of the mathematics we have taught them to do so.

So, this book is really about teachers' motivation. To what extent will we choose to make changes in our own practices that reflect the best evidence available about motivation's role in teaching students? If we can help students learn to motivate themselves in mathematics, we have won more than half the battle; we have won the war. A teacher has choices to make. We wrote this book to guide and orient those choices toward your own success as reflected in that of your students.

PART 1

What Is Motivation?
Fundamental Principles

CHAPTER 1

All Students Are Motivated: Why It Matters to Understand the Reasons Students Do What They Do

T*his chapter begins with a story about a middle school student named Grace. Her story illustrates that students are neither motivated nor unmotivated; they are both. Under certain conditions, a student may behave one way, but she may behave differently in another situation. A student's engagement can be seen to be a function of the classroom organization and social setting as much as her own beliefs about her abilities and about mathematics.*

After Grace's story, we will discuss the purposes and goals of this book. We begin each chapter in this book similarly to this chapter – with a story that illustrates either one of six principles of students' motivation or one of five research-based categories of teaching practices that can motivate students. Through Grace's story, we explore facets of three of the six principles of students' motivation: **Motivation is adaptive, motivation is social, and success matters**. *We examine Grace's story through these principles to illustrate how the principles can be used as lenses to think about students' motivation, and we entertain instructional dilemmas present in Grace's story to think about implications for teaching practice.*

A Typical Day in Grace's Mathematics Class
(Adapted from the Master's Thesis of Kateryna Ellis)

Today in third-period prealgebra, Grace wasn't really anxious, but she wasn't excited to be there, either. If you talked to her and asked her to describe herself as a mathematics learner, she would say that she was fourteen years old, outgoing, willing to try hard or challenging math problems, and liked to explain her answers. Grace also would say that she liked to work with numbers and liked to learn more about math. When she was most open and honest, she would tell you that solving a difficult math problem not only helped her learn, but it helped her show other people that she was smart, which mattered to her. She would share that she would always try every problem on her math homework and would offer to participate during discussions in math class. However, she also would acknowledge that she would get in a rush sometimes. She was sometimes inattentive when reading problems, and sometimes this carelessness led her to solve problems incorrectly. Mr. Lawson, her mathematics teacher, never admonished her for being incorrect, but sometimes she was embarrassed when she was asked to explain her reasoning when she was wrong.

Mr. Lawson thought that Grace was quite smart. She frequently showed sophisticated methods when solving problems. She talked about how she planned to go to college, and these future goals seemed to motivate her to try to be successful in mathematics class. Grace's motivation showed especially when the material was of great interest to her or when she was learning something she felt strongly about, like the environment. Mr. Lawson noted that if he could get Grace curious about something, she would put out effort and work hard to learn.

Grace's eighth-grade prealgebra class consisted of students in an accelerated track, fairly evenly divided between boys and girls. Earlier in the year, Mr. Lawson had established clear norms for participation; students appeared to understand that anyone could be called on to justify any answer at any time during the period. Mr. Lawson did not give students a lot of time to work in their small groups, and he encouraged class members to help one another. There was no penalty for not understanding—if you could not get a handle on the problem, the teacher would stop by and give you some assistance. The students could be seen gazing around the room, writing, or looking at the book in front of them. Some students talked to one another, some called out to the teacher, and some sat silently at their tables waiting for someone to give them the answer.

Although the atmosphere within tables was of cooperation, the feeling among tables was definitely of competition. Students would rush to be the first to solve any given problem and loudly proclaim to be "the smartest kids in the class!" This need for social recognition was a hallmark of this high-ability class. Students believed that being in an accelerated class separated them from the other students in the school, and they tried to find ways to win recognition both from their teacher and their peers.

Grace usually sat at a table with Nacho, Adam, and Janey. On this particular afternoon, Grace came into class as she usually did, talking with Nadia and Jenn. She split from her two friends to join Nacho and Adam at their table. Janey arrived just before the bell rang, puffing because she had to run all the way across campus from the gym.

"Jeez, Janey, you are sweating like a pig!" Adam commented.

"Oh you love it!" said Janey, putting Adam in a sweaty headlock. "Weee! Weee!"

"Ahem," coughed Mr. Lawson. "I have heard that pigs are quite intelligent. It doesn't seem as if you are of that family, given that you are on the verge of detention."

The group eyed each other, laughing, but calmed down and tried to pay attention. Mr. Lawson continued, "I think I am going to have to split you up. Janey and Grace, come over here and sit with Monica and Marisol. Adam, you and Nacho sit with Carlos and Terrell. Okay? Here we go." He proceeded to hand out a worksheet with the following problem.

> A group of students want to share a cake shaped like a cube. (This is a mathematical cake: It is frosted on all six sides). They want to cut it into portions of 1-unit cubes. Each student receives one small portion. Being smart students, they notice rather quickly that the number of people who have no sides frosted is *exactly* 8 times the number of people who have pieces with three sides frosted. How many students got a piece of cake?

Each of the girls in her group, including Grace, first tried to solve the problem separately. They knew that their teacher expected them to try the problem on their own before discussing the problem with their peers. Individually, the girls took notes and wrote down their thoughts. After they each made some progress on the problem, Grace and her new tablemates shared their ideas with each other in quiet conversations.

"I drew a picture of the cube. I saw that the 8 corners had 3 sides frosted, so the total number of unfrosted pieces is 8 times 8 equals 64. From my picture, the middle cube has to have 64 little pieces, so I thought what times itself 3 times is 64?" Marisol offered. "So that has to be 4 times 4 times 4. So I drew in 4 by 4 in my picture. Then I saw it had to be two more on each side so the whole cube had to be 6 by 6 by 6 equals 216 cubes."

Grace said that she did a similar drawing (see fig. 1.1) but then said, "I saw the 4 by 4 by 4, but then I saw two sides which were 6 by 6, and another two sides that were 6 by 4. So 4 times 4 times 4 equals 64, plus 2 times 36 equals 72, plus four 24s equals 96. 64 plus 72 plus 96 equals 216."

"No it doesn't! That equals 232."

"You can't both be right if your answers are different," broke in Mr. Lawson. "Can you prove your answer?"

Argument ensued, with Grace defending her point and Marisol countering. Eventually they discovered a small mistake in Grace's counting. The surface of the cube had to have 2 sides of 6 by 6, 2 sides of 6 by 4, and 2 sides of 4 by 4; otherwise some of the cubes were double-counted.

All three girls participated in solving the problem and had been involved in active teamwork discussions. When they worked on these problems, the girls first used their own individual strategies and solutions to find the answer. Only then did the group look over the proposed strategies and choose the correct answer. This practice encouraged the girls to discuss the answers that they had found and the methods by which they generated them. These conversations and discussions

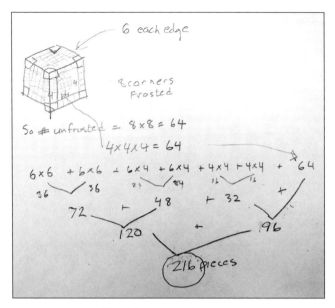

Fig. 1.1. Grace's drawing

were expected to increase the likelihood that girls would detect and correct one another's errors. Once errors were detected, students made attempts to remediate those errors for themselves, with a *little* prodding by the teacher. This group of girls showed a strong, positive dynamic among themselves in cooperative learning and understanding mathematics.

During the whole-class discussion after group work, Mr. Lawson asked Grace to explain her reasoning. She gave her answer and explained the steps she used to solve it. She spoke in a clear voice that expressed confidence in her reasoning. Grace's choice of strategy and her solution were logical, building on her understanding of volume and surface area.

Following this portion of the lesson, Mr. Lawson moved Grace from the homogeneous group of girls to a newly formed, heterogeneous group, because he hoped that Grace's enthusiasm would catch on with the members of her new group to involve themselves and discuss their thinking with one another more thoroughly. This class, like many middle and high school classes, had a variety of behavior issues related to personality clashes, friendship groups, and random mood swings among its members. Mr. Lawson often switched membership in groups, attempting to obtain better overall classroom behavior. But Mr. Lawson did not share that rationale with Grace. She was the only girl in her new group, mixed with three boys. Grace was not excited about the change in the seating arrangement. She walked slowly from her desk to the new group and made a couple of comments to her earlier group of girls and the teacher that she would prefer to stay at her desk. Once new mathematics tasks were presented to the class, Grace's behavior changed dramatically, as if she perceived the move as a punishment. Grace seemed to lose her interest in the mathematics problem. In her new group, students did not interact with one another and did not participate in an open discussion. Nevertheless, each of them did write some examples in their notebooks. When some of the students in the group did not understand a given question, they did not try to ask their teammates for help. They did not share their thinking; they simply tried to match their answers to the correct ones. During the rest of the class period, Grace sat quietly behind her desk and withdrew herself from participation. Rather than positively influencing the quality of participation in her new group, she adopted their approach of keeping to themselves. Grace twice tried to interact with her earlier group of girls instead, but the distance between tables made it impossible for her to do so effectively. As soon as the bell chimed to signal the end of the class period, Grace jumped and rushed toward her original group, where the girls were discussing the whole "relocation" deal.

Principles of Students' Motivation in Mathematics Classrooms

Teaching mathematics is a wonderful job, but it is a tough job. Children come to us with a variety of abilities and interests, reflecting a myriad of cultures and values. These individual characteristics are so varied that no two children are exactly alike, so much so that the strategies we devise to support one student often fail when applied to another.

From your time as a student, perhaps you can remember a day like the one Grace experienced, one where you have conflicting emotions, conflicting goals, definite opinions about the role of mathematics in your life, and definite opinions about your role in the mathematics class. Sometimes life seemed to conspire to make you grumpy, even in a class where you had friends, where the teacher assigned challenging problems and was careful to listen and support your learning.

Of course the goals, abilities, and opinions of teachers and students need to work together somehow for a productive learning environment to exist. This book addresses this issue. We are intent on helping teachers reflect on the goals they have for instruction, matching them with the knowledge, beliefs, aspirations, and emotional needs students bring to the classroom. We then make instructional decisions that increase the probability that the student will buy into the argument that engaging in mathematics is *important*, *useful*, *interesting*, *safe*, and *socially productive* in a personal sense. In other words, we believe that teachers can begin to change their practice so that it builds students' mathematical interest, self-interest, and self-confidence as an integral part of building their mathematical knowledge and skills.

Throughout this book, you will meet mathematics teachers and mathematics learners like Grace with her conflicting motivations, in stories. We believe that stories are an important tool for professional learning in that they present realistic people, in all their complexity, trying to do what is best, what is expedient, or what will help them just get through a situation with their self-confidence intact. Stories show how a person's behavior reflects both their internal beliefs and the environment within which they must negotiate life's presses. Time plays a special role, helping us think strategically about how to affect students' motivation, because events that appear earlier in a story relate causally to events that appear later. Mr. Lawson's actions, along with those of Janey, Marisol, and the other classmates, together affected the decisions Grace made to engage in a rather substantial mathematical task on the one hand, and to disengage on the other. Grace's decisions, therefore, can be seen as much a function of the classroom organization and social setting as of her own beliefs about her abilities and the role of mathematics. Through these stories, we can illustrate pivotal principles that reflect the best research on motivation as they play out in real classrooms with real teachers and real students.

Each chapter in this book will begin with such a story. After each story, we will discuss the salient features of motivation to learn mathematics through six essential principles. These six principles are general, drawn from the wide range of research on students' motivation, self-regulation, social behavior, and learning, and we can thus adapt them to a wide range of academic subject matter. But research also shows that mathematics is a special case. The social benefits and stigma of being "good" or "poor" in mathematics, the role of success and failure, and the impact of societal attitudes and personal beliefs about the subject's importance are more pronounced for mathematics. The resulting impact on future engagement in mathematics courses and mathematics-related occupations is therefore more dire than that of other subjects. These principles, then, make up what we know affects students' feelings, engagement patterns, and long-term valuation of mathematics with reasonable certainty.

Briefly, the five principles of motivation to learn mathematics, and the chapters in this book to which they relate, are the following:

1. **Motivation is learned (chapter 2)**. No inherent reason exists for mathematics to be considered any more difficult, confusing, or okay to perform poorly in than any other school subject. The fact that mathematics in general is viewed this way is a function of the learning environment where students grow up—the classroom, school, and home environments and the larger culture within which these institutions exist.

2. **Motivation is adaptive (chapter 3)**. If, at its most basic level, we can define motivation as the reasons people have for behaving a certain way in a certain situation, then we can see that children are always trying to adapt meaningfully to the features of the environment in which they find themselves. Even maladaptive behaviors—such as not doing homework— can be useful to help us design productive learning environments, if we ask *why* the student chose to engage in the maladaptive behavior and to what personal goals this behavior appealed.

3. **Motivation is "in the moment" (chapter 4).** We learn to be motivated by mathematics through engagement in tasks that pique our imagination, challenge our abilities, and afford us the opportunity to learn at an optimal level. Without such tasks and a classroom culture that supports engagement in them, a student likely will never have the opportunity to learn to recognize that mathematics *can* be interesting, that it *can* be useful, and that he or she *can* do it at a prodigious level.

4. **Motivation creates long-term attitudes (chapter 5).** The evidence that people tend *not* to value mathematics in a personal sense is all around us. Proportionally, few students choose to take mathematics courses beyond minimum requirements in high school or college. Fewer still choose mathematically intensive careers. The statement "I've never been good at mathematics" is acceptable in social circles. People tend to have reasonably consistent experiences in school mathematics that continually reinforce that engaging in mathematics is a bad idea. Countermanding this general tendency is difficult; it requires that we work together as an educational *system* to change the way we talk and do business. What would your own attitudes be if you had had consistent, coherent, positive experiences in mathematics?

5. **Motivation is social (chapter 6).** Human beings seek relatedness with one another. To be part of a group with common goals, ways of talking, and behaving gives us a sense of belonging. It is a natural focus of our interaction. When people around us are nervous, perhaps before a test, we tend to mimic their anxiety. When people around us are having fun—for example, examining relationships among data—we tend to enjoy the task. Motivation to learn mathematics, therefore, isn't just a function of the child and his or her beliefs; we can see it as stemming from how people fit with their environment. Fitting in really matters, both intellectually *and* socially.

6. **Success matters (chapter 7).** Success is motivating, and failure is off-putting, right? Well, it is not so simple. Think about it. If you succeed in a situation of trivial challenge, the success really isn't very valuable. But if you succeed in a challenging task, that success bolsters your sense of competence, and you reap the good feelings associated with competence. Moreover, failure on challenging tasks, if it doesn't happen all the time, is expected. That is one thing that makes a challenging task worthwhile: some chance exists that you might not get it right. When people attribute their successes to hard work and ability, they tend to become more motivated to learn. But also, *other people* seeing us as competent motivates us, and we will try to demonstrate our competence when others value it. This dance between internal attributions and external comparisons to others plays out continually in mathematics class.

Although each story could describe each of these principles and others, we will highlight and reflect on a story's most salient principles, ones that have the best potential for intervention and support. In other words, we focus more on where a teacher has a good probability of successfully helping a child develop mathematical interest and positive dispositions than on where change is unlikely or impossible. After all, if you read this book and don't take away any ideas that help you change your own practice positively, then we largely have not achieved our goals as authors. Below, we discuss these principles in more detail as they apply to Grace's story.

Show Me Somebody Who Is Unmotivated, and I Will Drive You to the Cemetery Where They Are Buried

Before we jump in with both feet, we must acknowledge one overarching principle that guides our work as teachers, teacher educators, and researchers: *All students are motivated!* After all, if we think about motivation as a reason to do something (e.g., a wish, intention, or drive; Hulleman et al. [2008]), then everyone has a motive to engage in something! *But students are not always motivated to learn and do mathematics.* The corollary to this principle is simply stated: *To be alive is to be motivated.* This principle is important in that it places a burden on us as teachers to know our students. Like Grace, students will *appear* to be more or less motivated depending on the situation. For Grace, social interactions and interpersonal relationships affected her motivation to engage in the mathematics tasks assigned in Mr. Lawson's class. Instead of being unmotivated, Grace chose to focus her motivation on different goals and values, actively pursuing them. Sometimes they aligned with her goals for mathematics learning, and sometimes they didn't. In this story, Grace drew on the classroom's social rules and her own need for relatedness to make decisions about how to engage in the assigned tasks. Her behavior illustrates important facets of three of our six principles: *Motivation is adaptive, motivation is social, and success matters.*

Motivation Is Adaptive and Social

Students will appear to be more or less motivated depending on the situation. Students are motivated to participate in discussions in the mathematics classroom partially to demonstrate their mathematical competence and attain status associated with appearing mathematically competent. Conversely, they sometimes disengage to mask their feelings of incompetence.

As we look at Grace, she *appeared* to be a very different mathematics learner depending on the students with which she was working. She interacted differently in her two different groups, and this affected her learning in each group. Grace *appeared* to be more motivated with Janey, Monica, and Marisol than she did with the boys. In the homogeneous group of girls, Grace and her peers each tried the mathematical task, and they tried to understand one another's solutions out of a need to resolve which solution was correct.

We can view the engagement in the group of girls through the perspective of students' needs to seek relatedness while working on mathematics together with peers. When students work together on academic tasks, they are motivated not only to learn the content, but also to build and maintain relationships with their peers and to be recognized for what they know. In Grace's group, when the students sought to determine whether Grace's solution was correct, they may have been trying to resolve a social conflict—*whose* solution is correct—just as much as to resolve the mathematical conflict—*which* solution is correct. The students may have been trying to help Grace as much to build a relationship with her, if not more, than to solve the mathematical task. When we teach, we may not have access to how our students think about their engagement, but these principles of motivation can provide us with lenses for seeing why they might engage as they do.

Research literature describes adolescents' motivation as a process of simultaneously managing both academic and social goals (Dowson and McInerney 2003). When working together in mathematics, students not only try to learn mathematics, but also seek social affiliation, status among their peers, social approval, social responsibility, or they act out of social concern. These are just a few social motivations to which students might respond in a classroom. We can adapt each of these motivations positively to working well in a group—by which we mean the group works harmoniously toward common ends, not that the group necessarily works together to learn mathematics—and therefore to being prosocial. The extent to which this classroom's prosocial goals aligned with its goals for learning is a telling feature. In the homogeneous group, the social norms reinforced Grace's learning and that of the other girls. It maintained all the positive characteristics of cooperative learning (Slavin 1981).

An additional explanation for the difference in Grace's behavior between the two groups may be gender. A clear difference between the two groups was that Grace was the only girl in the group when she was less engaged, and she was among other girls when she was more engaged. This may have been coincidence, because Grace's engagement may depend on *which* girls and *which* boys were in the groups with her, as contrasted with whether or not Grace was with *all* boys or *all* girls. Her more subdued learning behavior may have been due to feeling like the only different group member; perhaps having one more girl in the group with her would have helped her want to engage. Again, if we were Mr. Lawson, we would not know for sure whether gender could explain the differences in Grace's engagement, but we might wonder about it.

Belenky and colleagues (1986) show us that some learners may be more interested in engaging in classroom activities to relate with their peers. This type of engagement has been described as "connected" knowing. Some researchers have found gender patterns, such that females prefer connected ways of knowing, but these preferences do not necessarily follow gender lines consistently. In a conversation with Jim about motivation, Randy Phillipp, a colleague from San Diego State University, made the analogy that for many children, doing mathematics is like doing dishes. "I hate doing the dishes," he stated, "but when I do the dishes with Margaret (Randy's wife), I *love* it." We have all somehow experienced this connected learning. Nonetheless, some young women are *less* motivated for relational reasons, and some young men are *more* motivated for them. However, through exploring women's ways of knowing, researchers have learned that allowing students to work in groups can help learners achieve connectedness and come to know through relating with others (Noddings 1989). The benefits for learning of well-orchestrated cooperative learning environments are well documented (Slavin 1981).

Another explanation for the difference in Grace's behavior could have been her level of familiarity with the girls compared to her degree of familiarity with the boys. This may not be the best explanation for her behavior, because both groups in the story were new to her. However, the group with girls included one person with whom Grace had worked recently—Janey. Having just one familiar group member could have helped Grace feel more comfortable engaging deeply in the mathematics in that group. Groups may not function at their highest potential when first formed, because of a lack of comfort with a novel group composition. Having one familiar group member with whom the student is comfortable might lead to stronger engagement with mathematics during the group work.

Finally, each group in a classroom will develop its own microculture, depending on the group members' dispositions and knowledge and how they interact. The group with boys appeared to value getting to the correct answer rather than trying to understand one another's thinking. This microculture differed markedly from that of the group of girls. The girls tried to understand one another's thinking, to the point where they did not mind engaging in mathematical argumentation with one another. So, Grace's behavior may have differed depending on the microculture that developed in each group.

In her attempts to fit in to the two groups' different social settings, Grace altered her behavior in remarkably adaptive ways. At one moment, social and mathematically engaged, Grace used the first group's rules to learn the content actively. In the next moment, after unsuccessfully attempting to reorganize her group by making contact with her friends, Grace resigned herself to the second group's rules to maintain order and status. As a consequence, her learning and attitude suffered.

We shared a wide range of possible explanations for Grace's engagement— through the principles that motivation is adaptive and social—to demonstrate how the principles can help us thinking about students' motivation. We also want to acknowledge that, if we were Mr. Lawson, we wouldn't know for sure why Grace behaved as she did. We want to demonstrate that the principles could allow us to think about Grace's behavior from multiple perspectives. Similarly, we will reflect next on Grace's engagement and Mr. Lawson's classroom through another motivation principle: success matters.

Success Matters

Students are motivated to participate in mathematics classroom discussions partially to demonstrate their mathematical competence and partially to gain status among their peers. When we introduced this principle, we referred to the tension between attributing success to hard work and ability and needing social comparison—specifically, to *feel* competent relative to our peers, not just to *be* competent—as a dance. Grace performed this dance typically for an adolescent girl in mathematics class. She wanted to show others that she knew and understood mathematics when she contributed to class discussions. When Grace worked with a group of girls and had a different solution from one of her peers, the group worked together to determine which solution was correct. The group found Grace's mistake, and Grace could be more certain about her solution once her peers helped her correct it. Working with peers to discuss her solutions gave her an opportunity (1) to understand whether and why her solution was correct and (2) to feel confident about her solution. When she shared her thinking aloud with the class, she spoke in a manner that allowed her to enact her sense of competence.

Research on students' motivation has discussed the motivation to appear competent under a variety of names. Two examples of terms that describe student's motivation to appear competent are *ego orientation* (Nicholls et al. 1990) and *performance-approach goals* (Midgley, Kaplan, and Middleton 2001). Ego and performance-approach goals govern when students actively work to *appear superior to others* by demonstrating competence. These goals contrast with mastery goals, when the student desires to *obtain understanding*. A third category of goals related to performance, *performance-avoidance goals,* show a disturbing pattern. Because students evoke performance-avoidance goals when they want to *avoid demonstrating a lack of understanding*, they tend to shut down, deflect attention, and engage in tasks only with tremendous anxiety.

Grace may have been motivated to work with her peers to resolve their mathematical conflict because she anticipated that her teacher could call on her. The students knew that their teacher could call on any student at any time. Students who were aware of this expectation and were interested in appearing competent would likely be motivated to seek reassurance that their answers were accurate and their solutions reasonable during group work. Grace wanted to be certain that she was correct so that she would be prepared to demonstrate her mathematical competence if Mr. Lawson called on her.

It is relevant to consider that Grace is an adolescent, and adolescents tend toward heightened desire to appear competent in front of others. David Elkind (1967) wrote about adolescents' construction of an *imaginary audience*. This is when adolescents, in the process of starting to think more about their own thinking, believe that others are thinking about them as much as they are thinking about themselves. So, we might expect someone at Grace's age to be concerned about appearing competent. When we think back on our own feelings as adolescents, we can empathize with Grace.

However, we can also see that Grace's interest in demonstrating competence makes sense when we think about the competitive culture of her classroom. Her classmates were all relatively strong in mathematics, and the students had established a sense of competition among groups. They attained social status in their classroom culture by efficiently achieving a sensible and accurate solution, and they maintained that status through opportunities to share sensible and accurate solutions publicly. Although adolescents may be concerned already with appearing competent in front of their peers and teachers, this classroom's culture potentially intensified these adolescents' needs to appear competent.

It is also possible that the performance-approach goals that motivated Grace were not necessarily problematic. On the basis of their review of research literature, Midgley, Kaplan, and Middleton (2001) described conditions that facilitated learning when students held performance-approach goals. One of these conditions included a competitive classroom in which mastery goals were also present. In essence, by emphasizing understanding and sense making, Mr. Lawson's pedagogy supported the development of mastery goals. This emphasis on understanding focused competition, at least in Grace's first group, on developing the best strategies and explanations as opposed to coming up quickly and efficiently with a numeric answer. In this classroom, students appeared to be motivated to appear competent *and* achieve mathematical understanding simultaneously.

Below, we discuss how, in light of these motivation principles, teachers might think about and respond to events in this story. We provide some implications for teaching mathematics. When we interpreted Mr. Lawson's classroom and Grace's behavior through the principles of students' motivation above, we did not give clear answers. Instead, we entertained multiple interpretations. Similarly, when we share how teachers might respond to or think about a situation similar to this classroom, with a student like Grace, we do not offer prescriptions for practice. Answers for how to respond to students are rarely clear. Instead, we explore a range of possible responses that a teacher might have to situations presented in our chapters' stories.

Grace's Story:
Implications for Classroom Practice

Throughout this book, we explore implications for practice inspired by each student's story. In our experience, teachers want to support students' engagement in a manner that both facilitates mathematical understanding and promotes longer-term engagement with mathematics. We discuss implications in this chapter in the form of presented dilemmas, because we believe that no easy answers exist when making instructional decisions. We want to honor the complexity of a classroom's dynamics and acknowledge that addressing one element of a student's experience may perturb another, equally important element. Such was true of Mr. Lawson's decision to move Grace from one small group to a second and then to a third.

Dilemma: Should Mr. Lawson keep Grace in the group in which she appears to be motivated or help Grace develop a more flexible engagement with mathematics that isn't tied to group membership?

In this instance, perhaps we should rephrase the question. If students can learn mathematics through engaging in dialogue with their peers, then Grace may not be the one who needs to change. Rather than try to help Grace be motivated in multiple contexts, Mr. Lawson could consider how to help other students engage like the members of Grace's group. A new question could be *How can more groups function to be more like Grace's group when she worked with the group of all girls?*

Marlene Scardamalia and Carl Bereiter (2006) talk about classrooms as "knowledge-building environments." Their belief is that the classroom's social makeup should be explicitly designed such that each student feels responsible to build a better, more coherent, more efficient knowledge structure, both for themselves and for the class. This ethic combines the best aspects of both mastery goals and connected-learning goals to create an environment where all individual, contributing class members' needs for competence, recognition, and relatedness actually support and enhance one another.

Mr. Lawson's new dilemma becomes how to support groups' interactions in a truly collaborative manner. (See chapter 12 for more on this topic.) Some teachers have tried to foster collaborative interactions through group assessments. Others have tried holding all group members responsible for the groups' thinking, such that no one could ask the teacher a question until all group members have thought about the question first; the teacher could call on any student to present the group's thinking during a class discussion. These are both good strategies that help, but do not solve, the dilemma by themselves.

The fourth motivation principle states, **Motivation creates long-term attitudes**. To accomplish this positively, Scardamalia and Bereiter (2006) suggest that the bulk of classroom practices must align in several important ways:

1. Understanding knowledge advancement as a community achievement rather than merely an individual one

2. Defining knowledge advancement as the improvement of ideas, rather than as progress toward true or warranted belief

3. Defining the knowledge *of* mathematical concepts and their applications as opposed to knowledge *about* concepts or applications

4. Promoting discourse as collaborative problem solving—argument rather than argumentation

Using strategies to promote these values for collaborative activity across groups could have a promising impact on students. Emphasizing the importance of collaboration can help students meet their social goals as they simultaneously work to meet academic learning goals. If a value for collaboration is in place across the classroom, then Grace's motivation to engage in mathematics is less likely to appear different depending upon the members of her group.

Dilemma: Should Mr. Lawson support Grace in her need to feel competent before participating, or should he encourage Grace and her peers to see the value in participating in mathematical discussion, even if they are not certain they are correct?

Resolving conflicts during small-group work allows students to feel more competent to display correct solutions and sensible strategies during whole-class discussions, but the larger group may have fewer opportunities to learn from one another if students resolve conflicts during small-group work. Teachers may believe that learning is a process of constructing meaning together through dialogue with others, but some students may be less open to learning from others during the conversation. They thus may present ideas to the class only after the ideas are fully developed. Students who prioritize the need to feel competent in front of their peers may want to avoid letting their peers know that they are uncertain about their thinking. Students could benefit from the teacher bringing uncertainty about a mathematical understanding to the large group for discussion, so that the class can work together and wrestle with the uncertainty as a group.

One way to resolve this dilemma is for teachers to push students on what counts as "mathematically competent" in the classroom. For instance, the students may think that competence in mathematics looks like sharing a correct strategy. Alternatively, mathematical competence might consist of asking thoughtful questions, such as "I wonder why these two answers are different? How did we solve the problem differently to get to these two different answers?" If asking a thoughtful question is a form of mathematical competence, then students do not need to be sure that they are correct prior to participating, and therefore participation has more positive rewards than potentially embarrassing mistakes.

If more ways to be mathematically competent exist, then more students have the chance to be considered mathematically competent. If teachers use multiple ways of appearing competent in mathematics, then they can tailor assigning competence to specific students individually and thus raise more students' status in the classroom (Boaler and Staples 2008; Cohen 1994).

Summary

The first author (Middleton and Spanias 2002) wrote, "teachers matter" when it comes to creating positive learning environments—knowledge building environments—that enable students to become motivated to learn challenging mathematical concepts and skills. Our future depends on teachers who are capable of seeing through all the potentially conflicting motivations students bring with them to the classroom, who are capable of designing tasks, of orchestrating discourse, of seeing the potential in each and every one of their students and matching that potential with learning experiences that stimulate the student to maximize what they have been given. Teachers matter. Students learn to like or dislike mathematics, to see it as part of their future, or to see it as an endeavor to be avoided, and that learning takes place, for the most part, in classrooms led by teachers. The principles and strategies we share in this book will provide opportunities for mindful teachers to change their practice and affect that learning to be positive, yielding mathematically proficient, mathematically disposed knowledge workers. Let us now jump right in and examine those principles and strategies in action.

References

Belenky, Mary F., Blythe M. Clinchy, Nancy R. Goldberger, and Jill M. Tarule. *Women's Ways of Knowing: The Development of Self, Voice, and Mind.* New York: Basic Books, 1986.

Boaler, Jo, and Megan Staples. "Creating Mathematical Futures through an Equitable Teaching Approach: The Case of Railside School." *Teachers College Record* 110, no. 3 (2008): 608–45.

Cohen, Elizabeth G. *Designing Groupwork.* New York: Teachers College Press, 1994.

Dowson, Martin, and Dennis M. McInerney. "What Do Students Say about Their Motivational Goals? Toward a More Complex and Dynamic Perspective on Student Motivation." *Contemporary Educational Psychology* 28, no. 1 (January 2003): 91–113.

Elkind, David. "Egocentrism in Adolescence." *Child Development* 38 (1967): 1025–33.

Hulleman, Chris S., Amanda M. Durik, Shaun B. Schweigert, and Judith M. Harackiewicz. "Task Values, Achievement Goals, and Interest: An Integrative Analysis." *Journal of Educational Psychology* 100, no. 2 (May 2008): 398–416.

Middleton, James A., and Photini Spanias. "Pedagogical Implications of the Research on Motivation in Mathematics Education." In *Lessons Learned from Research,* edited by Judith T. Sowder and Bonnie Schappelle, pp. 9–15. Reston, Va.: National Council of Teachers of Mathematics, 2002.

Midgley, Carol, Avi Kaplan, A., and Michael J. Middleton. "Performance-Approach Goals: Good for What, for Whom, under What Circumstances, and at What Cost?" *Journal of Educational Psychology* 93, no. 1 (March 2001): 77–86.

Nicholls, John G., Paul Cobb, Terry Wood, Erna Yackel, and Michael Patashnick. "Dimensions of Success in Mathematics: Individual and Classroom Differences." *Journal for Research in Mathematics Education* 21, no. 2 (March 1990): 109–22.

Noddings, Nel. "Theoretical and Practical Concerns about Small Groups in Mathematics." *Elementary School Journal* 89, no. 5 (May 1989): 607–23.

Scardamalia, Marlene, and Carl Bereiter. "Knowledge Building: Theory, Pedagogy, and Technology." In *Cambridge Handbook of the Learning Sciences*, edited by R. Keith Sawyer, pp. 97–118. New York: Cambridge University Press, 2006.

Slavin, Robert E. "Synthesis of Research on Cooperative Learning." *Educational Leadership* 38, no. 8 (1981): 655–60.

PART 2

Content Matters:
Motivation to Learn
Mathematics

CHAPTER 2

Motivation Is Learned

*I*n this chapter, Jim reflects on his own experience as a learner. His autobiography *illustrates that motivation is learned, not innate, in students. In his reflection, mathematics that he encountered in school did not always inspire him, but he was curious about mathematical ideas and relationships generally. Often what stays with us over time are not the specific mathematical facts or procedures we have encountered, but what embodies the dispositions and feelings we developed toward mathematics while in our classrooms or in other situations when mathematical ideas inspired us.*

I never liked math much as I experienced it in school. Aside from geometry, it was always pretty boring. I was always good at it, but I was never very interested in solving equations or computing square roots. But I always loved mathematics when I experienced it outside school. I remember being a little boy, sitting in church. The minister was speaking about heaven and how it would go on and on forever. It wasn't very riveting for a five-year-old, but as he was speaking, I was pretending like I was pinching my sister's head (she was sitting four rows up). I would place my hand in front of my face and line up her head between my thumb and index finger and pretend that, as I squeezed, her head would squish like a Nerf ball. As I was engaged in this activity, I noticed that I could pinch halfway, then halfway again, and so on, making my fingers closer and closer by half the distance each time. In and of itself this was fascinating. But what really got me was that I began to realize that I could continue this halfway pinching pattern forever—my fingers would *never* touch. Yet, by just closing my hand normally, they *would* touch. How was this possible? I later learned that Zeno of Elea discovered this paradox and wrote about it circa 490–430 BCE. It seems that whatever crucial problems mathematicians have encountered over the millennia recapitulate in the problems that children confront (Freudenthal 1991).

I also remember my first-grade teacher, Mrs. Mark. Mrs. Mark was 23 years old and had just finished her teacher preparation program. We were her first class. This was at the height of the New Math movement, and Mrs. Mark was responsible for teaching 35 six-year-olds set theory. I still remember her fumbling, trying to help students understand the difference between a *cardinal number* and a *numeral*. To us, the symbol 2 meant "two," so there was no difference conceptually between the quantity and its representation. Somehow—it has all gotten fuzzy after 40 years—it clicked. *The quantity is the amount*, "two" is its name, and 2 is how we write it. That means that two isn't a real thing. It is an idea that can be used to describe real things!

In both these situations, I would describe myself as fully absorbed in the challenge of understanding and abstracting the concept of infinity in the first instance and number in the second. I wanted more of these experiences, but I never got them again in mathematics class until much later, in calculus and advanced statistics, and even then it was pitifully rare. Although I am not a research mathematician, I continue to read mathematical texts, and I try to work through new mathematical ideas on my own. I love mathematics.

I also remember the remainder of my school mathematics experiences. I remember in the second grade, we did away with the New Math and went back to basics (*yawn*). Two-digit addition, subtraction, multiplication, and division were taught using a standard procedure—line up the digits, start at the ones place, and so on. In high school, we learned about the FOIL and **O**scar **H**as **A** **H**airy, **O**ld **A**rm mnemonics. The latter was my teacher's personal version of the SohCahToa mnemonic—**O**pposite over **H**ypotenuse, **A**djacent over **H**ypotenuse, and **O**pposite over **A**djacent). We learned Cramer's rule, which I promptly forgot, all except the name. We learned the side-angle-side theorem and the sine rule. So what? I did well in mathematics because I wanted to become a scientist of some kind, but mathematics wasn't anything to which I aspired or that I wanted to spend any additional time exploring for its own sake. Memorizing rules and applying them to problems that already had the answers figured out did not interest me.

When We Engage in Mathematics, We Learn Both Content *and* Motivation

The biography presented here illustrates perhaps the most obvious, but most important of all the principles we discuss in this book. We base all the other principles and strategies we discuss on the assumption that, aside from minor predispositions toward quantitative or spatial reasoning that may be associated with genetics or random variation in neonatal care, the vast bulk of our likes, dislikes, predilections, and dispositions form from our experiences. In other words, they are learned. Jim's biography holds two fundamentally different feelings about his mathematical experiences and mathematics as a pursuit, based on the different types of mathematical activities in which he was engaged as a young person. On the one hand, he reveres deep, important mathematical concepts. He enjoys his personal mathematical journey enough to continue to study mathematics even beyond his compulsory education. On the other hand, he shows a negative attitude toward facts and rules, although he admits that both have some merit and he most likely uses both greatly in pursuing his more valued mathematical understandings. To quote him, "How can this be?"

Perhaps we are all conflicted at times when confronted with difficult subject matter. Research shows that children, when asked whether or not mathematics is important, tend to respond affirmatively. They acknowledge that mathematics is useful and that understanding it is important for scientific reasoning, financial savvy, and other applications (Kloosterman, Raymond, and Emenaker 1996). Yet as they grow older, typically sometime in the middle grades, when we ask children whether or not mathematics is important *to them*, they state that they really don't want to take more mathematics courses (Wigfield et al. 2002)! The message of mathematics's importance appears to be sinking in, but the personal desire to pursue it is missing.

What Is Learning? A Thought Experiment

Psychologists define learning as change in behavior potential that results from experience. Put simply, learning is just a change in thinking. When we learn the Pythagorean theorem, we change our way of thinking about triangles and the relationships among the lengths of the sides. We may also connect this knowledge with our knowledge of distance, because we can find the distance between any two points in a coordinate system using the Pythagorean theorem, and of the relationship between a circle's radius and the locus of its points, because a circle's center-radius formula is a special case of the Pythagorean theorem. Whether we have just had our first experience with triangles or whether we are applying this understanding to trigonometry, we are changing the way we think about distance, coordinates, geometric objects, and formulas. Each successive experience adds to our understanding, changing our ability to think, reason, and solve problems.

But think back to when you were first learning the Pythagorean theorem, perhaps in middle school. When you try to recall that situation, what comes to mind? Perhaps you mentally see your class—the rows of desks, the chalkboard or whiteboard, the windows, posters on the wall. Perhaps you see your friends. Perhaps you recall a particular event—a conversation, or a problem you were trying to solve. Try to bring this event to the forefront and recall it in as much detail as possible.

If you are like us, you probably don't remember much of the mathematics in any particular event. What probably pervades your memories are feelings, emotions about being an adolescent engaging with other adolescents, in a classroom with a teacher with whom you identified somehow. Are your feelings about those memories positive or negative? What caused them to be that way?

In classes at the university, we ask aspiring elementary school teachers to think back in this manner and write about their early mathematics experiences. They overwhelmingly report negative feelings. Interestingly, teachers tend to report vivid memories of their teachers and the ways in which their teachers failed to support them as students when they were struggling with difficult ideas. Many elementary school teachers report having enjoyed mathematics until a single instance convinced them that they just were not good at it or that it was not interesting or useful to them. From that point, their attitude about mathematics began a downhill slide, and their achievement also began to wane. They learned to dislike mathematics.

It turns out that these memories are very useful. People can look back on earlier experiences and use their memories to guide their future engagement. Research on how human beings develop useful memories has long been a goal of educators from a variety of disciplines, including psychology, sociology, and mathematics education. In general, these disciplines agree that our concepts about any situation evolve with each new use (Bransford, Brown, and Cocking 1999). Because the environment in which we live is so complex, we have evolved an adaptive learning system that augments our initial understandings as new situations arise and classifies the results of our actions into general strategies, habits, and preferences.

Our initial understandings about an activity help us create strategies to orient our attention and select relevant information to solve problems on the basis of recognized facets of the task at hand (Newell and Simon 1972; Newell 1993; Lehman, Laird, and Rosenbloom 1996). What could be more helpful as an aid to directing behavior than a system of concepts that classifies previously encountered activities as being worthwhile or a waste of time? We call this system of concepts our *interests*, or our *preferences*. Paying attention to our interests enables us, as Thoreau put it, to "live deliberately." Our interests allow us to make intelligent decisions regarding the various choices life offers—to avoid unpleasantness, to optimize our efforts, and to maximize the benefit we receive from our hard work. The preservice teachers we poll each semester, on the whole, have classified mathematics as *not an interest.*

Our memory functions as a means for anticipating the future. We have memories because our future success depends on us being able to sort through past experiences to predict a course of action. Those of our ancestors who could anticipate the results of their actions better could coordinate their behavior better, and these survived long enough for their genes to be passed to us. That legacy, though less focused on basic survival today, still manifests in our classifying tasks, occupations, hobbies, and other potential ways of spending our time as being an *interest* or as *not an interest* (Middleton and Toluk 1999).

How, exactly, do we go about classifying potential tasks? Although the details of how we develop interests are not well known, the general pattern across individuals is reasonably clear. When we have the opportunity to engage in a novel task, we have to determine whether or not it is a worthwhile expenditure of our time.

Determining Whether an Activity Is Worthwhile

Suppose you are asked if you wanted to try *teremogy?*

You probably have no idea what teremogy is, and therefore have little to go on to determine whether or not you will enjoy it. What do you do? First of all, you have to *determine the context* in which you have been provided this opportunity. Is it school or home? Who is asking you, a friend or someone in authority? What have been your prior experiences with that person in that context? These are questions that you might be asking yourself. If you know, like, and trust the person suggesting the teremogy activity, you might be predisposed to saying "Well, it probably won't hurt me, and I might like it."

You might then ask, "What do I have to do?" This is an intelligent question, because *gathering information about the task* enables you to determine if it is too easy or too difficult, if it is useful for you or serves some valuable purpose, or if it just doesn't seem to fit you. Perhaps teremogy is similar to an experience you have already had before. If so, you might compare how worthwhile teremogy might be to how worthwhile that experience was. An example that Jim, the first author of this book, uses in his classes is *skiing*. In the desert Southwest where he teaches, many students have never skied. How would they determine whether they should go skiing if given the chance? Some students compare skiing to mountain biking, water skiing, or some other activity they had already done. The obvious conclusion to that comparison is that the more similar the two experiences, the more similar their interest or disinterest in skiing would be. Others compare skiing to their general predilections, saying things like "I don't like the cold," or "I like to go fast," and using this analysis of the activity's features to help them with their decision. In either instance, they must do some analysis of the requirements for participation in the activity, and some comparison of the envisioned activity with past experiences has to take place. One's *interests* help them make such a decision efficiently and effectively. If the task seems to fit one's interests, we can tentatively say "Well, that might be fun! I'll give it a shot." Some of the primary criteria for determining whether or not a potential pursuit classifies as an interest include the *challenge* of the activity and the extent to which the learner has *control* over his or her participation.

Challenge

When we ask students what kinds of mathematical tasks they would like to do, they list criteria such as *relevance, excitement, variety,* and *challenge* (Nardi and Steward 2003; Meyer, Turner, and Spencer 1997). Interestingly, challenge per se is not sufficient to motivate students. The student must see challenge as relevant to them somehow personally. The challenge must also be at an appropriate level so that students experience success, but not so much success that the tasks become boring. Too much challenge, however, can lead to frustration. So, they tend to compare their own need for challenge with the task requirements prior to making a decision about whether or not to engage. While they are engaged in a task, they continually monitor the challenge to see if it is close to some optimal level (e.g., Ma [1999]). If it falls too low or grows too frustrating, they look for ways to disengage and do something else.

The implications of challenge for mathematics instruction are pretty heady: tasks must fit the person for him or her to develop a positive interest in them. The challenge, therefore, must be tailored to meet each student's optimal level. But how can I do this, one might ask, with 35 students in my classroom?

Control

Control compliments challenge. When we are challenged at an optimal level, we are working at the edge of our abilities. Though we make mistakes, we have control over our actions, and we can use our mistakes to improve our performance.

We have three ways to establish control over a situation. The first is *choice*. When we are forced to do something, even if we like the activity, we automatically have reservations about it. Some level of freedom to choose from among different activities is a necessary condition for liking the activities. Of course, in mathematics education much of what we assign students is compulsory. *Do problems 32 to 48 and record your work* doesn't seem to offer much opportunity for choice. However, one may allow students choice within boundaries—letting them choose their own method for solution, or allowing alternative representations. Even these small opportunities for choice can raise students' feelings of control and increase their interest in the task.

The second way to gain control over an activity is to *reduce its challenge* to an optimal level. Sometimes (but not very often it turns out), we overestimate the readiness of our students to engage in an assignment. Perhaps they are still confused about the size of denominators when ordering fractions. Perhaps their number sense is still a bit fuzzy. Stepping back and trying an easier problem can make all the difference.

The third way of establishing control over an activity is to *work hard*—to learn. If a task is at an upper level of challenge for a student, he or she can gain control by acquiring knowledge and skill. This requires that a student develop positive self-efficacy (Schunk 1994) coupled with beliefs that their successes depend on how much effort they expend (Blackwell, Trzesniewski, and Dweck 2007). We will treat this crucial set of attitudes in depth in chapter 3.

If we engage in mathematics over an extended period of time, during which we experience an optimal level of challenge coupled with adequate control, we have the basic parameters spelled out for developing *interest* (Middleton 1995; Middleton and Toluk 1999). Think about the activities you really like. Those activities probably involve at least moderate challenge, complemented by a sense of efficacy and control. In mathematics, students tend to recall high challenge, but feelings of low ability, lack of choice, and little chance of hard work paying off typically compromise their control. These kinds of feelings can provoke students to disengage from mathematics forever.

As we stated earlier, people learn their motivations by comparing current opportunities to engage with prior experience. As mathematics teachers, we can use this to our instruction's advantage. If we understand our students' interests, we can contextualize tasks to include these interests. Students' motivation for those interests, then, rubs off onto the mathematics, making it at least more palatable for the students in the short run. That motivation also presents the opportunity that, if the challenge and control parameters are optimal over an extended time, the activity, and by extension mathematics itself, can become an interest.

What about Grades and Other Rewards?

"Yes," we hear you say. "Interest-based activities are the ideal motivator. But this is the real world. You can't like *everything*. Sometimes you just have to buckle down and do some hard work." The fact is, we don't do *anything* (let alone anything requiring hard work) without a reason. If interest isn't the primary reason for engagement, we must search the activity for some other inducement to engage. In circumstances where there is not compelling interest to work hard at mathematics, teachers are tempted to use rewards and other incentives to motivate students to achieve.

Extrinsic motivation is the generic term researchers use to describe any time we engage in something to either gain some reward or to escape some negative consequence. Ryan and Deci (2000; see also Lepper et al. [2005]) suggest that extrinsic motivation is much more complex than *intrinsic* (interest-based) motivation. Think of all the presses students must negotiate every day in mathematics. We do mathematics to please—or at least not anger—the teacher, or to escape punishment for bad grades. We do it because it is instrumental for us to become financially successful. We do it to reduce the chance that we might be labeled "dumb." We do it because our parents expect us to. Grades and other rewards are just the tip of the proverbial iceberg of motivations we must work through.

But there is a catch-22. (Beware: this the second metaphor in two sentences!) Anytime you engage in a difficult activity, your involvement will cause some mental and sometimes physical fatigue. It will cause some level of anxiety associated with looking foolish in the classroom social setting. It will induce some frustration associated with the challenge. These are *all* negative consequences of engagement. You can think of others that might arise depending on the situation. The problem is, they are inescapable for any task you might choose. At some point, if time is not a factor, the level of fatigue, frustration, anxiety—or boredom, if the task is too easy—or most likely a combination of these things will overcome any reward value the task may present in the moment, and we will look to end our involvement (Middleton and Toluk 1999).

Moreover, even if the teacher sets up the reward contingencies to be overwhelmingly positive, decades' worth of evidence shows that doing so may actually detract from the intrinsic motivation a student experiences in mathematics. This will make it *less* likely in the future that the student will engage willingly in mathematics in the absence of a substantial reward (Lepper, Corpus, and Iyengar 2005). Lepper and Greene (1978) call these "the hidden costs of reward." We take this issue up in depth in chapter 10.

It turns out that both intrinsic enjoyment and extrinsic rewards and punishments play off each other all the time in school instruction. A realistic approach to motivation is to design or choose activities that optimize intrinsic motivation by capitalizing on interest, challenge, and control, and to minimize using rewards and certainly punishments as inducements to engage. The research is clear: rewards can be useful to induce a student to do an activity he or she would not normally choose freely. But, doing so will reduce the chance that the student will enjoy the activity and engage in it willingly in the future. Use rewards sparingly and in such a manner that the student doesn't come to expect an extrinsic reward for their hard work.

So far we have shown that students learn mathematical motivation in much the same manner as they learn academic content. They learn to enjoy tasks by keeping track of the challenge and control aspects of tasks. They learn to associate mathematics content with their interests. They learn to negotiate the extrinsic motivators that exist in the school and social environments. The point of all this is that, as we shall explore in chapter 5, these experiences lead to long-term attitudes toward mathematics and its applications. How can we as teachers design learning environments that induce students to create positive mathematical attitudes, and to use these attitudes to direct their educational and occupational choices?

What we want to avoid, at all costs, is for students to develop debilitating, frightened, or bleak attitudes toward mathematics. When students continually experience frustration, lack of control, and lack of personal involvement or interest, they can develop what is commonly referred to as *math anxiety* (Tobias 1993). Math anxiety is exhibited as feelings of fear related to any mathematical situation, particularly those associated with some kind of performance, like a test or quiz (see also Selkirk, Bouchey, and Eccles [2010]). We all get anxious from time to time depending on situational factors like a lack of preparation, momentary confusion, or heightened challenge of a task. These reactions are natural, and we can develop coping mechanisms for dealing with them. Extra effort applied to studying or asking for help can resolve our anxiety reasonably quickly with no negative consequences. But, for some students, this anxiety can become so pervasive in mathematics that it can become *learned helplessness*, the tendency to give up easily when faced with challenge because of repeated and continual failure, and *learned hopelessness*, feelings of depression stemming from a belief that not only is the student unable to affect the outcomes of mathematics tasks, but that those outcomes will be highly aversive (i.e., not just negative, but harmful). Both these beliefs lead to negative personal and academic consequences, including lowering the student's academic self-concept, reducing the effectiveness of learning strategies, and ultimately leading to a downward slide in academic achievement (Au et al. 2009).

So What Have We Learned?

When we look at how people develop interest, we see that people learn both positive and negative patterns of motivation as a result of *anticipating the future* by *reflecting on past experiences*. If students have positive experiences in mathematics—

experiences that present an appropriate level of *challenge*, coupled with a sense of *control*—they begin to anticipate their future engagement in mathematics optimistically, with a sense of enjoyment. If, however, students are not challenged, they may perform well in mathematics but their interest will wane over time. If they lack a sense of control, they can develop seriously negative motivations, including math anxiety and learned helplessness. These, in turn, lead students to give up easily and avoid mathematical tasks, classes, and careers.

We can also see that the trend for most students is to learn negative patterns of motivation overall toward mathematics. This stems from a system that provides lots of challenge, but little personal control; that offers relatively little personal relevance; and that uses rewards and punishments often as the primary motivating features that define students' engagement. Continued positive experiences seem necessary over a long period to develop productive motivations to learn mathematics. It only takes a few negative experiences for students to begin to define mathematics as "not an interest" and to begin a pattern of avoidance that lasts the rest of their lives.

References

Au, Raymond C. P., David Watkins, John Hattie, and Patricia Alexander. "Reformulating the Depression Model of Learned Hopelessness for Academic Outcomes." *Educational Research Review* 4, no. 2 (2009): 103–17.

Blackwell, Lisa S., H. Kali Trzesniewski, and Carol S. Dweck. "Implicit Theories of Intelligence Predict Achievement across an Adolescent Transition: A Longitudinal Study and an Intervention." *Child Development* 78, no. 1 (February 2007): 246–63.

Bransford, John D., Ann L. Brown, and Rodney R. Cocking. *How People Learn: Brain, Mind, Experience, and School.* Washington, D.C.: National Academies Press, 1999.

Freudenthal, Hans. *Revisiting Mathematics Education: China Lectures.* Dordrecht, Netherlands: Kluwer, 1991.

Kloosterman, Peter, Anne M. Raymond, and Charles Emenaker. "Students' Beliefs about Mathematics: A Three-Year Study." *Elementary School Journal* 97, no. 1 (September 1996): 39–56.

Lehman, Jill Fain, John Laird, and Paul Rosenbloom. "A Gentle Introduction to Soar, An Architecture for Human Cognition: 2006 Update." http://ai.eecs.umich.edu/soar/docs/GentleIntroduction-2006.pdf.

Lepper, Mark R., and David Greene, eds. *The Hidden Costs of Reward: New Perspectives on the Psychology of Human Motivation.* Hillsdale, N.J.: Lawrence Erlbaum Associates, 1978.

Lepper, Mark R., Jennifer Henderlong Corpus, and Sheena S. Iyengar. "Intrinsic and Extrinsic Motivational Orientations in the Classroom: Age Differences and Academic Correlates." *Journal of Educational Psychology* 97, no. 2 (May 2005): 184–96.

Ma, Xin. "A Meta-Analysis of the Relationship between Anxiety toward Mathematics and Achievement in Mathematics." *Journal for Research in Mathematics Education* 30, no. 5 (November 1999): 520–40.

Meyer, Debra K., Julianne C. Turner, and Cynthia A. Spencer. "Challenge in a Mathematics Classroom: Students' Motivation and Strategies in Project-Based Learning." *Elementary School Journal* 97, no. 5 (1997): 501–21.

Middleton, James A. "A Study of Intrinsic Motivation in the Mathematics Classroom: A Personal Constructs Approach." *Journal for Research in Mathematics Education* 26, no. 3 (May 1995): 254–79.

Middleton, James A., and Zulbiye Toluk. "First Steps in the Development of an Adaptive, Decision-Making Theory of Motivation." *Educational Psychologist* 34, no. 2 (1999): 99–112.

Nardi, Elena, and Susan Steward. "Is Mathematics T.I.R.E.D? A Profile of Quiet Disaffection in the Secondary Mathematics Classroom." *British Educational Research* 29, no. 3 (June 2003): 345–67.

Newell, Allen. "Reflections on the Knowledge Level." *Artificial Intelligence* 59, nos. 1–2 (February 1993): 31–38.

Newell, Allen, and Herbert A. Simon. *Human Problem Solving.* Englewood Cliffs, N.J.: Prentice Hall, 1972.

Ryan, Richard M., and Edward L. Deci. "Self-Determination Theory and the Facilitation of Intrinsic Motivation, Social Development, and Well-Being." *American Psychologist* 55, no.1 (2000): 68–78.

Schunk, Dale H. "Self-Regulation of Self-Efficacy and Attributions in Academic Settings." In *Self-Regulation of Learning and Performance: Issues and Educational Applications*, edited by Dale H. Schunk and Barry J. Zimmerman, pp. 25–44. London: Psychology Press, 1994.

Selkirk, Laura C., Heather A. Bouchey, and Jacquelynne S. Eccles. "Interactions among Domain-Specific Expectancies, Values, and Gender: Predictors of Test Anxiety during Early Adolescence." *Journal of Early Adolescence* (May 2010). http://jea.sagepub.com.ezproxy1.lib.asu.edu/content/early/2010/05/19/0272431610363156.full.pdf+html.

Tobias, Sheila. *Overcoming Math Anxiety.* New York: W.W. Norton & Co., 1993.

Wigfield, Alan, Ann Battle, Lisa B. Keller, and Jacquelynne S. Eccles. "Sex Differences in Motivation, Self-Concept, Career Aspirations, and Career Choice: Implications for Cognitive Development." In *Biology, Society, and Behavior: The Development of Sex Differences in Cognition*, edited by Ann McGillicuddy-De Lisi and Richard De Lisi, pp. 93–124. Greenwich, Conn.: Ablex, 2002.

CHAPTER 3

Motivation Is Adaptive

Breanna's precalculus experience is a story that illustrates how motivation is adaptive. The motivation that a student exhibits reveals information about her history as a mathematics learner. Our experiences shape our motivational responses, and our motivation reveals information about our past experiences as much as about our present ones. Our experiences teach us what mathematics is, how we should respond to mathematics tasks, and who we are as mathematics learners. How we respond to particular situations can reveal what we have learned from prior experiences and the degree to which our current experiences align with our previous ones. Breanna's is a true story submitted by Eric Weber, one of her instructors.

Breanna walked into the first day of class with her schedule in hand and shoulders slumped. She was a hard worker who excelled in academics and sports, and she had a vibrant social life. She loved to be known as "the best" in all her endeavors. She sat down at the table in the back of the classroom, dropped her bag on the ground, and let out a big sigh. Precalculus was her first college course, and it was the one she dreaded the most. Breanna was the class clown in high school; she often made cynical remarks when asked to explain how she was thinking about a mathematics problem. Breanna intended to go for a bioengineering major in college. She had passed AP tests in biology, chemistry, and physics, but she did not take a mathematics course in her high school senior year. She was concerned about collegiate mathematics, and she often resorted to making jokes about what she called "the stupidity of math" in order to soothe her fears. Despite her antics in class, Breanna always completed her homework on time, earned perfect scores on every quiz and exam, and would come to class early, often asking deep, challenging questions about complex mathematical issues.

Though she understood the course's content, each day Breanna took her seat and complained to other students about the difficulty of the homework. She emphatically stated that she spent so much time on the homework that she finally had to give up on it in order to get some sleep. She was adamant to her classmates that the course was impossible, even though her mathematics questions sometimes stumped the university tutors. While in high school, Breanna said, all her math teachers considered getting the right answer the important part of it. None of her teachers ever gave credit for her insightful explanations to difficult problems. Breanna recalled her teachers telling her that they did not give partial credit for "writing," because it was a mathematics course. She said that her geometry teacher once used her ten-page proof homework, full of explanations, to show the class an example of what not to do in future homework. Although the teacher did not say it was Breanna's homework, a student in the first row saw her name on the paper and told the rest of the class. Her peers then referred to in-depth explanations as "doing a Breanna" for the rest of the geometry course. In her college precalculus course, Breanna often told other students she had not done the homework because it was "stupid," but she handed in the homework more than fifteen minutes before class started.

Breanna's college precalculus course focused on having students explain their thinking. The teacher was interested in understanding the students' process of solving complex problems rather than having them simply produce the correct answer. Breanna, however, did not think explaining what she was thinking was important, and she dismissed the teacher's goal as unrealistic. The teacher, who arrived just minutes before class each day, did not observe Breanna asking the tutors deep, meaningful questions before class. The teacher assumed from Breanna's negative disposition that Breanna disliked the course. The teacher rarely called on her for fear of receiving a snide remark about a question. Breanna soon became complacent in class and rarely paid attention to what the teacher was saying. The tutors' reports on students for the teacher, however, said that Breanna was having no problems. The teacher assumed the only conclusion was that Breanna did not care about math and wanted to do the bare minimum to pass. Breanna, who noticed the teacher avoiding calling on her, started acting out. She interrupted the teacher, asking why what they were doing in class was relevant to anything in the real world. Her peers, who found it entertaining, laughed along and encouraged her.

Six weeks into the semester, the teacher handed back quizzes from the previous class period. Breanna looked at her score, a 7 out of 15. She looked to see what she had done wrong and noticed she had all the right answers. Fuming, she walked up to the teacher. She yelled emphatically, "Why did I get a 7 out of 15 when I got every single answer right?"

The teacher responded, "The directions stated that you need to explain your answer and show your work to receive full credit. You did get all the correct answers, but you did not give any explanation for your work."

Breanna retorted, "This class is so stupid! I have never had to show my work before, and it is just a huge waste of time to write a paragraph about what I was thinking. Who cares what I am thinking—I got the right answer!"

Breanna sat down and asked her group members, "Did all of you lose points for not explaining too?" All the group members shook their heads, and Breanna looked at their quizzes. They had all received a 15 out of 15, and they had written detailed explanations justifying their solution. They stated that they found it valuable to write out what they were thinking so that their grade was not solely based on answers. They told her that they thought it was stupid at first, but that they could actually say what they were thinking as opposed to producing a number. Breanna was dumbfounded. She had always been at the head of the class in sports, academics, and social life, but that day, she was out of her comfort zone. As she left class that day, she knew she had to change.

The next day, Breanna came to class with all her old quizzes and worked with the tutor an hour before class began. She approached the teacher before class, and handed her all the quizzes from the semester with a simple note that said, "I hope this makes up for it." Breanna had gone through every quiz from the semester, and whether she had received full credit or not, added detailed explanations to each question. During the eight weeks left in the semester after that, Breanna came to class early, not only to be tutored, but also to tutor fellow peers. The teacher remarked at how Breanna sought to help all her group members in class, often having completed the reading for that day's lesson the night before. Breanna began handing in homework with the other students, and she raised her hand every time the teacher asked a question. Some students chided Breanna for being "fake dumb" at the start of the semester, but she simply ignored these comments.

Near the end of the semester, Breanna approached the teacher. The teacher asked, "Breanna, what or why did you change so much this semester?"

Breanna responded, "Well, I came in to the class being scared of mathematics. Really, it terrified me more than biology, physics, and chemistry combined. I always liked thinking about problems, and physics and chemistry, there I could explain how I was thinking, and the right answer was not as important. I always thought math was about getting the right answer, at least formally. It was easier for me to make fun of the problems where we had to explain because I did not think it was real math. I just figured it was an experimental thing, and then we would start doing real math later. Then I realized it was okay to talk about how I was thinking about problems, and it became more like physics and chemistry, which I love!" Two years after she completed precalculus, Breanna became a mathematics major; she hoped to become a secondary school teacher.

Why Be Motivated in the First Place?

In our story, Breanna was a good student. She did her work, understood the content, and by all accounts was successful at a pretty high level. But she didn't like mathematics. Moreover, she had developed (i.e., *learned*) a disposition to think of mathematics as computing correct answers to problems, not about inventing new medical procedures, designing prosthetic devices to help others, or engineering new vegetable hybrids to synthesize sustainable biofuels. In her mind, mathematics had ceased to be *instrumental* to her life goals and aspirations.

If we examine Breanna's high school experiences, we see that her beliefs fit the message she had been given. Her teachers emphasized correct answers, so she tailored her motivational set to give them correct answers. Her geometry teacher discouraged extensive writing in proofs, so Breanna tailored her motivation to devalue writing. Mathematics class appeared, in this instance, to be just another one of those hoops you jump through to get to college so you can do what you really want to do in life.

When Breanna got to college, she found the norms and expectations in her precalculus class quite different from those set by her high school teachers. Mathematics became more than correct answers. Unlike Breanna's high school teachers, her university instructor valued written documentation of her solution methods and written arguments regarding the logic of her approaches to problem solving. What happened when Breanna first confronted these new rules and expectations is not atypical. She first became confused, then frustrated and maybe a bit angry. She thought the teacher was playing with her mind. It wasn't fair. It was all stupid. But Breanna had a good core *academic self-concept*. She believed she was smart and capable. She believed that *hard work* would both help her be successful and demonstrate to her teacher that she was smart and successful. The extent to which she came to see mathematics as instrumental for bioengineering wasn't clear, but her instructor clearly inspired her enough to change her career aspirations to include mathematics teaching as a viable option.

In Breanna's instance, we see how students' motivations are *adaptive*. They help us *anticipate* the appropriate kinds of behaviors we need to bring to a situation, *initiate* new behaviors to fit the situation, and *regulate* our behaviors to insure our success. Although Breanna's story is a positive one, less positive outcomes can happen. Students can also *anticipate* behaviors that they don't want to do, *initiate* avoidance behaviors, and *regulate* their actions by keeping an eye out so that they *don't* get put in mathematical situations again. Both are examples of adaptive behavior. The first is perhaps more socially desirable, but the second clearly helps students who have had bad experiences in mathematics avoid continued frustration and failure.

The thought that we take away from Breanna's situation is that motivations allow us to regulate our actions in the world, seek out positive opportunities, and avoid potentially negative ones. They work in the short term by monitoring our performance as we immerse ourselves in tasks, and they provide general templates by which we can see our immediate actions as contributing to longer-term life goals and values (Miller and Brickman 2004).

But why be concerned about students' ability to self-regulate? Why not just worry about their mathematical knowledge and understanding? After all, Breanna would most likely have ended up just fine with her level of skill, regardless of whether or not she liked her mathematics classes.

Adaptive Expertise

Motivation's adaptive function is not just an interesting aside in mathematics education. Given the kinds of changes in science, engineering, economics and other mathematically intensive fields, we need to develop a new kind of mathematical student. Giyoo Hatano in 1982 anticipated this change and announced that schooling needed to foster a different kind of expertise in students. He labeled this *adaptive expertise* to differentiate it from just plain ability to do what you have been taught. Adaptive expertise is characterized by knowledge that is *organized* around the fundamental concepts and principles of the discipline. It is not just a list of facts and rules. Adaptive experts' knowledge allows them to see things in new, *creative* ways. Moreover, adaptive experts have knowledge *applicable* across different domains, and they have the *disposition* to apply it—to transfer their knowledge to solve important problems (Pandy et al. 2004).

It is to these dispositions that motivation most readily applies. DeCorte (2007) argued that adaptive expertise involves several additional types of knowledge: *metacognitive knowledge*, such as knowing that one's intelligence can be augmented through learning and effort; *metavolitional knowledge*, being aware that one is has fears and frustrations around mathematics or that one loves geometry; *positive mathematics-related beliefs*, stressing mathematics as valuable and interesting, and *self-regulatory skills*, such as planning, monitoring, and persistence.

Motivation is implied three ways in the goal of helping students develop adaptive expertise. The first concerns why one learns subject matter in the first place. One can see mathematics as a hoop to jump through, as Breanna did in high school; a barrier; or an obstacle to overcome. Alternatively, one can see it as a set of skills to be mastered, some of which will be instrumental to one's future career or life goals. But we can also see mathematics as a way of thinking about patterns in the world, as part and parcel of an engineer's mindset or of a businesslike approach to administration. Any number of desirable jobs can use mathematics, but a mathematical mindset or disposition can transform one's job into a creative, productive life's work. Positive, mathematics-related beliefs can direct students' attempts at self-regulation. When we feel positively toward a pursuit, we will try to motivate ourselves to work through some of the small frustrations for the larger goal of developing understanding and expertise.

The second implication of motivation for developing adaptive expertise lies in the notion that we develop general beliefs about the world and what is important. In chapter 2, we discussed how our *interests* shape whether or not we judge available tasks as worthwhile for expending effort. Here, we broaden this concept to include other kinds of *values*, such as *being a good person*, *having a family*, and *technology helps me do my job*. Because interests define who we are to a great extent, we can see them as very important for establishing academic and professional goals. They constitute much of our metavolitional knowledge. But these broader values are also crucial for channeling our thoughts and actions into a reasonably consistent, coherent *self concept* (Harackiewicz and Sansone 1991, 2000). We can see that all our goals derive from our values as our best guesses at how to make our values real in our lives. Mathematics may seem somewhat removed from most people's values, but when we factor in the importance of interests and mathematics's perceived instrumentality to those interests, we can see that we *can* position mathematics within our goals, and that if we can, then we *can* enhance our broader values by developing adaptive expertise in mathematics. So, developing a positive mathematical self-concept is crucial for students to engage in mathematics willingly over the long haul. It is a necessary, but not sufficient, condition for persistence and choices of advanced mathematics coursework and career.

Academic Self-Efficacy

Most learning in life is not guided by a teacher, but is instead self-directed (de Corte 2007). If we examine school mathematics, we see that students actively make choices about the amount of effort, time, and emotional energy they are willing to spend on mathematics assignments. These choices are results of their self-regulation system.

We have already seen in Breanna that students make choices of what activities to engage in to obtain anticipated and valued outcomes such as interest or social recognition. We have also seen that students choose to avoid activities where they believe their actions will result in frustration, failure, or loss of status. Such outcome expectations are projections of the future—imagined scenarios where they anticipate the outcomes of their actions. They relate strongly to the personal value the outcome has for the individual, and they serve as target goals for constructing strategies (Bandura 1986). It stands to reason that the more valuable the expected outcome is, the more effort students will willingly spend to obtain it. For interests, the more central the interest is to their self-concept, the more likely they will be to seek it out and invest a lot of effort in it. The same could also be said for extrinsic outcomes. The more valuable they consider the outcome (e.g., the more they are being paid to do a job, or the more praise they will likely get from a person they respect), the more likely they will expend effort to obtain it (Miller and Brickman 2004).

But self-regulation involves more than merely creating a hierarchy of outcomes and choosing which ones are most valuable. Students also have abilities, knowledge, skills, and opportunities, such that some outcomes are just more attainable than others. They also must anticipate the outcomes of their actions related to these abilities and opportunities. Sometime in the first century CE, Seneca wrote, "Luck is what happens when preparation meets opportunity." Human beings apparently try naturally to bolster their "luck" by evaluating the opportunities that present themselves relative to their perceived abilities. Researchers often call our ability perceptions *self-efficacy* (Bandura 1993).

Briefly, self-efficacy is our personal view of our ability to affect our future. People need generally efficacious beliefs to have an optimistic perspective on life. Academically, students need to believe that their efforts will produce increased learning, skill improvement, and positive social outcomes (Usher and Pajares 2008). We use four sources of information to help us create these beliefs. The first and most important source of information we use is what Bandura (1997) called *mastery experiences*. When we engage in challenging tasks, overcome obstacles, and gain significant knowledge and skill, we tend to chalk up our efficacy for the domain that includes the task. In our mathematics example, Breanna experienced continual success in high-level mathematics, and as a consequence, she rightfully believed that she could be successful in anything mathematical if she only worked hard at it. The lesson here is that the tasks must be *challenging* (i.e., they must have value and potential interest-level), students must expend *effort* (i.e., make a personal investment of time and energy to increase their sense of *control*), and they must experience success *because* of their expenditure of effort (i.e., their mastery can't just be considered a fluke or random chance). If the task is so challenging that all the hard work a student invests *can't* pay off, perhaps because the content is just too advanced for the student's current level of understanding and skill, it can seriously undermine efficacy, and learned helplessness can result.

A second source of information from which we construct our self-efficacy beliefs is what Bandura called *vicarious experiences*. We don't actually have to engage in a task to make an educated guess about whether or not we would be successful. We can observe others and make some predictions about our own success based on (1) our perceived similarities with them and (2) the perceived competence of the person being observed. Having a successful *role model* with whom a student identifies can be a pivotal motivator, showing them that they also can succeed. Moreover, by watching another person solve a particularly hard mathematical problem, for example, students can "appropriate" (you might use the word *borrow* or *steal*) the problem solver's solution strategy. This gives students a new ability that further increases their probability of success. If students perceive the role model as competent, they will tend to steal the role model's ideas in order to become competent themselves. Often we have students in our classes share their strategies for solving mathematical problems. We do this to allow struggling students to see different strategies they can use. But an additional benefit of such discourse is for students to see that other students, who are just like them in most attributes, are successful, so they can succeed as well. Students in a community learn to identify with the community, and they take on the efficacy beliefs of the community by and large by observing others and through the messages they receive from teachers and their peers (Dorman 2006). We learn from one another this way all the time, by example.

The third kind of information we use to build our self-efficacy beliefs is the *encouragement and support* we receive from others. Exhortation, if we direct it at a realistic goal, really does induce a student to expend more effort. The *effort*, not the exhortation, causes students to be successful, but the students may not expend the effort without the exhortation, particularly if the students have not had a history of success in an area (i.e., their self-efficacy beliefs are low). Moreover, as we shall see when we look at chapter 7, students' efficacy must be directed at personal growth and learning and not on social comparison against others. If our success depends on beating others, then much of the time we cannot consider ourselves successful, and that will undermine our efficacy severely (Wolters 2004).

Lastly, like interest, efficacy is affected by *psychological and physiological states*. When we are tired, we just don't perform as well as when we are fresh. When we are discouraged, we have difficulty building up our confidence to expend the necessary effort. The advice of "wait a bit and get some rest" is often good counsel. We can rejoin the activity with renewed enthusiasm and energy. If, however, lack of nutrition, poor study and sleep habits, or other nonacademic distracters have students continually tired or depressed, their ability to perform well can be undermined and their resulting efficacy diminished.

Positive self-efficacy correlates strongly with students' academic achievement (Pajares and Miller 1994; Multon, Brown, and Lent 1991). Motivationally, beliefs that one has moderately high competence and skills associate with higher value for academic tasks, lower mathematics anxiety, better and more productive academic goals, optimism, and an overall better self-concept. Cognitively, students with higher self-efficacy engage in metacognitive behaviors like productive help-seeking, time management, and self-evaluation of their progress more than students with lower self-efficacy. Lastly, students with high self-efficacy are more efficient problem solvers, are more persistent, and tend to seek out challenge more than students with low self-efficacy (Schunk and Pajares 2005). Mathematics self-efficacy has shown relation to students' taking higher mathematics coursework and choosing mathematically intensive careers (Hackett and Betz 1989; Lent et al. 2008).

"Ah," you are saying. "Doesn't this create a vicious cycle in some students? Won't low self-efficacy lead a poor student to choose less challenging tasks, which will reduce their ability to be successful, thus reducing their self-efficacy?" If self-efficacy is a major template by which we regulate our actions, this vicious cycle has to be a possibility. In fact, to preserve a sense of efficacy, students will often make such self-defeating choices, ultimately removing them from the possibility of experiencing any meaningful success in mathematics.

Summary

One of the primary goals of mathematics education should be nurturing adaptive experts. We can see that students adapt inherently to the conditions under which we expect them to perform in the classroom. But what we have failed to do as a field is inspire our students to adapt *using mathematics*. To facilitate developing a positive mathematical self-concept, we need to help students develop positive mathematics-related beliefs and self-regulatory skills.

A key among these beliefs and skills is developing a positive mathematical self-efficacy, the belief that one can be successful in mathematics, and that, by applying effort, one can improve one's performances. Four sources of mathematical self-efficacy exist: (1) experiences where we achieve success on some moderately challenging task; (2) vicarious experiences, where we watch others perform and judge our own capacity to succeed against their performance; (3) verbal persuasion from the teacher, students, or others in society; and (4) emotional and physiological states during engagement. We, as teachers, can't affect emotional and physiological states directly, but we can (1) think carefully about how we initiate and sustain challenge in the classroom, (2) watch carefully the messages we give to students, and (3) adjust our actions to model the kinds of affect and engagement we expect from our students. The result will be a productive classroom environment in which students can adapt their values and content knowledge—the will *and* the skill—to learning and applying mathematics now and in their future.

References

Bandura, Albert. *Social Foundations of Thought and Action: A Social Cognitive Theory.* Englewood Cliffs, N.J.: Prentice-Hall, 1986.

———. "Perceived Self-Efficacy in Cognitive Development and Functioning." *Educational Psychologist* 28, no. 2 (1993): 117–48.

———. *Self-Efficacy: The Exercise of Control.* New York: W. H. Freeman, 1997.

De Corte, Erik. "Learning from Instruction: The Case of Mathematics." *Learning Inquiry* 1, no. 1 (March 2007): 19–30.

Dorman, Jeffrey P. "Associations between Classroom Environment and Academic Efficacy." *Learning Environments Research* 4, no. 3 (2006): 243–57.

Hackett, Gail, and Nancy E. Betz. "An Exploration of the Mathematics Self-Efficacy/Mathematics Performance Correspondence." *Journal for Research in Mathematics Education* 20, no. 3 (May 1989): 261–73.

Harackiewicz, Judith M., and Carol Sansone. "Goals and Intrinsic Motivation: You Can Get There from Here." In *Advances in Motivation and Achievement*, vol. 7, edited by Martin L. Maehr and Paul R. Pintrich, pp. 21–49. Greenwich, Conn.: JAI Press, 1991.

———. "Rewarding Competence: The Importance of Goals in the Study of Intrinsic Motivation." In *Intrinsic and Extrinsic Motivation: The Search for Optimal Motivation and Performance*, edited by Carol Sansone and Judith M. Harackiewicz, pp. 79–103. New York: Academic Press, 2000.

Lent, Robert W., Hung-Bin Sheu, Daniel Singley, Janet A. Schmidt, Linda C. Schmidt, and Clay S. Gloster. "Longitudinal Relations of Self-Efficacy to Outcome Expectations, Interests, and Major Choice Goals in Engineering Students." *Journal of Vocational Behavior* 73, no. 2 (October 2008): 328–35.

Miller, Raymond B., and Stephanie J. Brickman. "A Model of Future-Oriented Motivation and Self-Regulation." *Educational Psychology Review* 16, no. 1 (March 2004): 9–33.

Multon, Karen D., Stephen D. Brown, and Robert W. Lent. "Relation of Self-Efficacy Beliefs to Academic Outcomes: A Meta-Analytic Investigation." *Journal of Counseling Psychology* 38, no. 1 (January 1991): 30–38.

Pajares, Frank, and M. David Miller. "Role of Self-Efficacy and Self-Concept Beliefs in Mathematical Problem Solving: A Path Analysis." *Journal of Educational Psychology* 86, no. 2 (June 1994): 193–203.

Pandy, Marcus G., Anthony J. Petrosino, Barbara A. Austin, and Ronald E. Barr. "Assessing Adaptive Expertise in Undergraduate Biomechanics." *Journal of Engineering Education* 93, no. 3 (July 2004): 1–12.

Schunk, Dale H., and Frank Pajares. "Competence Perceptions and Academic Functioning." In *Handbook of Competence and Motivation,* edited by Andrew J. Elliot and Carol S. Dweck, pp. 85–104. New York: Guilford Press, 2005.

Usher, Ellen L., and Frank Pajares. "Sources of Self-Efficacy in School: Critical Review of the Literature and Future Directions." *Review of Educational Research* 78 (2008): 751–96.

Wolters, Christopher A. "Advancing Achievement Goal Theory: Using Goal Structures and Goal Orientations to Predict Students' Motivation, Cognition, and Achievement." *Journal of Educational Psychology* 96, no. 2 (June 2004): 236–50.

CHAPTER 4

Motivation Is in the Moment

*Whether or not students appear to be motivated depends on what we ask them to do. Students may appear to be more motivated in some situations over others. Rachel's story illustrates this idea. Her story comes from research done on using stories to situate mathematics curriculum (Middleton and Roodhardt 1997). The story problem's context, redistricting, generally but not universally interested the students. We changed the context from seventh grade to high school Algebra 2 because that is when linear programming most often appears as a topic. The take-away idea from this chapter is that teachers can construct classroom situations that motivate students more, and we should not assume that we cannot ever motivate students if they sometimes appear to lack motivation. Stating this positively, we **must** assume that we **can** motivate students, even when they appear listless, bored, or distracted, because these behaviors are momentary and adjusting norms and practice can have a dramatic effect on students' interest.*

Rachel began Algebra 2 with a bad attitude. She had done well in Algebra 1 and geometry, but mathematics had become successively less interesting over the years. She just didn't care about *x* and *y*. The relationships they got into were not nearly as interesting as those of biology or history. Mathematics held little meaning for her. As a result, she received average grades, did enough to get by, but never went beyond the assigned work and rarely showed any enthusiasm for class discussions.

In Algebra 2, after a week or so of review, she was ready to resign herself to the fact that math was just not her thing. It was something she had to get through if she wanted to go to college, but if she could avoid math after high school, she would. She was hoping to major in political science, because she had an interest in human rights legislation. In week 3, Mr. Iverson, the algebra teacher, said that they were going to learn linear programming. Rachel was not impressed. The words sounded like some computer thing, and that was even worse, if you can imagine it, than math.

But it wasn't computer programming. It was using linear systems to help make decisions regarding plans' feasibility under different, often competing constraints. What got her interested wasn't the linear programming itself, but the topic to which it was applied. The class started the unit focusing on a story about how an urban center and a suburban town were fighting over how to redistrict some vacant acreage that lay between the two communities. The urban community wanted to build multifamily, high-rise condominiums, whereas the suburban community wanted single-family homes. Neither side wanted to budge, but both recognized that the only way to get past their impasse was to compromise. High-rise condos were cheaper per family unit and had a smaller overall footprint per person. Single-family homes were more expensive per family unit and had a greater footprint. To complicate things, for the land taken up by each house built, condos could be built to accommodate four families. But condos were more expensive to build. What was the optimal mix that would accommodate both sides?

Now *this* was interesting. Rachel had an interest in politics. She was intrigued by the fact that condos had a better environmental profile and were more affordable for poor families, but she liked living in a detached house with her family. Using linear programming, she could graph the different plans, determine where the linear systems intersected, and examine those plans that were feasible for both sides. After choosing the plan that was the best compromise given her group's specifications, she arranged for her group to come to her father's workshop and build a scale model of their plan to present to the class.

After the presentation, Mr. Iverson met with Rachel's parents. He remarked, much to their surprise, "Rachel is an amazing student. She is self-motivated and a leader, helping others in the class understand the material. Her group's scale model showed that she fully understood the mathematics and its application."

Situational Interest

Rachel is probably a typical student in Algebra 2, viewing mathematics as a necessary evil as opposed to a personal interest. Most students in high school will admit that mathematics is important to get into college and to obtain a higher-paying job, but most will also admit that they personally believe that mathematics isn't important *for them*. After all, many college majors only require one mathematics course—College Algebra, or its equivalent—and the prevailing rhetoric about algebra is that no one ever really uses it in real life. To set a pedagogical goal for all our students to develop mathematics as a personal, long-term interest is pretty ambitious. It would require concerted effort from each and every teacher children encounter in their school career. But even if this goal is impractical, we can each set the goal for our students to see mathematics as personally relevant by helping them learn mathematics in useful contexts that tap into their established interests. Doing so is important for two reasons. The first is that we teach mathematics as a school subject *because* it is useful. Emphasizing this usefulness and developing important skills is necessary so that students can apply mathematics now and in their future careers. The second reason concerns how we adapt to circumstances. We devote more time, attention, and cognitive resources to situations that pique our interest. We actually think better when tasks have personal relevance, novelty, and utility.

In chapter 3 we discussed how motivation is adaptive—an evolved way of processing information that orients us toward engaging in activities beneficial to us, or at least to minimize any psychological damage our engagement may engender. We can see that the choices students make to become interested or to disengage are adaptive responses. Such responses maximize students' enjoyment and minimize their discomfort at any moment, given the various opportunities and difficulties life might throw at them. In chapter 2, we examined interests in particular as important determinants of the choices students make. We showed how we could encourage interest by developing challenge while at the same time allowing students appropriate personal control over their involvement in academic tasks. Over the long haul, we can expect students' attitudes—their long-term values related to academic subject matter—to become stable, predictable orientations.

But students live and learn *in the moment*. Each learning opportunity is unique, giving the student varying degrees of challenge and control or differentially addressing their interests and expertise. Of course, most classes will develop routines and norms that allow students to function smoothly, most mathematics texts have a predictable format for presenting concepts and exercises, and students will use a standard set of representations and symbols in their studies that distinguishes mathematics from other subjects. But in spite of all this standardization, some moments are just better than others. What explains this? Sometimes a discussion turns on the most recalcitrant students in the class and reveals that they are not as disengaged as the teacher has come to expect. Likewise, sometimes the most diligent student becomes distracted and bored. These momentary variations that we see can give us hope that we can make a difference as teachers. Through careful instructional design, appropriate feedback and attention to students, or the management of a discussion to incorporate input from a variety of learners, we can change students' learning experiences from neutral or negative to positive.

These positive moments are crucial in our development as learners. We use them as inspiration to pursue future goals and direct our actions so that we can experience more of the good than the bad. The negative moments are also crucial. People who avoid advanced mathematics in high school and college, and who avoid mathematics-related careers, tend to recall specific instances where they decided, once and for all, to avoid mathematics (Hackett 1995).

Researchers have coined the term *situational interest* for this phenomenon, by which we mean a short-lived, emotional urge to approach or avoid specific characteristics of an event in a specific circumstance (Murphy and Alexander 2000; Krapp 2002; Hidi 1990; Schiefele 1991). Situational interest, then, is a peculiar relationship between a person and a task, which is typically characterized by positive emotional experiences and feelings of personal relevance. Although we almost always characterize situational interest as positive, we would like to stress that it resembles more a continuum by which we can assess an activity's fit to an individual's immediate needs. So a person's situational interest can possibly be low as opposed to high, indicating that they are less than enamored with the prospect of engagement. Situational interest contrasts with the more long-term, individual interest we discussed in chapter 2 because of this time-and-topic specificity. The two interact significantly in that we can use the set of long-term interests students bring to the class as contexts for building situational interest in a topic with which students do not yet have experience (Middleton and Toluk 1999). Over time, as students develop situational interests in a variety of similar topics and circumstances, those situational interests can become long-term, stable attitudes across varying situations (Bergin 1999; Pintrich and Schunk 2002). So how can teachers encourage their students to develop situational interest in mathematics?

Suzanne Hidi (1990), one of the leaders in interest research, identified two classes of task characteristics that contribute to situational interest. The first class consists of the activity's general organization, including factors such as the degree of novelty, intensity, or ambiguity a task holds. These characteristics are factors of almost any task one might engage in, and they thus make good design parameters for selecting and modifying classroom tasks to enhance interest. The second class consists of content features such as human activity, life themes, and the degree of overlap the task parameters have with students' individual interests. Situational interest is particularly important for the teacher confronted with students who have no particular interest in the topic at hand, like Rachel in our story. Tapping into themes proven to interest students of a particular age or culture and introducing novelty and intensity enhance the possibility for developing situational interest and, along with it, the benefits of interest, which include enhanced cognitive processing of the material, persistence, and enjoyment. With some degree of situational interest under their belts, students *can* develop more long-term individual interests in the mathematics (Bergin 1999; Ainley, Hidi, and Berndorff 2002).

In a research study examining students' learning expository text, Ainley, Hidi, and Berndorff (2002) found that interest in the topic being read about contributed to an emotional response to the topic. This affective reaction influenced students' persistence; when they liked the topic, they tended to spend more time and effort learning the material. This persistence increased learning (Krapp 2002). The lesson we can take from this study, although not directly related to mathematics teaching and learning, regards how powerful a problem's context is for students. Choosing appropriate, interesting topics in which to situate mathematics instruction is crucial to getting buy-in from students. The more relevant the topics, the more situational interest students will exhibit.

We can also state that meaningfully applied contexts offer cognitive benefits apart from motivation, among them increased retention and transferability of concepts and critical thinking skills (Bransford and Schwartz 1999). Moreover, Ainley, Hidi, and Berndorff's (2002) study shows us that emotions play a unique role in helping human beings manage their motivations. We use emotions to encourage ourselves to achieve, reward ourselves for a triumph, or escape some potential disappointment.

Goal Theory and Situational Interest

Throughout this document, we emphasize using *learning goals* over *performance* or *ego goals*, partly because setting goals orients behavior to a task's most relevant, important aspects. Having set specific, challenging learning goals regarding the learning moment, students tend to display more interest in the task (Locke and Bryan 1967). An example of this occurred in a fifth-grade class. The students were learning the logic behind the traditional long-division algorithm. The teacher worked with them first, discussing the distributive property, and helped them develop a goal for learning how the distributive property helps them solve multidigit division problems. With this specific learning goal in hand, the students began, using the principle of distributivity, to split the dividend into easily divisible chunks (see fig. 4.1 for a typical example). The students used this goal to focus on ways to split the dividend, 1039, easily into simple multiples of the divisor, 56. Their proof shows that they conceived of the division through their understanding of the distributive property and could state their answer as a multiplication problem, also using the distributive property.

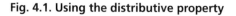

18 31/56

56	1039	
	560	10
	280	5
	840	15
	168	3
	1008	18

31 Left

Proof:

$$56 \cdot (10 + 5 + 3 + 31/56) = 1039$$
$$(560 + 280 + 168 + 31) = 1039$$

Fig. 4.1. Using the distributive property

The affect that students displayed was not uniformly positive. But as students focused on the goal of figuring out how the distributive property applied to long division, they began to see, and their teacher encouraged them to see, that they could choose any easy multiple of the divisor so long as they kept a running record of the cumulative total they were building. *This* provoked situational interest. In the end, the quotient was merely the sum of the factors they had chosen! Now—unlike Rachel's situation, where the context provided the situational interest—the personal relevance became focused on how the students could easily solve any division problem using remembered facts. As if to prove the point, students' solution strategies to this problem differed; some groups used multiples of 2 and then 1, and some tried to split the remainder, 31, into 1/2 (28/56) plus an additional 3/56. Having a specific learning goal focused on discovering the logic behind what was heretofore a rote-memorized procedure clearly enhanced the class's general demeanor, engagement, and resulting learning.

In the research literature, we find that learning goal orientations consistently predict students' task-specific interest and their subsequent enjoyment (Harackiewicz et al. 2000, 2002). Does this mean that all students will do backflips when asked to examine long division? Of course not! But this does say that *most* students will see *more* relevance to their mathematical activity, and they will subsequently show *more* interest and *more* enjoyment. This helps students engage more deeply in the task, giving the opportunity to discover an activity's pleasurable aspects. Again, the more personal importance students accord to tasks, the more situational interest the tasks generate (Czikszentmihalyi 1997).

Phases of Interest Development

Ann Renninger (2009) provides an excellent framework that summarizes the research that we can use for understanding the progression students undergo as they move from situational interest to what she calls *well-developed individual interest*. She presents four phases students go through. We will use Rachel's case throughout this section to illustrate how students' motivations in the moment can cumulate and grow into long-term, productive attitudes. Also, Renninger's model is a general one, applicable to many content domains. For practical purposes, we focus our discussion on developing mathematical interest.

Phase 1: Triggered Situational Interest

Renninger characterizes the first phase of students' interest development, *triggered situational interest*, by students' attention being devoted to how interesting the context or topic is instead of to the activity's actual content, which is the teacher's goal for instruction. Students do attend to content during this phase, but their attention is often fleeting or undifferentiated. For example, Rachel may have found it difficult to separate linear programming's mathematical content from the context of urban planning. This is understandable. In this first stage, Rachel may not have had enough knowledge to identify other situations where linear programming would apply, or she may not have even understood that linear programming is a generalizable technique.

To help them develop situational interest, students need support from others. Rachel received support from her group, her teacher, and her parents in pursuing her situational interest. Students also need to receive support from the instructional design. We can teach linear programming as a set of concepts and skills isolated from urban planning, economics, optimization, and other applications. But, as we see in Rachel's case, the context really did matter. She would not have developed interest had Mr. Iverson not selected a situation that appealed to his students. Students may develop both positive and negative feelings as they negotiate their interest in the context and—perhaps—their reticence to engage in difficult mathematics, and they may not even be conscious of the fact that the two feelings conflict. The teacher's role in this instance is to respect the students' ideas and help them gain an appreciation for mathematics's usefulness for helping students pursue these ideas.

Phase 2: Maintained Situational Interest

The second phase in interest development is what Renninger calls *maintained situational interest*. This phase re-engages students with content associated with their previously triggered interest. Rachel's teacher might take what Rachel learned from linear programming, for example, and use that context to teach systems of linear equations. In that instance, the teacher could extend the triggered situational interest developed in the urban planning context to other areas, such as determining the costs and benefits of different economic policies or examining the benefits and constraints for installing third-generation solar collectors. The teacher could extend the interest Rachel displayed in her first encounter with linear programming to both these new contexts, as well as to the new mathematical content that those contexts will teach.

Rachel needed help in this phase actually making those connections. The teacher could help her actively explore the connections between her personal interests and the applications to which she could apply the linear systems. Additionally, because Rachel is beginning to see the mathematics as productive in this phase—that is, as contributing to her enjoyment of learning and growth in knowledge about things she cares about—she develops a sense of the content's value, both to society and to herself. Lastly, in part because of this interest, Rachel will develop more positive feelings toward the content, persist in learning the content, and ultimately learn more and achieve better. Concrete suggestions here from the teacher will help orient her to contexts and pursuits that align with her interests, as well as pointers on how to see situations where the mathematics she is learning can apply productively.

Phase 3: Emerging Individual Interest

In the third phase of interest development, students begin to see mathematics as being relevant to their lives. They will likely re-engage with the content itself when they see opportunity for its application, develop questions regarding the content and its application because they are genuinely curious, and build some knowledge and skills that make them more efficacious mathematically. But they may still focus on their own questions of interest as opposed to those of mathematicians. They have not yet gone over to the "dark side," so to speak, and incorporated mathematics into their personal and professional identity. Mathematics is still just a tool—a useful one that has some interesting aspects, but still just a tool, not a pursuit in and of itself.

This phase can become a tightrope walk for the teacher: students are willing to expend effort when activities support their own interests, but the teacher has Standards and goals of her or his own. Let us say that Rachel has moved to this third stage. She is still reluctant to admit that mathematics interests her at times, but she has developed an appreciation for its utility to help her pursue her interests. The teacher must both continue to support this position and introduce new mathematics that makes the whole of Rachel's knowledge more powerful. One of the techniques the first author uses with teachers is to help them step back and look at how the mathematics they have been using all fits together into a coherent whole. Teachers are often amazed that skills they learned as discrete rules are in fact only instances of larger, more interesting, broadly applicable concepts. Like the fifth-grade students in our example of long division stepping back to look at the distributive property—or like Rachel, who now has to think about systems of linear equations more formally— the coherence and connectedness of the mathematics students have learned can motivate them in and of itself at times.

Phase 4. Well-Developed Individual Interest

If your students have progressed to this fourth stage, you have a different set of challenges before you than we currently tend to struggle with. With well-developed individual interests, students independently seek out mathematical activities. They self-regulate to motivate themselves through difficult challenges, displaying persistence both in a task and across tasks in the domain. They deal with frustration positively, applying effort, and they actively seek feedback so that they can improve. Curiosity, creativity, and quantity of questions are this phase's hallmarks. We all get a student or two periodically who displays these characteristics. With just one or two, we can usually manage by providing extra challenge or steering them to advanced topics or enrichment activities. If Mr. Iverson helps Rachel develop to this level, even if it is for a narrow band of mathematics, she will have not only the mathematical knowledge and skills to be successful in her chosen field of political science, but also the attitude and discipline to go into a host of other fields, some mathematically sophisticated and others less so.

But what would happen if Mr. Iverson's class had five or six Rachels? How could he manage this? We really don't know. The first author had this unique problem with a dozen or so students when they first used the basics of linear programming to think about urban contexts. They just couldn't get enough. He tried writing problems using different scenarios. The students came back with answers. He tried writing problems with seven or eight interacting constraints. Ditto. The seventh- and eighth-grade students he was working with ended up doing high school–level systems of inequalities as a matter of course. The only thing that saved him was that, after a month of work, the class had to go on to other topics. And, at that time, the students' motivation stayed generally high. He did not, however, get the same level of situational interest in a unit on regular polyhedra (*sigh*).

Needless to say, we should set our goals for developing students' interest high. What would happen if students actualized those goals every time is unclear— probably something very, very good. But, in the meantime, we can think of each of these phases as positive in its own right, serving as a potential springboard for developing mathematical interest over a relatively long time.

A Quick Homily

We hope that you have caught our intent in this chapter to illustrate that situational interest, and through it individual interest, develops best in school mathematics through careful instructional design. Interest is too important a variable in predicting future life courses for us to leave it completely to chance. We will speak more about the teacher's role in developing interests in the second section of this book, in chapter 11. But, in the meantime, remember this: students can only learn in the moment. No other moment but now exists. How will you organize and tailor this moment to be worthy of the intellect and potential that each student brings to the learning situation? Rachel is in your class right now. What will you do for her?

References

Ainley, Mary, Suzanne Hidi, and Dagmar Berndorff. "Interest, Learning, and the Psychological Processes That Mediate Their Relationship." *Journal of Educational Psychology* 94, no. 3 (September 2002): 545–61.

Bergin, David A. "Influences on Classroom Interest." *Educational Psychologist* 34, no. 2 (March 1999): 87–98.

Bransford, John D., and Dan L. Schwartz. "Rethinking Transfer: A Simple Proposal with Multiple Implications." *Review of Research in Education* 24 (January 1999): 61–100.

Czikszentmihalyi, Mihaly. *Finding Flow: The Psychology of Engagement with Everyday Life.* New York: Basic Books, 1997.

Hackett, Gail. "Self-Efficacy in Career Choice and Development." In *Self-Efficacy and Changing Societies,* edited by Albert Bandura, pp. 232–58. New York: Cambridge University Press, 1995.

Harackiewicz, Judith M., Kenneth E. Barron, John M. Tauer, and Andrew J. Elliot. "Predicting Success in College: A Longitudinal Study of Achievement Goals and Ability Measures as Predictors of Interest and Performance from Freshman Year through Graduation." *Journal of Educational Psychology* 94 (September 2002): 562–75.

Harackiewicz, Judith M., Kenneth E. Barron, John M. Tauer, Suzanne M. Carter, and Andrew J. Elliot. "Short-Term and Long-Term Consequences of Achievement Goals: Predicting Interest and Performance over Time." *Journal of Educational Psychology* 92 (June 2000): 316–30.

Hidi, Suzanne. "Interest and Its Contribution as a Mental Resource for Learning." *Review of Educational Research* 60, no. 4 (Winter 1990): 549–71.

Krapp, Andreas. "An Educational-Psychological Theory of Interest and Its Relation to SDT." In *Handbook of Self-Determination Research,* edited by Edward L. Deci and Richard M. Ryan, pp. 405–27. Rochester, N.Y.: University of Rochester Press, 2002.

Locke, Edwin A., and Judith F. Bryan. "Performance Goals as Determinants of Level of Performance and Boredom." *Journal of Applied Psychology* 51, no. 2 (April 1967): 120–30.

Middleton, James A., and Anton Roodhardt. "Using Knowledge of Story Schemas to Structure Mathematical Activity." *Current Issues in Middle Level Education* 6, no. 1 (1997): 40–55.

Middleton, James A., and Zulbiye Toluk. "First Steps in the Development of an Adaptive, Decision-Making Theory of Motivation." *Educational Psychologist* 34, no. 2 (1999): 99–112.

Murphy, P. Karen, and Patricia A. Alexander. "A Motivated Exploration of Motivation Terminology." *Contemporary Educational Psychology* 25 (2000): 3–53.

Pintrich, Paul R., and Dale Schunk. *Motivation in Education: Theory, Research, and Applications.* 2nd ed. Upper Saddle River, N.J.: Prentice Hall, 2002.

Renninger, K. Ann. "Interest and Identity Development in Instruction: An Inductive Model." *Educational Psychologist* 44, no. 2 (2009): 105–18.

Schiefele, Ulrich. "Interest, Learning, and Motivation." *Educational Psychologist* 26 (1991): 299–323.

CHAPTER 5

Motivation Creates
Long-Term Attitudes

The story below describes a group of high school students as they discuss how they think about themselves as mathematics learners. They share how their experiences in school mathematics classes affect how they think about themselves as learners, and they share implications for their future, long-term career paths. The students in this story represent high school students that Mandy followed through their first two-and-a-half years of high school as a part of a research project (Smith and Star 2007; Star, Smith, and Jansen 2008). The research project's purpose was to study students' experiences in their transition into high school and college mathematics programs. The students at this high school had come from a middle school where their teachers used the Connected Mathematics Project (Lappan et al. 1997). The high school's teachers used more conventional materials. Many of the students preferred their middle school's mathematics program, but some of the students preferred the high school's. The students at this site inspired the story's ideas. The story illustrates how experiences in school can influence how students think about themselves as mathematics learners, and, in turn, how longer-term attitudes toward mathematics can affect students' futures.

The bell rang, dismissing students to second lunch at Two Rivers High School. Brianna, Jordan, Kelsey, and Tanisha left their mathematics classroom together to walk to the cafeteria. Jordan held up his math quiz to share his grade with his friends.

"Another quiz, another C for me. I'm so tired of feeling like I can't do this stuff. I used to be good at math. Now I'm a failure." Jordan shoved his quiz into his backpack.

Brianna said, "The last time I checked, a C wasn't a failing grade."

"It might as well be," Jordan replied. "I just don't understand this stuff anymore. And on top of this quiz grade, I have an appointment with my counselor this afternoon. I know we all have to go to these meetings, but I really don't feel like going to see my counselor about that career aptitude test that we had to take in English."

They got in line to order their food for lunch. Kelsey said, "Oh, our English teacher gave us that career assessment thing, too. I think all the juniors have to take it. That's what Ms. Hernandez said."

"I answered the questions so differently than I think I would have answered them in middle school," Jordan said.

"Me, too," Kelsey nodded.

Tanisha said, "Mine probably wouldn't be too different."

"I have trouble thinking that far ahead," Brianna contributed. "I mean, I like thinking about and doing so many different things. I can't imagine trying to narrow down ideas for a future job. I haven't even thought very much about college at this point."

"I don't even want to think about it," Jordan said.

Kelsey glanced up quickly at Jordan as she put away her money, gathered her food from the counter, and said, "Well, we kind of should think about it. I'm excited about college, actually. Let's find a place to sit."

Once they found a table in the cafeteria, Brianna turned to Jordan and said, "Are you really that upset about your math quiz? I mean, it's just one grade. You can make it up. You can go for after-school help. We can study together. You can do this."

Jordan sat quietly for a minute and ate a few fries. Then he said, "You know, I don't even know if I can do it. I am starting to think that I'm just not a math person."

"What do you mean? For one thing, we all remember that you were so into math a few years ago, back in middle school," Tanisha said.

"Yeah, I was there, too," Brianna said. "You can't act like that didn't happen. You sure did seem like a math person then."

Jordan replied, "Maybe it was just the teacher."

"You mean back in junior high? Back in eighth grade? I had Mr. Jameson, and you all had Ms. Donavan," Kelsey said. "We all heard that Ms. D was the best math teacher. Mr. Jameson was pretty good, but everyone who had Ms. D seemed to really love math."

Brianna lit up at the very mention of Ms. D. "Oh! I still go visit Ms. D sometimes after school. She's my favorite teacher of all time."

"Remember how she would let us instant message her?" Jordan asked.

Brianna laughed. "Remember?! I was just chatting with her last night! I was really annoyed at our math teacher yesterday, and I thought she'd cheer me up. I mean, math seems so boring lately, and Ms. D really made things fun. She would ask us what we thought. She would ask us for our own strategies. Our teacher now? He doesn't even care what we think about the problems. I'm so bored in class this year by the way the teacher just talks at us the whole time. I mean, let me try the problem myself, you know? Let me see if I can come up with another solution. But no. The teacher doesn't ask us for other ways to solve the problems like Ms. D did. Last night, Ms. D told me to hang in there, and she said that math could get cooler and more interesting as we take different classes, and she reminded me that different teachers have different approaches. I mean, Mr. J wasn't like Ms. D, either. She kept saying that she couldn't wait to see what I thought about calculus next year."

Jordan said, "I'm done with math. I mean, if it were totally up to me, I wouldn't take calculus next year. I'm tired of feeling this dumb. My parents want me to go to college, but I don't really care anymore. I used to want to be an engineer. But why? Wouldn't I make enough money if I got an apprenticeship and went into tool and die?"

Tanisha said, "Well, my uncle does that, and, yeah, he makes money, but there is math involved with that, too. Are you sure that you're not interested in college anymore?"

Jordan sighed. "I don't know what I'm interested in."

"You need to know math for a lot of jobs. You might as well keep taking math classes. If you don't know what you want to do, you might as well take more math just in case. The job you're thinking about now.… Well, there's nothing wrong with it, and you might like it, but if you're not sure about it, it seems like you'd want to give yourself options."

"Well, that's easy for you to say, Tanisha," Jordan replied. "Your quiz grade was fine."

"I guess," Tanisha said. "I mean, for me, it's not really about what grade I get. Sometimes I feel like I understand more than what my grade says, but, for me, I know that this stuff that we're doing is useful. My mom, she's an architect, you know? I want a job like hers. She gets to do fun stuff, like be creative, work with computers, work on teams with other designers, and think about making the buildings good for the environment, as well as cool designs. I know that math is a part of what she does every day. I want to get a degree in architecture, so I am going to keep trying even when I'm having a tough time in one of these chapters in the math book, because I need a good grade in math to get into a good college, and I know that I need to understand this stuff if I am going to be an architect like my mom."

"I used to want to be an accountant or even a math teacher," Kelsey said. "But now I think I don't really like to be around numbers too much. Maybe I still want to be a teacher, but probably a band or music teacher. Well, I mean, I think it could be fun to do something with math, but not if it's like what we're doing now. It used to seem easier, and back in middle school, we were able to work with other people and put our work on the board and talk about it. Now our teacher just talks *at* us, not really *with* us, which is kind of boring to me. Usually when I get bored, I don't try as hard as I should or could. I'm doing okay in math, but I think I could be doing better. I used to think that math was really fun, but now I'm not really sure that it is."

Jordan said, "Yeah, math class with Ms. D was pretty great. She never made me feel like I couldn't do this stuff."

"Well, it's not like our teacher is telling you now that you can't do it. He's not the one telling you that you can't do it. You're the one telling yourself that," Brianna said.

"Yeah, but Ms. D would tell me that I could do it when I would feel like I couldn't. She didn't give up on me. She encouraged me to keep going. I'm not sure that this teacher cares either way."

Tanisha said, "That's not true. Our teacher cares. He always tells us exactly what is going to be on the next quiz. He's always fair about how he assigns partial credit, too. You know what? I actually like math in high school better than in junior high."

"You had Ms. D, right?" Kelsey asked. "Didn't she have everybody do problems on the board? Mr. Jameson would do that, and I wish that I had a teacher now who did that, too. Sometimes the students who put it in their own words can explain it better than what the book or the teacher says. I liked that better."

"All that talking!" Tanisha laughed. "That got old after a while for me. I'd rather just get the assignment and go read the chapter if I have more questions. Just let me get my work done! My high school math classes have been better for me, because we don't spend as much time talking about how everybody solved it. Your way and your way, who cares? I just want the quickest way that works."

"I've heard that Ms. Gordon does have people talk about their work and put their work on the board in her calculus class. I think that's what Ms. D meant when she talked about it getting better in upcoming math classes. I think Ms. Gordon is teaching calculus again next year," Brianna contributed. "So, Kelsey and I will be happier in that class. Jordan, does it help to hear that?"

Tanisha replied instead, "That doesn't help me, but it doesn't really matter, because I know I need to know it, so I'm going to take the class and still do what I need to do to get the grade I want."

"I think that it would be better for me to have a class more like Ms. D's again. If Ms. D vouches for this calculus teacher, maybe I should try to take it. I have a lot of work to do to bring my grade up so I can be ready for that class, though," Jordan reflected.

"I know that you can bring your grade up," Brianna said, "but you were saying a few minutes ago that you're not a math person."

"I'm just not feeling it today. I want to believe you when you say that I can raise my grade, but it feels so out of reach right now." Jordan started to gather his trash from the lunch table, and the group of students got up from the table together.

"Just because you get some quiz grades that you don't like, it doesn't mean that you can't do this. You can still learn this stuff in time for the final. We can meet in the library after school before track practice, if you want, and do some of tonight's homework," Brianna encouraged her friend.

"I'll be there!" Tanisha said.

Kelsey waved to her friends as she turned the corner. "See you after school!" she said.

Quiet Desperation

In 1854 Thoreau wrote, "The mass of men lead lives of quiet desperation." It is a fact that most students want to grow up, learn, and apply their learning to a useful and productive occupation. Why? To be happy. Our pursuit of happiness has many roadblocks. Unfortunately, for many students, school mathematics has become a serious roadblock. We can witness students like Jordan, developing a "quiet desperation" stemming from a lack of connectedness with the teacher, continued frustration, and a lack of a sense of efficacy—that is, a lack of perceived ability to change their situation. What this amounts to in the long run is that students' liking of mathematics continually declines and their choices, both conscious and unconscious, point their life's compass as far away from mathematical inquiry as possible.

Mathematics can be a useful tool for future occupations and future life pursuits. It can provide insight into interesting scientific phenomena. It can help us understand the political and economic forces that shape our society. We can use it as an engine for artistic and creative activity. It can also be interesting in its own right. But any of these reasons to engage in mathematics beyond the compulsory requirements of public education require extended, positive experiences to develop. So, a major reason to promote students' motivation to do mathematics is to prevent them from opting out of engaging with mathematics in the future. When students imagine their lives beyond our classrooms as Jordan and Kelsey were considering, we would like for them to not rule out mathematically intensive professional work. We do not want to devalue other types of experiences, but we want students to have real choices from among a plethora of good options. If bad feelings associated with school mathematics hinder students' willingness to follow a life's dream, our system of education has done them a disservice.

As students envision their future, we hope for them to imagine a *possible self* (Markus and Nurius 1986) that includes mathematics. Possible selves are images of how people perceive their future selves—who they might become, who they would like to become, or even who they are afraid of becoming or do not want to become. Possible selves relate to motivation because they manifest a person's goals, values, aspirations, and motives (Cantor et al. 1985).

The value of such projected self-images is that they provide incentive either to avoid or engage in behavior in a manner that supports the person's goals, values, aspirations, and motives (Markus and Nurius 1986). In this chapter's story, Jordan saw his future as an engineer as out of reach and less valuable than the monetary return that becoming a tool-and-die technician offered. Students who feel like Jordan likely will not choose higher-level mathematics coursework or to pursue a career related to mathematics. Of particular concern nationally are those who remain underrepresented in careers involving mathematics, including women (National Center for Education Statistics 2009). Again, the issue is not the particular choice, but the ability to make the choice without having mathematics be the deciding factor.

In this chapter, we discuss how motivation can create long-term attitudes toward mathematics, both pro and con. We examine how students' motivation influences their choices to continue studying mathematics or pursuing mathematics-related careers. Some relevant aspects of motivation that can influence these choices may include (*a*) interests, (*b*) values, (*c*) what students expect and believe about themselves and the school subject of mathematics, (*d*) how students cope with challenge, and (*e*) their needs for relatedness with others. We also, however, acknowledge that students' motivation does not entirely shape their choices to continue taking courses in mathematics or their career aspirations. Real barriers to opportunity exist for many Americans, including poverty, associated material resources, and lack of opportunity to experience high-quality instruction. Just because a student does not pursue a career in mathematics or continue their education in mathematics does not mean that the student is not motivated to do so.

Interests: Beyond Situational to Long-Term Interest

When they have options, people will choose to do what interests them. So, interest influences whether students continue taking mathematics courses and pursue careers involving mathematics. Some students' interest in school subjects improves in high school. Unfortunately, evidence indicates that in general, students' interest in academic subjects, including mathematics, tends to decline steadily over time. This decline is even more prevalent for lower-achieving students, with students' decline in interest hitting its lowest point early in high school (Eccles and Wigfield 2002). The timing of most students' declining interests happens to coincide with when students have more choices about which courses they take or whether to continue to pursue education at all. So, a student whose interest in mathematics declines into their high school years may choose to take the least amount of mathematics possible. To address this, teachers could purposefully attempt to increase students' interest in mathematics.

Interest affects our judgments about academic tasks; we like to think about interest as having both *situational* and *personal* facets (Harackiewicz and Hulleman 2009). Situational interest is an in-the-moment reaction, stemming from the task's relative excitement, novelty, and the extent to which it piques a person's curiosity. Personal interest develops over the long term, as people begin to classify pursuits by their likes and dislikes, evaluating their successes and failures, and negotiating the social pressures to conform to particular pursuits over others. Continued experiences of situational interest can potentially promote personal interest. So, promoting opportunities for students to see that mathematics is beautiful, intriguing, useful, worthwhile, or otherwise interesting can give students an experience of situational interest. Such an experience, in time, can lead to students developing more long-term interests in mathematics. Likewise, personal interest can make an ordinarily dull task more palatable because it can redefine the task as contributing to the area of interest. Contextualizing mathematical curriculum in students' areas of interest can give them the opportunity to connect their interests with their mathematical motivations. These experiences can happen in classrooms, after school, or in summer activities. (See chapter 11 for more about promoting students' interest.)

What Do Students Value?

Values can indicate a student's interest. Jacquellyn Eccles (1983) described four values a task can afford: attainment value, intrinsic value, utility value, and cost. *Attainment value* refers to the relative importance an individual assigns to being successful at the task. All things being equal, if students do not value the task's successful completion highly, they likely will not put much effort into completing it. If, however, completing the task has high value, the student will tend to expend more effort toward successful completion. *Intrinsic value* refers to personal enjoyment derived from the task—the sense of satisfaction, pride, and joy that one experiences from engaging. *Utility value* refers to whether the task helps the individual achieve short- or long-term goals. *Cost* refers to negative consequences resulting from engaging in the task.

The value students place on an activity or school subject will influence their engagement, both short- and long-term. When students have choices, they spend time on what they enjoy (intrinsic value), what is important to them (attainment value), and what they think is useful (utility value). They avoid the activities that they perceive will have negative consequences (cost). Note that each of the first three values has a negative pole: one can consider tasks unimportant, boring, and useless, each of which contributes to negative interest. In essence, when a student's engagement in mathematics does not satisfy the first three values, the cost of said engagement can outweigh its benefits.

The key here is that students' values influence their interests and career choices. In Kelsey's instance, as mathematics became boring to her in high school, she became less interested in it, and mathematics became less important to her. She also became less sure that she wanted to pursue a career related to mathematics. In contrast, Tanisha found mathematics useful, that she was interested in it, and that she also wanted to pursue a career that involved doing mathematics. Tanisha illustrates that it is possible to increase students' interest in an activity by promoting its utility value—by helping students see connections between mathematics course content and their lives outside school (Harackiewicz and Hulleman 2009). Utility values also influence career choices. Watt (2006) found that high school students with high utility values for mathematics would likely plan for highly mathematics-related careers. Also, it may be true that students like Tanisha, who view themselves as likely to pursue a highly mathematical career, can see better how their mathematics classes can be useful to them. Utility, then, influences a positive cycle of behavior where students see mathematics as useful and important to their future lives. They thus engage in it more deeply and learn it more fully, opening themselves up to even more opportunity to perceive its utility, restarting the cycle once more.

What Do Students Expect from Themselves and Mathematics? Or, *You Get What You Expect*

If students expect to succeed in mathematics, they will more likely be willing to put forth effort and persist when working on a challenging mathematical task. If they expect to perform poorly or not to succeed, they may avoid the task to protect their self-esteem or self-concept. These expectancies—whether students believe that they can succeed at a mathematical task or understand a mathematical concept—are called students' *self-efficacy* in mathematics, or their *competence beliefs,* because at heart, they are students' opinions about their own abilities in the subject.

Like their values, students' expectancies about themselves in mathematics are enduring, difficult but not impossible to change, and major determinants of their future choices. Similarly to the research findings on interest, evidence regarding students' competency beliefs and self-efficacy in school subjects shows that these attitudes tend to decline over students' time in school (Chouinard and Roy 2008). We have found that self-efficacy in mathematics influences career aspirations; high school students who believe themselves capable in mathematics will more likely aspire to a mathematically related career (Farmer 1997) or mathematics-related college major (Hackett and Betz 1989). Students who believe themselves good at mathematics will more likely be interested in it and continue to pursue that interest.

Our student Jordan's sense of competence in mathematics was faltering. Frustrated by continually earning low quiz scores, he started to take these grades as a sign that he could not do well in mathematics. Consequently, he started to reconsider pursuing careers that would involve doing more mathematics. Illustrating the prevailing trend in the United States, his drop in sense of competence coincided with a time when he was considering whether to continue taking more mathematics courses, as well as whether to pursue college or a trade.

Abilities are not fixed! Whether students believe that their competence can improve or not affects their effort and engagement in mathematics. If students believe that they are not good at mathematics, we can try to improve their beliefs about their competence by giving them experiences with a moderate degree of challenge and helping them work through the experiences successfully. But some people will still believe their ability in mathematics to be a fixed quantity, that they either are a "math person" or they are not. Think about this. If I think that I am not very good at mathematics, and I encounter a difficult problem, why should I work hard? Hard work will not improve my ability, nor will it increase my chances at succeeding. It will only increase my frustration at my lack of mathematical intelligence. The logical conclusion for students with such beliefs is to disengage from mathematics, whether or not they are truly able in it, and to redirect their efforts to other subjects. This preserves feelings of self-efficacy and competence, increases enjoyment they receive from their activities, and, unfortunately, denies them mathematical success.

Conversely, if, one believes oneself essentially able in mathematics, but that to do well, one must work hard—that hard work makes one smarter—then it makes sense to work hard, to persevere. This builds self-efficacy, personal enjoyment, and competence in mathematics, and it promotes mathematical success over the long run.

Promoting the ideas that (1) ability is not fixed, but instead grows incrementally over time; and (2) effort can make a difference in improving one's competence is significant for improving a student's achievement and sense of competence in mathematics. This mindset of incremental growth in ability over fixed ability is important for students to see themselves as able to do mathematics, so that they do not attribute their failures or challenges to their own lack of ability (Dweck 2007).

Brianna tried to confront Jordan about his view of himself as "not a math person." She remembered when he was successful at mathematics, so if he defined himself by his performance, she wanted him to see that he had a prior history of succeeding. Also, neither she nor Tanisha believed that their grades defined their abilities to do mathematics. Brianna wanted Jordan to believe that his effort would matter, that if he studied more or sought different support, he would be successful. Presumably, his teacher had not noticed Jordan's drop in sense of competence; otherwise, his teacher could also talk explicitly with Jordan about how his ability is not fixed and how seeking different support and investing effort differently would help him improve.

If That's What You Think Math Is, I Understand Why You Don't Like It

What students believe about mathematics will likely influence whether they expect to be good at mathematics, interested in it, or even successful in it (Muis 2004). Students' image of mathematics may be primarily about memorizing and reproducing calculations that they have been taught. If they do not enjoy or feel effective at doing this kind of work, then they will not be as interested in mathematics or believe themselves to be competent in it. Jo Boaler's research (1998) found that if students experience mathematics differently—through an instructional approach that involves engaging students in solving open-ended, interesting tasks and promotes the belief that success in mathematics does not depend on memorization—then students may become more interested in mathematics. What students think doing mathematics means influences whether they want to continue engaging in it.

Tanisha expressed different expectancies about mathematics from those of her friends. Brianna, Kelsey, and Jordan talked about wanting to talk about their own solution strategies and to hear about those of their peers, and for their teacher not to talk *at* them so much. They wanted to discuss mathematics with their peers and feel more engaged during class. As a result, when their expectancies about mathematics and preferences for how mathematics should be taught did not align with their experiences in a mathematics class, they lost interest in the class. In contrast, Tanisha expected and preferred the opportunity to work more efficiently and independently. Her expectancies aligned with how their current teacher taught mathematics, so she became more interested and engaged in the class. Both types of preferences, in differing proportions, will be present among students in any classroom.

Coping with Challenge

How students cope with challenge will influence whether they continue taking mathematics courses or pursuing a career related to mathematics. A motivated mathematics student is a persistent student. Persistent students do not see challenge in mathematics as evidence that they, themselves, lack ability. Instead, they view the challenges as temporary setbacks to overcome. Brianna viewed Jordan's situation as a temporary challenge that support could help overcome, whereas it overwhelmed Jordan.

Students who cope with challenge productively will be less likely to avoid taking advanced mathematics courses, and they could become more willing to confront complex mathematical tasks in future careers.

Martin and Marsh (2008) coined the term *academic buoyancy* to describe everyday academic resilience, such as students' abilities to deal successfully with academic setbacks and challenges typical of students' school experiences. Their research showed that less anxious high school students had higher academic buoyancy. They also found that higher self-efficacy and positive relationships with teachers led to higher academic buoyancy. In upper elementary school mathematics classrooms, Meyer, Turner, and Spencer (1997) also found that students who avoided challenge had lower self-efficacy in mathematics, whereas those who did not avoid challenge had higher self-efficacy. So, aspects of students' motivation, such as their self-efficacy, relate to how they cope with challenge. When students believed that they were likely to succeed, they tended to cope with academic setbacks more effectively. Those with strong mechanisms for coping with setbacks in mathematics would more likely persist in mathematics.

One reason why Brianna may have had strong academic buoyancy could have been her strong relationship with her previous mathematics teacher, Ms. D. In Brianna's experience with Ms. D, the teacher believed in her, showed her that mathematics could be interesting and engaging, and continued helping her see that mathematics could be that way again in the future. This relationship with a previous teacher helped Brianna persist in a mathematics classroom that she claimed not to enjoy as much.

Relatedness: Wanting to Be with or Like Others

Issues of relatedness, including wanting to spend time with others to build relationships or wanting to be like others, affect students' short-term choices about mathematics course-taking and long-term decision making about their future careers.

Regarding shorter-term choices, Frank and colleagues (2008) found that high school students' choices about which courses to take were influenced in part by their friends. They chose to take the same courses, including mathematics, that their current friends and friends they wanted to have also chose to take. This tendency was stronger for girls, but it held for both male and female students. What may be most important to adolescents is what is most immediate to them, such as whom they will see on a daily basis in class. However, these choices carry long-term implications. If students choose not to take an advanced mathematics class, they will not have the same opportunities to learn about mathematics as those who do take such a course.

Because Brianna encouraged Jordan to study with friends and take calculus with friends, if relatedness motivated him, he might end up making choices that support his learning of mathematics to meet his need for relatedness. Brianna encouraged Jordan to continue taking mathematics—to go on to calculus and to take it with the rest of them, with some of his friends. In this instance, taking classes that friends take could benefit Jordan mathematically. Managing the class's social atmosphere to tie relatedness goals to mathematical pedagogy can positively influence students to take on better study habits from their peers: provide extra, more productive time for learning; and promote generally positive motivations.

Vicarious experiences, or thinking about other people you want to be like (Zeldin and Pajares 2000), will likely influence long-term choices, such as career aspirations. Individuals hypothetically may be able to imagine any variety of possible selves, but their social experiences also shape the pool of possible selves (Markus and Nurius 1986). If you see someone accomplish a goal that you would like to accomplish, it could give you a vicarious experience that helps you imagine that you could conceivably accomplish a similar goal (Bandura 1997). Moreover, apart from believing that you might succeed in a similar situation, you also gain information regarding *how* to succeed. Such a vicarious experience is particularly valuable if you somehow relate to or identify with the person you observed being successful.

Adults and peers in students' lives give them access to vicarious experiences. Tanisha saw her mother become a successful architect. Tanisha's relationship with her mother provided her with a vicarious experience of a family member succeeding in a career involving mathematics. She could see in detail what such a career entailed, which helped her decide whether she would value or enjoy that sort of work. She could imagine a possible self as an architect because of this access to a vicarious experience. However, our life experiences shape which vicarious experiences we might encounter. No one in Mandy's (the second author of this book) family had pursued graduate school, so she did not see this path as an option for her until some of her peers pursued it. Students' relationships with adults and peers give them cultural capital (Bourdieu 1977). Different relationships can offer unique vicarious experiences, and not all students have access to similar vicarious experiences.

Motivation Is Not the Only Explanation

Saying that motivation is the most significant reason students choose not to continue taking mathematics courses or pursue mathematics-related careers, however, would be a mistake. Mathematics motivation is part of a large network of motivational presses that students negotiate. Students do not opt out of these mathematical paths simply because they are not motivated enough. Social influences also strongly affect why students would *pursue* these paths. Students who like mathematics and can succeed in it may choose paths that do not involve mathematics. Women remain underrepresented in some mathematics careers, even though research indicates that women do not achieve worse than men in mathematics (Hyde et al. 2008). Below, we discuss women's long-term decisions about participating in mathematics-related careers, to illustrate that their motivation was not necessarily the primary factor in their career choice.

Research results on gender differences in students' motivation have not been conclusive. Some researchers (e.g., Meece, Glienke, and Burg [2006]) document consistent gender differences in competence beliefs, with boys having higher mathematics self-efficacy than girls, but no difference in the degree to which boys and girls value mathematics. Other researchers (e.g., Bornholt and Möller [2003]) found minimal gender differences in motivation. Still others (e.g., Chouinard and Roy [2008]) observed that if gender differences in motivation existed when boys and girls were younger, the differences converged in high school, so that boys' and girls' motivation became more similar. If male and female students do not necessarily have different levels of motivation in mathematics, then other reasons must explain why women do not pursue mathematics-related careers as frequently as men.

One way to think about this question is instead to consider the experiences of women who *have* pursued mathematics-related careers; for these women, relationships and social support made the difference, from verbal encouragement and support to the examples of those who went before them. Zeldin and Pajares (2000) interviewed women in mathematics-related careers and learned about the importance of mentors or teachers, family members, and peers. The women cited family members as providing them a vicarious experience or an example of what pursuing such a profession could look like. Family members, mentors, and teachers all offered encouragement to pursue a mathematics-related profession. Relationships mattered for these women, not only because believing in themselves was important, but also because it mattered that others believed in them, too. Additionally, their peers provided a support system for them as they pursued a mathematics-related career. Women who have chosen to stop their graduate studies in mathematics said that a lack of mentoring and support influenced their decision (Herzig 2004). Among high school students, girls who had positive relationships with teachers and mentors in a science and mathematics activity program would more likely see themselves as people who chose to engage in mathematics and science (Lee 2002). Emotionally satisfying, supportive relationships affect choices to continue engaging with mathematics.

A former teacher encouraged Brianna, and Tanisha had a significant example in her mother. Tanisha wanted to pursue a career related to mathematics, whereas Brianna was unsure about her career choices and remained open to considering a mathematics-related field. In both instances, these young women had supportive relationships and examples that helped them avoid ruling out careers that involved mathematics.

What Can Teachers Do to Promote Positive Long-Term Motivation to Engage in Mathematics?

Supporting students' motivation in the short term, so that they choose to continue taking mathematics courses, can support students' choosing to engage in mathematics more in the long term, as they decide to pursue a career involving mathematics. The relationships and support that teachers give play an important role in helping students develop their sense of competence in mathematics and see value in it. Below, we highlight important ideas from this chapter for teachers to consider as they work with their own students.

Teachers Can Provide Support and Positive Relationships

Relationships with mentors and teachers make a difference for those who choose to pursue mathematics-related careers; by encouraging students, teachers can give them supportive opportunities to engage in mathematics. We saw this in Brianna's relationship with her former teacher. Close bonds with mentors or teachers support students when they work through challenging tasks or academic expressions (Martin and Marsh 2008). Satisfying relationships with mentors or teachers can help students see that they can engage in relation-supporting experiences while doing mathematics (Lee 2002). This is important because some people might avoid engaging in mathematics-related careers if they prefer relational experiences but do not associate them with doing mathematics. A mentor's acceptance and encouragement can help students believe that they can fit in with or belong in mathematics-related careers (Herzig 2004; Zeldin and Pajares 2000). For more on how teachers can foster productive relationships in the mathematics classroom, see chapter 6 for our thoughts on the importance of building such relationships and chapter 12 for how to do it.

Teachers Can Foster Students' Sense of Competence in Mathematics

We find positive self-efficacy or a strong sense of competence in mathematics among those who have chosen mathematics-related educational paths and careers, because people choose to spend more time and effort on something if they believe that they can succeed. Teachers can promote a strong sense of competence among students by communicating beliefs that all students can succeed in mathematics in general and individual students can succeed in it in particular (Gresalfi and Cobb 2006; Zeldin and Pajares 2000). When teachers communicate a high regard for students and provide specific praise about strengths in students' thinking, skills, and performance in mathematics, students will likely develop stronger self-efficacy in mathematics. Brianna and Jordan spoke about their junior high mathematics teacher, Ms. D, as someone who expressed high regard for them, which, in turn, fostered positive mathematical experiences for them at that time. Additionally, communicating to students that their abilities to do mathematics are not permanently fixed, that they can improve in their abilities to do mathematics, will make a difference in students' sense of competence in mathematics (Dweck 2007). If students believe that they are not "math people," teachers can help them see the fallacy in this belief. Teachers can help students see that whether or not they are math people is not predetermined, that each student can become more of a math person over time. Peers can do the same. Brianna, for example, tried to help Jordan see that his characterizing himself as "not a math person" was unproductive.

Teachers Can Help Students See the Value in Mathematics

People spend time engaging in activities that they value. If we want students to choose to engage in mathematics on their own, through future coursework and their career choices, we need to help students value mathematics and become more interested in it. Tanisha demonstrated an awareness that mathematics could be useful to her, which helped her cope even if she was not always successful. That awareness gave her motivation to work hard even if the classroom was not structured in a way that she preferred. Helping students see how mathematics is useful and related to their lives outside school can lead to increasing students' interest in mathematics (Harackiewicz and Hulleman 2009). Giving students opportunities to think about and see the aesthetic beauty in mathematics can also promote students' interest in mathematics (Sinclair 2009). If teachers engineer opportunities for all students to see that mathematics is more than memorizing procedures (Gresalfi and Cobb 2006), students will likely see it as more valuable and interesting to them. For more on how teachers can help students value mathematics, see chapter 8 about judicious use of contexts.

Summary

Motivation plays a role in long-term decision making—deciding whether to continue taking mathematics-related coursework or pursue a mathematics-related career. Students' interests, values, and senses of competence influence their long-term decision making. Their relationships with significant mentors, teachers, family members, and peers also affect their long-term engagement with mathematics.

How these interests, predilections, desires, and supports align in their academic lives matters if students are to have choices among good collegiate and occupational pursuits. We hope that students grow to include mathematical activity among the options for their visions of their possible selves so that these choices do not become unnecessarily curtailed.

References

Bandura, Albert. *Self-Efficacy: The Exercise of Control*. New York: Freeman, 1997.

Boaler, Jo. "Open and Closed Mathematics: Students' Experiences and Understandings." *Journal for Research in Mathematics Education* 29, no. 1 (January 1998): 41–62.

Bornholt, Laurel, and Jens Möller. "Attributions about Achievement and about Further Study in Social Context." *Social Psychology of Education* 6, no. 3 (2003): 217–31.

Bourdieu, Pierre. "Cultural Reproduction and Social Reproduction." In *Power and Ideology in Education,* edited by Jerome Karabel and Albert H. Halsey, pp. 487–511. New York: Oxford University Press, 1977.

Cantor, Nancy, Hazel Markus, Paula Niedenthal, and Paula Nurius. "On Motivation and the Self-Concept." In *Development during Middle Childhood: The Years from Six to Twelve,* edited by W. Andrew Collins, pp. 147–83. New York: National Academies Press, 1985.

Chouinard, Roch, and Normand Roy. "Changes in High School Students' Competence Beliefs, Utility Value, and Achievement Goals in Mathematics." *British Journal of Educational Psychology* 78, no. 1 (March 2008): 31–50.

Dweck, Carol. *Mindset: The New Psychology of Success*. New York: Ballantine Books, 2007.

Eccles, Jacquellyn S. "Expectancies, Values, and Academic Behaviors." In *Achievement and Achievement Motives: Psychological and Sociological Approaches,* edited by Janet T. Spence, pp. 75–146. San Francisco: W. H. Freeman, 1983.

Eccles, Jacquellyn S., and Allan Wigfield. "Motivational Beliefs, Values, and Goals." *Annual Review of Psychology* 53 (2002): 109–32.

Farmer, Helen S. "Women's Motivation Related to Mastery, Career Salience, and Career Aspiration: A Multivariate Model Focusing on the Effects of Sex Role Socialization." *Journal of Career Assessment* 5, no. 4 (Fall 1997): 355–81.

Frank, Kenneth A., Chandra Muller, Katheryn S. Schiller, Catherine Riegle-Crumb, Anna Strausmann Mueller, Robert Crosnoe, and Jennifer Pearson. "The Social Dynamics of Mathematics Coursetaking in High School." *American Journal of Sociology* 113, no. 6 (May 2008): 1645–96.

Gresalfi, Melissa Sommerfeld, and Paul Cobb. "Cultivating Students' Discipline-Specific Dispositions as a Critical Goal for Pedagogy and Equity." *Pedagogies: An International Journal* 1, no. 1 (January 2006): 49.

Hackett, Gail, and Nancy E. Betz. "An Exploration of the Mathematics Self-Efficacy/Mathematics Performance Correspondence." *Journal for Research in Mathematics Education* 20, no. 3 (May 1989): 261–73.

Harackiewicz, Judith M., and Chris S. Hulleman, "The Importance of Interest: The Role of Achievement Goals and Task Values in Promoting the Development of Interest." *Social and Personality Psychology Compass* 4, no. 1 (December 2009): 42–52.

Herzig, Abbe H. "'Slaughtering This Beautiful Math': Graduate Women Choosing and Leaving Mathematics." *Gender and Education* 16, no. 3 (September 2004): 379.

Hyde, Janet S., Sara M. Lindberg, Marcia C. Linn, Amy B. Ellis, and Caroline C. Williams. "Gender Similarities Characterize Math Performance." *Science* 321, no. 5888 (July 2008): 494–95.

Lappan, Glenda, James T. Fey, William M. Fitzgerald, Susan N. Friel, and Elizabeth Difanis Phillips. *Connected Mathematics Project.* Palo Alto, Calif.: Dale Seymour, 1997.

Lee, James Daniel. "More than Ability: Gender and Personal Relationships Influence Science and Technology Involvement." *Sociology of Education* 75, no. 4 (October 2002): 349–73.

Markus, Hazel, and Paula Nurius. "Possible Selves." *American Psychologist* 41, no. 9 (September 1986): 954–69.

Martin, Andrew J., and Herbert W. Marsh. "Academic Buoyancy: Towards an Understanding of Students' Everyday Academic Resilience." *Journal of School Psychology* 46, no. 1 (February 2008): 53–83.

Meece, Judith L., Beverly Bower Glienke, and Samantha Burg. "Gender and Motivation." *Journal of School Psychology* 44, no. 5 (October 2006): 351–73.

Meyer, Debra K., Julianne C. Turner, and Cynthia A. Spencer. "Challenge in a Mathematics Classroom: Students' Motivation and Strategies in Project-Based Learning." *Elementary School Journal* 97, no. 5 (May 1997): 501–21.

Muis, Krista R. "Personal Epistemology and Mathematics: A Critical Review and Synthesis of Research." *Review of Educational Research* 74, no. 3 (Fall 2004): 317–77.

National Center for Educational Statistics. *Digest of Education Statistics.* 2009. http://nces.ed.gov/programs/digest/, July 23, 2010

Sinclair, Nathalie. "Aesthetics as a Liberating Force in Mathematics Education?" *ZDM—the International Journal on Mathematics Education* 41, no. 1 (2009): 45–60.

Smith, John P. III, and Jon R. Star. "Expanding the Notion of Impact of K-12 *Standards*-Based Mathematics and Reform Calculus Programs." *Journal for Research in Mathematics Education* 38, no. 1 (January 2007): 3–34.

Star, Jon R., John P. Smith III, and Amanda Jansen. "What Do Students Notice as Different between Reform and Traditional Mathematics Programs?" *Journal for Research in Mathematics Education* 39, no. 1 (January 2008): 9–32.

Watt, Helen M. G. "The Role of Motivation in Gendered Educational and Occupational Trajectories Related to Maths." *Educational Research and Evaluation* 12, no. 4 (August 2006): 305–22.

Zeldin, Amy L., and Frank Pajares. "Against the Odds: Self-Efficacy Beliefs of Women in Mathematical, Scientific, and Technological Careers." *American Educational Research Journal* 37, no. 1 (Spring 2000): 215–46.

CHAPTER 6

Motivation Is Social

*S*tudents' interests in building relationships may conflict with learning mathematics in school, but we intend to demonstrate that students can meet their needs for relationships while engaging productively in opportunities to learn mathematics. *Teachers can set up their classrooms so that this will more likely occur. We have written the story in this chapter to illustrate how a teacher structured her classroom so that students could meet their social goals and learn mathematics simultaneously. A student that Mandy met when talking with middle school students about participating in group work during mathematics class inspired Alejandro, one of the story's focal students (Jansen 2011). Consider how social motivations can support students' learning when reading about Ms. Targett's mathematics classroom. After all, as teachers, we all see how hard our students work to find their place socially, to fit in, to make friends, or to get or avoid attention. Ms. Targett tries to consider these needs of her students while teaching.*

As the seventh-grade students entered Mrs. Targett's math class during first period, Alejandro noticed his group's poster hanging in the hallway. Last year, he would not have expected to see his work from math class on display. At his old school in sixth grade, he hadn't been successful in math. He felt some pride seeing that Mrs. Targett valued his group's work. He was glad that he was finally doing well in math. He turned to Jacob and said, "Hey, man. Math's my thing." Then he pointed at his group's poster. Jacob said, "Yeah, okay, but what's really new about that?" Alejandro smiled and thought that moving into a new neighborhood really changed what he thought about himself and what others thought about him.

Students picked up their math notebooks from the shelf as they walked into class and sat down with their groups. Mrs. Targett turned on the SMART Board and displayed a page from their math books.

Mrs. Targett said, "Okay, so let's get started with today's problem here on page 8 in the book—is everyone on that page? It says that some people are planning on participating in a run to raise money for a charity."

"Ugh. I hate running. I wouldn't do that," Kelly groaned.

"Yeah, I agree. I'm not good at running," Tina said, as she turned to Kelly for an air high-five.

"Yes, Eliza, are you going to get us back to the math?" Mrs. Targett asked, noticing that Eliza had raised her hand.

"Hey, running is good for you. I like staying in shape," Eliza contributed. "You know, like Mrs. Passiatore said in P.E., it's an aerobic exercise. You've got to keep up your heart rate to keep your heart healthy."

"Well, I like that you're making connections between math class and another one of your classes, but let's make some progress on this problem together. I hear you that not everyone loves running, but this is for charity, so some people might run to raise money. Also, some people walk in these events. Some of these events are even called walk-runs, so you don't necessarily have to run. The charity benefits if you collect pledges as donations. You can collect money based on either the distance you go or you can collect one flat pledge no matter how far you go. With the flat pledges, people give you the money even if you don't complete the walk-run." Mrs. Targett noted that the idea of a run could disengage some of the students from the task, as they didn't see themselves as runners, so she turned the problem around to emphasize the charitable contribution of the event, and on the possibility of walking, not just running, hoping that more students would become engaged in the problem.

"Yes, Jacob?" said Mrs. Targett, having noticed him looking at her quizzically.

"You said this was for charity. What charity? I mean, maybe people would pay more or less depending on the charity."

Mrs. Targett replied, "We could either go with the name of the charity in the book—actually, I don't remember if the book gives us a name for it—or I guess we can name one. It's a good point that the choice of charity could affect people's donations."

Jacob said, "My granddad had Alzheimer's disease. Maybe the walk-run could be for that."

Alejandro added, "What if it was, like, the American Cancer Society? Isn't that, like, a thing? A real charity name? I saw a commercial. I think that one would be good, because a lot of people have family members who've had cancer, and something like that could work for a lot of different people, no matter what kind of cancer. I mean, I'm not saying that I don't want to support Jacob's family...."

"Whatever, man!" Jacob turned his back on Alejandro, but then it became apparent that Jacob was joking, because he turned toward Alejandro again and laughed, "Nah, I mean, just kidding. I hear you. Maybe not everyone's family has someone with Alzheimer's, but maybe more people know someone who has had cancer."

"Actually, each group can choose their own charity," Mrs. Targett said, and the students started mumbling to each other in their groups. "No, I should I have clarified. Each group can choose their own charity *later*. Later, each group can choose their own charity. For this problem, the name of the charity isn't really the point. The point is, which pledge plan would be the best to recommend to a sponsor and why?

We want to compare and contrast different pledge plans and decide which plan is better, for what reasons."

During this initial conversation about running and charities, Mrs. Targett did not view the students' talk as off topic. Instead, she hoped that students would personally connect with the mathematics problem. The students' reactions to the problem's situation served an instructional purpose. She wanted to give her students space to share and relate to the context before they got into the problem's mathematics; then, she redirected them toward the task's mathematics.

Ben raised his hand and said, "I have an idea for a plan!"

Mrs. Targett looked at Ben and said, "Good. I'm glad that you're thinking of possible plans. But in this case, I want to start with three plans recommended by the book. Ben, since you were thinking about plans, why don't you read what the book says about the plans on page 8."

"Where do you want me to start?" Ben asked.

"Right at the part where it begins with 'Mrs. Chang says.'"

Ben read aloud the following, modified from a Connected Mathematics unit, "Moving Straight Ahead" (Lappan et al. 2002):

> Ms. Chang says that some sponsors might ask the students to suggest a pledge amount. The class wants to agree on how much they ask for. Leanne says that each sponsor should pay $10 regardless of how far a person walks. Gilberto says that $2 per kilometer would be better, because it would bring in more money. Alana points out that if they ask for too much money, not as many people will want to be sponsors. She suggests that they ask each sponsor for $5 plus 50 cents per kilometer.

Then Ben asked, "Do you want me to keep going?"

Mrs. Targett replied, "No, that's good, Ben. Thanks. Do we see the different pledge plans suggested?"

Maritza asked, "No, I don't get it. What are we supposed to do with these plans? Somehow compare them?"

"Maritza, I like how you are thinking about the goal. Being clear about our goal will help us remember what we are doing and not get confused in the middle of the problem. We *are* going to compare the plans. The book is going to ask us to compare the pledge plans using different representations. The representations should help us notice different qualities of each plan. Ben, would you continue reading?"

Ben read:

> For each pledge plan:
>
> 1. Make a table showing the amount of money a sponsor would owe if a student walked distances from 1 to 6 kilometers.

2. Graph the three pledge plans on the same coordinate axis. Use a different color for each plan.
3. Write an equation that can be used to calculate the amount of money a sponsor owes, given the total distance the student walks.

Mrs. Targett said, "Great, thanks, Ben. Right, so let's notice that we have to do all three of these for each pledge plan. For every plan, we need a table that expresses the pledge amounts for 1, 2, 3, 4, 5, or 6 kilometers. We need a graph. And we need an equation. Three pledge plans. Three representations for each pledge plan. Nine things in all. Three tables, one for each pledge plan. Three graphs, one for each pledge plan. Three equations, one for each pledge plan. Use what you know. Work with your groups. I want to hear math talk. Talk about the math problem. And if you get stuck, ask your group members before me. I'll give you 10 minutes and then we'll check in as a group."

Mrs. Targett's instructions directed students' attention to the goals of the mathematics task. She provided some social scaffolding when she talked about how she wanted students to talk with one another.

Once students started to work in groups, Mrs. Targett went over to a group of students: Alejandro, Maritza, and Jasmine. Jasmine and Alejandro were working together and leaning over a graphing calculator. Mrs. Targett could hear them laughing. Maritza was working alone and sketching graphs on paper. Mrs. Targett was concerned that Alejandro and Jasmine could be off task and that the group might not be working together cohesively.

Mrs. Targett was impressed with the improvement she noticed in Alejandro's engagement in mathematics class over the past six months. She had seen him do mathematics for fun outside school and play the 24 card game with his friends while waiting for the bus after school. She was concerned about Maritza because Maritza had struggled in mathematics last quarter. Sometimes a group of students had treated Maritza like a bit of an outsider, perhaps because she had struggled in class. Her peers thus might not have turned to her for suggestions or solution strategies. Jasmine tended to get her work done quickly—perhaps too quickly—and could be a bit more attentive to details such as showing her work, but she had a history of success in mathematics.

Mrs. Targett put her hand on Maritza's shoulder lightly and asked, "What are you noticing in your graphs?"

Maritza looked up and said, "I'm confused. I don't know whether to connect these dots or not."

"What do you mean?"

"I'm making a graph for Gilberto's plan. It's $2 for each kilometer. That's easy. One kilometer is $2. Put a dot." Maritza gestured toward a point at (1,2) on her graph. "Two kilometers, $4, put a dot. Three kilometers, $6, put a dot. Keep going to 6 kilometers, $12, another dot. Now, I don't know. Connect the dots or not?"

Mrs. Targett asked, "So why would you and why wouldn't you connect the dots?"

Maritza looked down at her paper and started tapping her pencil. "Um,…"

"Would you ever need to know the amount of money for a distance that doesn't have a dot?" the teacher inquired.

"Yeah, kind of. If I got tired between kilometers, like, if I walked two and a third kilometers and didn't want to keep going until three kilometers. If I connect the dots, I could see the amount of money I would get for two and a third."

"And if you didn't connect the dots?"

Maritza said, "Then I guess it could be harder to see how much money I would get if I didn't walk for the entire next kilometer?"

Mrs. Targett responded, "That's the kind of thing you should be thinking about. Good question. Maybe you want to compare the plans for a distance that is not a whole number. Connecting the dots could be a way to go in that situation. I wonder what your group members think." Mrs. Targett looked over at Maritza's group members.

Jasmine nudged Alejandro and said, "Oh, I think she's talking to us." Jasmine and Alejandro looked over at Maritza and Mrs. Targett, and moved their chairs a bit closer to Maritza.

Mrs. Targett said, "Maritza has a good insight about the graphs for the pledge plans. She was thinking about whether or not to connect dots on the graph."

Jasmine rolled her eyes and said, "That's obvious. You connect them."

Maritza looked down and blushed.

Mrs. Targett said, "Wait a minute, Jasmine. How do you know for sure that is what you should do?"

Jasmine replied hesitantly, "Um,… because that's what the calculator did?"

"Well, that's trusting the calculator a bit too much, really. In this situation, Maritza has more insight than the calculator. I think you should talk about the graphs with her." Mrs. Targett looked at Maritza and gestured as if to encourage her to talk with Jasmine and Alejandro. The teacher's intention was to empower Maritza and to help her group members see that they could learn from Maritza's thinking.

Jasmine looked up at the ceiling, thought for a minute, and then looked back at Maritza and said, "Huh. I guess I don't really know why you connect the dots."

Alejandro shrugged and said, "Yeah, I didn't really think about graphing any other way than connecting the points, because that's what the calculator did."

All three of the students started talking with one another about the graphs. They compared Maritza's paper graphs with their graphs on their graphing calculator.

After a few more minutes circulating the room and talking with other groups of students, Mrs. Targett brought the class together. "Okay. I want to see your eyes. Eyes on me, please. I want to bring us together to talk about how you're doing on the problem so far. Remember the point of this problem? You want to think about which pledge plan you should use and why. You may have a different favorite pledge plan depending on your reasons, and the book wants you to look at the different representations and compare plans with each one. Any thoughts so far? Jasmine?"

Mrs. Targett purposefully called on Jasmine to allow the rest of the class to learn from that group's conversation.

"Yeah. We were looking at the graphs. You can really see, like, where they cross. Some plans start out higher, like with more dollars, for just one or a couple of kilometers, but as you walk more, another plan gives you more money. The lines cross over," Jasmine explained.

"It would probably help if we could see what you were talking about. Can someone in your group come put your group's graphs into the graphing calculator up here at the overhead?" Mrs. Targett asked.

Alejandro immediately got up and went to the front of the room. He liked getting to go up to the front of the class sometimes, because he was proud of his recent successes in math. Then he looked over and waved at Maritza to ask her to come to the front with him, too. He said, "I want Maritza here, too, because she really helped me on this problem." Maritza smiled as she joined Alejandro at the overhead. (To continue reading about Mrs. Targett's classroom and their conversation about this mathematics task, see chapter 12, Building Relationships: Characteristics of Knowledge-Building Communities.)

Students Can Meet Their Needs for Relatedness During Mathematics Class

Beside the beautiful cave paintings in southern France and northern Spain, tally marks inscribed with bone and numerical counters made of clay constitute human history's first attempt at recording thoughts. Humans have needed to communicate quantitative and spatial information from our earliest days as fully modern (Marshack 1972; Lakoff and Núñez 2000). From this early evidence we can reach two important conclusions: (1) human beings, attempting to communicate and connect with other human beings, invented mathematics for this purpose; and (2) even the simplest forms of mathematical inquiry are complex cognitive activities that arise from interaction with both other people and the environment. So why does school mathematics generally minimize this social aspect, instead emphasizing the individual in isolation of others? We shall see that this minimizing is futile, only detracting from students' inherent relatedness needs as opposed to building positive interdependence and individual initiative simultaneously.

As the story of Mrs. Targett's classroom illustrates, learning in school classrooms occurs through interactions with people—teachers and peers—as well as interactions with mathematical objects, including books and tools. Classrooms are both academic and social settings, and they motivate learners to achieve both intellectual and social goals simultaneously (Dowson and McInerney 2003; Jansen 2006; Walter and Hart 2009). As students share their mathematical thinking in classrooms publicly, in either whole-class or small-group interactions, they encounter social implications for their interactions as well as academic or intellectual motivations. Motivation to engage in school tasks is not only an individual phenomenon, but also a social phenomenon.

In this chapter, we highlight how students' needs for relatedness shape their motivation to engage in school mathematics. In doing so, we acknowledge that students' needs for relatedness intersect with their needs for autonomy and competence. For instance, students who feel a strong sense of belonging—connection with their teacher and peers—in their classroom may feel more secure taking intellectual risks. Students thus can develop *autonomy* fruitfully only if some kind of *positive interdependence* exists. Students' sense of belonging relates to other aspects of students' motivation as well, such as increased interest and higher achievement in mathematics (Martin et al. 2007; Roeser, Midgley, and Urdan 1996). After all, we like being around others, and we naturally learn more when we have the opportunity to bounce ideas off of each other in the process of generating solutions to challenging problems.

Needs for Relatedness Can Either Interfere with or Support Mathematics Learning

Some aspects of students' needs for relatedness may plague teachers, but positive aspects of students' efforts to meet their own needs for relatedness can support mathematics learning. We may think about students who don't participate because they don't want to be wrong in front of people. We may think about students who would rather talk about anything other than mathematics during class. In these examples, the social dimension of the classroom can interfere with mathematics learning.

But sometimes the social dimension of the mathematics classroom can initiate and support engagement with mathematics. Consider a student who may otherwise keep to herself during a class discussion, who decides instead to participate to help her friend, who is stuck while trying to explain her thinking. Consider a student who decides to take a break from raising her hand during class, because she realizes that she's been volunteering frequently lately and she wants to hear and think about what her classmates are thinking. In both instances, students adjusted their engagement with mathematics for social reasons, and they received a positive academic benefit. The student who chose to help her friend also took an opportunity to engage in mathematical discourse. The student who decided to give other people a chance to talk also took an opportunity to learn a new solution strategy or way of thinking about mathematics by choosing to listen to someone else's thinking. The classroom's social dimension can have positive implications for learning.

Below, we describe several relatedness needs or social goals that students may pursue in their mathematics classrooms that can affect their engagement with school mathematics tasks: (1) avoidance and fear of disapproval, (2) need for social affiliation, (3) need to demonstrate competence to others and to seek approval, (4) need for social concern, and (5) need to build shared meaning. We will describe these relatedness themes, both relative to research on students' motivation and as they apply to the story of Mrs. Targett's classroom described above.

Avoidance and Fear of Disapproval

Some students, like Maritza, may purposefully avoid taking intellectual risks, particularly in public, because they fear that others will judge them negatively if they are incorrect. When students appear to avoid engagement with mathematics, they may be attempting to save face. In particular, we commonly characterize middle school students as highly self-conscious. See this quote from the Communication Standard for the grades 6–8 band in NCTM's *Principles and Standards for School Mathematics* (NCTM 2000, p. 268):

> During adolescence, students are often reluctant to do anything that causes them to stand out from the group, and many middle grades students are self-conscious and hesitant to expose their thinking to others. Peer pressure is powerful, and a desire to fit in is paramount.

Although this quote may align well with many mathematics learners' experiences, in middle school and otherwise, not all middle school students feel equally reluctant to avoid sharing their thinking with others. In Mrs. Targett's classroom, Maritza did not have a history of strong success in mathematics, so she was a bit nervous about being incorrect in front of her classmates. In contrast, her peers Jasmine and Alejandro were more willing to share their thinking about mathematics out loud with the entire class, and they were both confident about their mathematical thinking.

Middle school students who are acutely aware of their fear of losing face in front of peers may more likely participate in mathematics classroom discussions out of social concern for others (Jansen 2006). A student who wants to avoid being wrong in front of others may be empathetic to others who might feel this way, too. This student may attempt to help their peers feel and be successful in mathematics class. One's own fear of lack of approval can lead to helping others avoid having to face the same fear. This was Alejandro's experience. Consider the situation at the end of the story when Alejandro asked Maritza to join him in the front of the room. At one time in his history as a mathematics learner, prior to moving to that school, he hadn't been as successful in mathematics. He felt a sense of pride in his own improvement in math in the current year, and he wanted to help Maritza have a moment like that, to show what she knew.

Additionally, when students look like they are avoiding work, they may be engaging in thinking mathematically. Sometimes what may appear to a teacher to be an off-topic conversation and work avoidance could be a helpful route for students to make progress together. We must spend considerable time and effort coming to understand the context, to determine the relevant mathematical information and relations, particularly with contextualized problems. When the students at the story's beginning talked about disliking running and about various charities for the walk-run, the teacher could have dismissed this talk as students wanting to avoid work. Instead, the teacher incorporated their ideas into discussing the problem to help students connect with the context. (Chapter 8 in this book goes further into discussing how to support students with mathematics problems in context.) Additionally, we do not know whether Alejandro and Jasmine's socializing at the beginning of small group work added any mathematical components to the talk. Students can laugh with one another and balance their talk between social topics and math topics and still make progress on mathematics tasks.

Need for Social Affiliation

We tend to think about students' efforts to develop affiliations with their peers, such as cliques in school, as interfering with their learning, but this is not always true. Granted, plenty of instances exist in which students' desires to fit in with peer groups can affect their engagement with mathematics negatively. They may be concerned about how peers outside mathematics class will interpret their behavior, as "geeky" or dumb or any number of imagined slurs. A student may not want to appear "nerdy" or "geeky" in front of her friends in class, so she may hide how much she understands. Students may prefer to work with their friends, so they resist engaging with peers in groups who are not their friends and do not benefit as much from the opportunity to learn in groups.

In contrast, students' efforts to develop affiliations with their peers can support mathematics learning as well. Some social groups can encourage peers' success in school. Consider Alejandro. His teacher was proud of him for the growth in his mathematics performance and his improvement in his explanations during math class. He was not only getting higher grades now than he earned a few months ago, but he also had grown such that he provided rationales for why solution strategies worked when explaining his thinking during class. Earlier in the year, he described only the steps he used when solving the problem. Part of his back story is that this was his first year living in this neighborhood. He told Mandy in an interview,

> "When I moved over here, I ran into this group, and they were mainly like my kind, Latino. So, we, we like math. Like, all of a sudden, I didn't, like, know I liked math, so we just started playing 24. And then I started adding everything, and I realized I was good, so that, I started to like math more."

Out of affiliation with a group of students that he considered "mainly like my kind," he had an opportunity to do recreational math. This experience raised his confidence in mathematics and helped mathematics feel like an acceptable way to spend time. If a student's peer group values mathematics, then that student's effort to meet his need for affiliation can converge with developing productive engagement with mathematics.

We can see other instances when students acted on their need for affiliation during the problem's introduction in Mrs. Targett's class. For instance, when Tina connected with Kelly's lack of interest in running, she wanted to identify as someone who shared a similar perspective as Kelly. Also, when Alejandro wanted to present an alternative idea to Jacob's suggestion of a charity, he took care to support Jacob's idea for a charity as well. When students interact in class, they tend to their relationships, not just academic learning.

Students' needs for affiliation can support their success in school. Recent research (Witkow and Fuligni 2010) among high school seniors indicated that students who had relatively more in-school friends, compared to their number of out-of-school friends, had higher grade point averages, and students with higher grade point averages had more in-school friends. These results did not differ depending on gender or race. Having relatively more friends at school can reinforce academic and school-related values, particularly if students who are interested, engaged, and successful at school find peers at school who are similarly motivated. Students who are not interested in school, however, tend to look outside their school settings for their friends, and they may find friends who are similarly not as engaged at their schools. But out-of-school relationships do not necessarily interfere with achievement. For instance, if a student interested in school struggles to find similarly engaged friends at school, he or she may find friends interested in school outside his or her own school, and the student will likely do better at school. Students' sense of belonging to and affiliation with their school community affects their academic success.

Need to Demonstrate Competence to Others and to Seek Approval

Students will sometimes say that they want to share their thinking because they want other people to know that they know mathematics. They want others to think that they're smart. This is not inherently problematic for that individual student's mathematics learning, because if a student wants others to see his or her competence, then he or she will strive for competence in mathematics. This perspective can become problematic if one student's need to appear competent interferes with other students' similar needs. If a student who wants to appear competent dominates the floor during whole-class discussions, then other students do not have a chance to show what they know.

All students need to feel competent, but not all students may need to appear competent to others in the same ways. When engaging with mathematics, students want to believe that their effort makes a difference. They want to focus their efforts in a way that helps them learn and succeed in mathematics class. If they believe they have no opportunity to feel competent in mathematics class, they will be less likely to put forth effort. Maritza had an opportunity to demonstrate her graphing competence to the class, because her teacher helped her do so during small-group work and Alejandro helped her do so during the whole-class discussion at the end of the story. She beamed with a sense of pride because the opportunity to show her classmates that she knew something helpful about mathematics hadn't come her way in a while.

A student's need for approval can be counterproductive for mathematics learning if he or she seeks approval from people who do not value doing well at mathematical tasks or understanding mathematics. In this way, students' needs for approval can converge with their need for affiliation with a group of peers. For instance, if Alejandro had *not* gotten involved with a group of peers who engaged in recreational mathematics and decided that being good at mathematics was socially appropriate, he may not have started to like mathematics as much.

A student's need for approval can support mathematics learning, however, if she or he seeks the approval of those who do value success in mathematics class or depth of mathematical understanding. Perhaps a student admires a particular teacher or academically successful peer. They may choose to behave in ways that seek their approval. When Eliza spoke about the value of running, it appeared that she valued the opinion of her physical education teacher, and perhaps that of other teachers as well. Students may be motivated to work harder or differently in school by a desire to earn others' approval, and they may get more out of mathematics class as a result.

Need for Social Concern

In the classroom community, students may act out of a desire to help and support others. Students may put forth extra effort to explain solution strategies or mathematics concepts more elaborately out of goodwill for their peers. As students achieve such a prosocial goal, they benefit from developing their mathematical communication and reasoning skills. Students who can explain mathematics well to others will probably understand mathematics better. Additionally, students may have a need to be concerned *for* in the classroom, by their teachers.

Students may be concerned about fairness in the mathematics classroom. One way to think about fairness could be in terms of getting the floor during classroom discussions; they may be concerned about all students having opportunities to participate. They may choose to volunteer a bit less often during class discussions to give their peers a chance to contribute. Through the process of letting other students contribute, they may learn something new by listening to other students' perspectives. Another way to think about fairness could be in access to resources, such as when Jasmine and Alejandro were working together over the same calculator. Jasmine's calculator was broken, so Alejandro offered to share his with her. Sharing in the classroom could inspire opportunity for dialogue with a peer about mathematics over the shared calculator. In these ways, students' concerns about fairness can support their mathematics learning. Of course, the students perceive the teacher's attitudes and behaviors, and these develop into classroom norms.

A teacher who expresses *genuine* interest in what a student knows and can do will generate interest among others. In a study of first-grade classrooms, Middleton and colleagues (1998) found that the students appropriated the language that the teachers used, including the teachers' peculiar ways of asking questions and evaluating others' responses to questions. Moreover, because the classrooms studied valued students' sharing their strategies regardless of whether the answers were correct or not, students felt free to share their thinking, to get help from others and to help others. The conversation treated all contributions as potentially helpful and meaningful. These students appeared to engage productively in mathematics when their teachers expressed interest in and concern for them.

Need to Build Shared Meaning

Students who ask questions of their peers, such as "I don't understand why you …" or, "What do you mean by…?", are working to build shared meaning among themselves. This negotiation of meaning has both an intellectual and a social component. Through trying to understand what another person is saying, students can extend their own thinking. This effort to build shared meaning can lead to developing new ideas together by using a peer's ideas as a jumping-off point, such as asking, "I wonder what would happen if we tried…?" When Jasmine and Alejandro worked together to compare their graphs with Maritza's, they examined what was similar and different in each, such as whether to connect the points or, perhaps, what to choose for scaling the axes, such as by ones or twos. Working to understand a peer's thinking builds relationships, because this process communicates that another person's thinking is valuable and important.

Students Simultaneously Seek Multiple Needs, Both Social and Intellectual

The point that we are trying to illustrate throughout this chapter is that when students pursue their needs for relatedness in the mathematics classroom, they can learn mathematics simultaneously. Needs for relatedness do not necessarily inhibit opportunities to learn mathematics. Instead, we can build tasks and norms that take advantage of students' relatedness needs and orient them toward building mathematical knowledge. One way a teacher can understand this kind of behavior is through *self-determination theory* (Deci et al. 1991). According to self-determination theory, three needs drive learners—for competence, relatedness, and autonomy. To meet needs for competence, students must know what it means to succeed (in mathematics, in their mathematics classroom) and believe that they can do what is expected of them. Recall that in chapter 5, we discussed how expectations of success are crucial for building positive long-term values toward mathematics. These competency-efficacy-related beliefs provide the basis for a students' *agency* in mathematics. To meet needs for relatedness, students must develop secure, meaningful connections with others. Teachers, peers, parents, and authority figures are all essential actors in a student's network of relations. Different people become more important at different levels of the child's development, but teachers, peers, and parents are all important throughout childhood and adolescence (Patrick, Ryan, and Kaplan 2007; Wentzel 1998). To meet needs for autonomy, students must have opportunities to initiate (e.g., ask questions, create their own solution strategies) and self-regulate (monitor and assess their own engagement when learning). Students seek all three of these needs in their mathematics classrooms.

How Can Teachers Support Students' Needs for Relatedness and Help Students Learn Mathematics?

Teachers have more autonomy to influence the structure of classroom social interactions than students have. Below, we briefly describe some instructional choices that can support both students' needs for relatedness and their mathematics learning. Chapter 12, Building Relationships: Characteristics of Knowledge-Building Communities, builds on and extends the ideas presented below and describes additional instructional practices.

The Choice of Mathematical Tasks Matters

Mathematical tasks that support students' mathematics learning can enhance or constrain opportunities to meet their needs for relatedness. To provide students more opportunities to demonstrate their competence and build shared meaning and to prevent students appearing not competent, tasks need to be open, with multiple entry points and solution strategies. If more than one way exists to begin or solve a problem, then more than one student can contribute to a small-group or whole-class discussion about that problem. These more open tasks are considered to be "group worthy tasks" (Boaler and Staples 2008).

In Mrs. Targett's classroom, the walkathon task had several different entry points: students could start with any representation or any plan, and the rationales for determining which pledge plan was most appropriate could vary. This sort of task is more group-worthy than a problem in which students are asked, "For this system of equations, what is the point of intersection?" The walkathon task had more to discuss. Moreover, the context allowed students to connect their everyday understandings, and their own experiences raising funds for charity, with the mathematics. Some students have this everyday understanding and some do not. Students experienced with walkathons or similar events can use discussion to show their competence, directing it to helping others in the class understand the mathematical models being compared.

If mathematics classroom interactions focus on narrow tasks, or ones that students can only solve through one procedure, then opportunities to appear competent belong to the first students who share the single correct solution. These sorts of tasks constrain interactions more because students are either correct or incorrect. If only one possible solution exists, then one possible way to appear competent exists, so fewer students can appear mathematically competent. Students may be able to help others achieve correct solution strategies for these sorts of tasks during classroom interactions, so it is possible that students could meet needs for relatedness through social concern, but these tasks just present fewer opportunities to meet needs for competence.

How Teachers Treat Students' Errors or Imprecise Solutions Matters

When teachers explore students' errors or imprecise solution strategies as an opportunity to learn mathematics, determining why they are incorrect or could be improved, they can help students see mistakes as valuable opportunities for learning. This helps students avoid feeling less-than-competent during classroom interactions, saving face. Mrs. Targett could have just told Maritza that the points needed to be connected—or not—and not explore her thinking. Talking with Maritza to make sense of her thinking, and validating that thinking, supported the potential that Maritza could learn from her uncertainty. Teachers who explore errors and imprecise solution strategies with their students take care to create a safe space where students feel comfortable taking intellectual risks and being incorrect. They make students feel valued by taking their thinking seriously and demonstrating that their peers have something to learn from their ideas.

The Nature of Evaluations Matter

How students are evaluated in mathematics class can affect opportunities to meet needs for relatedness. For instance, Slavin (1991) advocates a balance between group goals and individual accountability, to encourage students to collaborate and listen to one another during mathematics class. Some believe that group quizzes can promote students' willingness to help their peers, as grades would depend on what the group could do. However, more recent research by Esmonde (2009) notes problems with this approach; her research indicates that when group products have highly evaluative consequences, as quizzes would, some students will more likely be positioned as authorities than others. Students may attempt to meet their social concern needs by helping, for example during group quizzes, but that help can be somewhat unidirectional. Highly evaluative group products often position students as if some students know, others do not, and those who know must pass the knowledge to those who do not. These interactions are not equitable in that not all students will have equal opportunities to contribute to the mathematical discussion.

As an alternative, Esmonde explored groups working together on presentations, in contrast to working together on quizzes, and she found these interactions more equitable. Students worked together to achieve shared meaning; the task did not have such highly evaluative consequences. With presentations, students can focus on building shared meaning rather than quickly transferring knowledge to one another. Students who attend to issues of fairness, such as wanting to hear from peers instead of dominating discussions, can enact this social-concern need even better during group presentations.

Reduce Competition and Social Comparison

In chapter 3 we briefly alluded to negative consequences of focusing students' outcome expectations on social comparison—the tendency of some students to define personal success only by doing better than someone else. In some classrooms, the teacher may quickly post students' test grades or examples of students' high-quality work. Posting test grades could promote competition and social comparison, emphasizing performance over understanding, so we recommend avoiding this practice. Posting high-quality work can give students examples, helping them see what counts as high-quality work, so in the future, they will be better able to produce such work themselves. In Alejandro's instance, it helped him develop and maintain a positive identity as someone who can be successful in school mathematics. The practice of posting students' work can have benefits, but teachers should watch whose work they post. If teachers post the same students' work time after time, they may inadvertently send a message that they value some students' thinking more than others'.

Teachers Can Purposefully Raise the Status of Individual Students

Cohen (1994) advocates for teachers to engage purposefully in status raising, so that more students have opportunities to be valued as mathematically competent in the classroom. One way to do this is posting the work of a student whose work is not frequently highlighted, as mentioned above, but status-raising treatments can take place during small-group and whole-class interactions as well.

Teachers can purposefully raise a student's status during small-group interactions. For instance, Mrs. Targett noticed that Maritza's group might have marginalized her. Maritza and Mrs. Targett talked about Maritza's thinking, and the teacher explicitly told Jasmine and Alejandro that they could benefit from hearing her ideas. This sort of status raising can occur when students are wondering about an interesting question that the group should consider, or when they investigate an alternative strategy, among other ideas. Teachers can play an active role in widening the scope for what sort of mathematical thinking—and whose thinking—is valued in the classroom. Through such status treatments, more students can feel mathematically competent and learn from one another. These kinds of exhortations enhance feelings of self-efficacy, but only if the students see them as valuable *and* if they focus on some substantive contribution like Alejandro's as opposed to a peripheral comment.

This sort of status-raising conversation can happen during whole-class discussion as well. Alejandro tried to raise Maritza's status by publicly sharing that he learned from her perspective. If the teacher values many different ways of thinking about mathematics, students will often do the same.

When making efforts to raise students' status, teachers play a role in making sure more students are positioned as competent, particularly by using problems that include multiple ways to demonstrate mathematical competence (Boaler and Staples 2008). Status raising (1) helps address students' needs for acceptance by, and for appearing competent in front of, their peers and (2) can facilitate opportunities for students to hear more ways of seeing and thinking about mathematics, thus promoting mathematics learning.

Developing Positive One-on-One Relationships with Individual Students Matters

The work that teachers put into getting to know their students, treating them with respect, treating them as individuals, and connecting with them interpersonally can have positive benefits for students' mathematics learning. Mrs. Targett took care to take her students' contributions seriously during whole-class discussions, even when they appeared to be off-topic, and connected them back with the mathematics investigation. She also took time to understand the thinking of learners who appeared to be marginalized from their small groups and explicitly attempted to raise their status. She tried to learn about students' histories as mathematics learners prior to coming to her class and about their lives outside school. She displayed students' work without grades on it, and she purposefully tried to vary whose work was displayed so that every student would have her or his work displayed at least once a semester. Mrs. Targett believed in the importance of building positive relationships with her students.

Adolescents who perceive that their teachers care about them will orient themselves positively toward learning in school, behave prosocially, and have a more positive self-concept; in research, this effect appears to be stronger for girls and weaker for older students (Wentzel et al. 2010). Adolescents have a need to bond with adults other than parents. Relationships with teachers often matter more than relationships with parents for promoting academic outcomes such as success in school and interest in school subjects (Martin et al. 2007).

Summary

Mathematics classrooms' social dimension can support students' learning of mathematics, particularly when teachers purposefully structure opportunities for social needs to converge with academic needs. All students' needs for relatedness— among them avoiding disapproval, achieving social affiliations, demonstrating competence, acquiring social concern, and building shared meaning—can become channeled into opportunities to engage with mathematics. Teachers' efforts to support students' mathematics learning—how they choose mathematical tasks, treat students' errors, evaluate students, reduce competition, raise status, and build positive relationships with students—can help students meet their needs for relatedness as well. Rather than assuming that socializing should be kept to a minimum in the mathematics classroom, we can instead capitalize on students' interests in socializing to promote their learning.

References

Boaler, Jo, and Megan Staples. "Creating Mathematical Futures through an Equitable Teaching Approach: The Case of Railside School." *Teachers College Record* 110, no. 3 (2008): 608–45.

Cohen, Elizabeth G. "Restructuring the Classroom: Conditions for Productive Small Groups." *Review of Educational Research* 64, no. 1 (Spring 1994): 1–35.

Deci, Edward L., Robert J. Vallerand, Luc G. Pelletier, and Richard M. Ryan. "Motivation and Education: The Self-Determination Perspective." *Educational Psychologist* 26, nos. 3–4 (1991): 325–46.

Dowson, Martin, and Dennis M. McInerney. "What Do Students Say about Their Motivational Goals: Towards a More Complex and Dynamic Perspective on Student Motivation." *Contemporary Educational Psychology* 28, no. 1 (January 2003): 91–113.

Esmonde, Indigo. "Mathematics Learning in Groups: Analyzing Equity in Two Cooperative Activity Structures." *Journal of the Learning Sciences* 18 (2009): 247–84.

Jansen, Amanda. "Seventh Graders' Motivations for Participating in Two Discussion-Oriented Mathematics Classrooms." *Elementary School Journal* 106, no. 5 (May 2006): 409–28.

———. "Listening to Mathematics Students' Voices to Assess and Build on Their Motivation: Learning in Groups." In *Motivation and Disposition: Pathways to Learning Mathematics*, 73rd Yearbook of the National Council of Teachers of Mathematics (NCTM), edited by Daniel J. Brahier, pp. 201–13. Reston, Va.: NCTM, 2011.

Lakoff, George, and Rafael E. Núñez. *Where Mathematics Comes From: How the Embodied Mind Brings Mathematics into Being.* New York: Basic Books, 2000.

Lappan, Glenda, James T. Fey, William M. Fitzgerald, Susan N. Friel, and Elizabeth Difanis Phillips. *Connected Mathematics: Moving Straight Ahead.* Glenview, Ill.: Prentice Hall, 2002.

Marshack, Alexander. *The Roots of Civilization: The Cognitive Beginnings of Man's First Art, Symbol, and Notation.* London: Weidenfeld and Nicolson, 1972.

Martin, Andrew J., Herbert W. Marsh, Dennis M. McInerney, Jasmine Green, and Martin Dowson. "Getting Along with Teachers and Parents: The Yields of Good Relationships for Students' Achievement, Motivation, and Self-Esteem." *Australian Journal of Guidance and Counseling* 17, no. 7 (December 2007): 109–25.

Middleton, James A., Leslie Poynor, Paula M. Wolfe, Zulbiye Toluk, and Lisa A. Boté. "A Sociolinguistic Perspective on Teacher Questioning in a Cognitively Guided Instruction Classroom." Paper presented at the Annual Meeting of the American Educational Research Association, Montreal, Canada, April 19–23, 1999.

National Council of Teachers of Mathematics (NCTM). *Principles and Standards for School Mathematics.* Reston, Va.: NCTM, 2000.

Patrick, Helen, Allison M. Ryan, and Avi Kaplan. "Early Adolescents' Perceptions of Classroom Social Environment, Motivational Beliefs, and Engagement." *Journal of Educational Psychology* 99, no. 1 (February 2007): 83–93.

Roeser, Robert W., Carol Midgley, and Timothy C. Urdan. "Perceptions of the School Psychological Environment and Early Adolescents' Psychological and Behavioral Functioning in School: The Mediating Role of Goals and Belonging." *Journal of Educational Psychology* 88, no. 3 (1996): 408–22.

Slavin, Robert E. "Synthesis of Research on Cooperative Learning." *Educational Leadership* 48, no. 5 (February 1991): 71–82.

Walter, Janet G., and Janelle Hart. "Understanding the Complexities of Student Motivations in Mathematics Learning." *Journal of Mathematical Behavior* 28, nos. 2–3 (June–September 2009): 162–70.

Wentzel, Kathryn R. "Social Relationships and Motivation in Middle School: The Role of Parents, Teachers, and Peers." *Journal of Educational Psychology* 90, no. 2 (June 1998): 202–9.

Wentzel, Kathryn R., Ann Battle, Shannon L. Russell, and Lisa B. Looney. "Social Supports from Teachers and Peers as Predictors of Academic and Social Motivation." *Contemporary Educational Psychology* 35, no. 3 (July 2010): 193–202.

Witkow, Melissa R., and Andrew J. Fuligni. "In-School versus out-of-School Friendships and Academic Achievement among an Ethnically Diverse Sample of Adolescents." *Journal of Research on Adolescence* 20, no. 3 (September 2010): 631–50.

CHAPTER 7

Success Matters

We use this story about Kristine to illustrate that we, as adults, are not so different from our students. The principles we communicate in this book are as relevant to our own development as mathematics learners and teachers as they are to our students. Jim met Kristine when she was a student in his university class. We hope to encounter more students like Kristine and to encourage other students to cope with academic struggle as she did—to believe that effort matters more than ability, realize that struggling to understand is a normal part of learning rather than evidence of intellectual deficit, and be persistent in the face of struggle and challenge.

Kristine is an eighth-grade teacher. She works in a diverse school district in a rapidly urbanizing suburb of Phoenix, Arizona. In recent years, the shortage of mathematics specialists in her district forced her to move from a self-contained classroom to a situation where she teaches both mathematics and science to seventh and eighth graders. To help her develop her mathematics skills, she enrolled in a master's degree program that focuses on developing teachers' content knowledge in a pedagogical environment that engages teachers in modeling data in science and engineering contexts. Jim recently saw Kristine working on an assignment dealing with rate-of-change as a way to compare the behavior of different functions. The context she was studying was Newton's law of cooling, which describes how the rate of a fluid's cooling is proportional to the area of the fluid open to the atmosphere and to the difference between the fluid's initial temperature and that of the surrounding environment (see fig. 7.1).

Newton's Law of Cooling:

(Rate of cooling over time) = (heat transfer coefficient) × (exposed area) × (temperature difference)

$\Delta Q / \Delta t = h \times A \times (T_{\text{initial}} - T_{\text{at time } t})$

Fig. 7.1

The class had finished collecting data for two conditions where the students had poured two containers full of water at 100°C, one of which had a smaller opening than the other. Thermometers in each of the containers recorded the temperature of the water over a 30-minute period (see fig. 7.2).

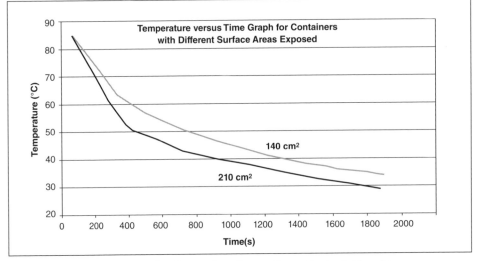

Fig. 7.2. Graphs illustrating the mathematical relationship with which Kristine was struggling

The students were grappling with how to describe the fact that the two curves began at the same temperature (approximately 85°C at the time when they first began recording), but ended up at different temperatures (approximately 35°C for the container with the smaller opening, and approximately 29°C for the container with the larger opening). Clearly the container with the larger opening had cooled off significantly more in the half hour in which Kristine's group had taken the data. But the curve wasn't linear. How could she describe a rate, which she thought of as a line with a constant slope, when that rate was changing?

Throughout the activity, the professor observed Kristine frowning and looking back and forth in her notes as she attempted to compare the two sets of data. When he asked her to send him a note detailing her difficulty, she responded with the self-evaluation in figure 7.3.

Kristine's actions and comments show that she was having a difficult time experiencing success given all the different and difficult concepts she was building. Additionally, like most teachers, Kristine probably has limited time, which can add to frustrations. What is noteworthy about Kristine's comments is that she attributes her struggles to a lack of knowledge, the amount of material she is processing, and other factors *not* related to her inherent mathematical ability. Quite the opposite, her response indicates that she believes that if she works hard and reviews material that she has forgotten, she can tackle these concepts. In addition, her last comment clearly

What I Am Struggling With

1. My algebra skills. I often feel that I can't follow along in class or in the book, not because I don't understand the topic, but because I don't understand and/ or can't remember the algebra that is taking us from point A to point C.

2. Sometimes I feel that it is not so much one particular idea or concept, but rather that my brain is struggling to assimilate too many different ideas and concepts at once. I am digesting the new concepts in class, struggling to attach them to schema that at this point are very limited, while at the same time digging through my brain files for algebraic information that is present, but filed way in the back and very dusty. At the same time I am also learning how to use Excel, learning how to use a graphing calculator, and learning how to type math equations on the computer, or figuring out how to scan them without the file being so big that I can't upload it. Then I am also trying to connect this information with the science involved in our weekly modeling problem. I kind of feel like I have moved to another country and am now trying to survive while learning the new language, cultural norms, customs, etc.

3. I don't know that I really understand what a function is.

Fig. 7.3

indicates that Kristine comprehends the major source of her troubles—the concept of function. Each of these sources of difficulty are what motivation researchers would call *healthy attributions* of causes for her lack of success.

In the weeks following Kristine's self-assessment, the professor created new assignments designed to help her and others in the class who were struggling, dusting off little-used knowledge from back in their high school days. He wrote specific tutorials for using spreadsheets and other technologies so that the students would spend less cognitive load learning the technology and use more to examine the important features of exponential functions, their overall behavior, and, specifically, their rate of change. They also examined the most common and important classes of functions, focusing on how one would recognize a quadratic or exponential relationship by analyzing a set of data.

During this time, Kristine kept asking questions, persistently asserting her right to learn. When, three weeks later, she and the professor discussed her plans for a final project, her affect was positive, and she showed that although she was still struggling with the ideas, she was learning and trying to apply them to her current teaching practice (see fig. 7.4).

The extent to which students are motivated to work hard to learn mathematics concepts and skills depends on how they define success in mathematics (Urdan and Schoenfelder 2006; Ames 1992; Maehr and Midgley 1991). These definitions of success come from their experiences being successful or not in the mathematics curriculum, seeing how others react to success and nonsuccess, and the messages they receive from teachers, parents, and society in general regarding how each one values mathematics. We should note that success in and of itself is not a determining factor

For my final project I am thinking that I would really like to do something with convection. As part of the 7th grade curriculum, I have to teach about the convection currents as the driving force for tectonic plate motion. Ideally, I would like to create some experiment that I could eventually use with my students to demonstrate the process of convection. The classic example that is always given in the textbooks is the example of boiling water. They always discuss how the water on the bottom heats up, becomes less dense, and rises, and at the surface it cools, becomes denser, and sinks. This, however, is still hard for the students to grasp because the water is boiling, so it is all hot to them. It would be interesting do something where they could take the temperature near the bottom and near the surface, but that is where I am stuck. Not really sure how to design an experiment that models convection in the earth....

Fig. 7.4

of motivation. Instead, it is what success *means to the student*. If a task is trivial, for example, the student will not value success with it. If a task is challenging, success has more meaning. If a student works hard, success provides a sense of accomplishment. We must thus look at success and its counterpart, nonsuccess, in conjunction with students' beliefs about themselves and the task.

In general, when a student expects to be successful in a moderately challenging task, they tend to expend more effort. Effort provides a greater chance of success, and success breeds more success. An expectation of failure often leads to low effort levels, or worse, a lot of effort spent avoiding mathematics. Acting out, withdrawing, feeling sick, and other task-avoidance behaviors will likely lead to failure, and just as success breeds success, failure tends to breed more failure. Ultimately, the long-term patterns of success and nonsuccess that students experience consolidate into a general feeling of mathematical competence called *self-efficacy* (Schweinle, Turner, and Meyer 2006; Nurmi et al. 2003).

Kristine, for example, illustrates that although success is a crucial factor in determining what motivates us, a healthy appreciation for nonsuccess is equally crucial. After all, success only has value if we have some difficulty attaining it. Notice that we are using the word *nonsuccess* here in lieu of *failure*. As we established in the first two chapters of this book, motivation is really an attitude. If we want to change our attitude, then we need to change our vocabulary regarding that attitude. Changing *failure*, with its negative connotations, to the more neutral *nonsuccess* reorients us to the positive aspects of challenge as opposed to its negative ramifications. Challenge implies that we will be nonsuccessful in a significant portion of the tasks we perform. A healthy attitude, therefore, toward nonsuccess is crucial for developing persistence, grit, and ultimately, greater success than would be possible if nonsuccess were defined as *failure*.

From an educational perspective, success in mathematics matters in three ways: (1) we want students to be successful, and we have an ethical responsibility to support them academically so that they can *become* successful in life; (2) students' successes and nonsuccesses drive interests and predilections; and (3) students' beliefs about their probability of success in academic tasks—their sense of efficacy—influence their choice of tasks in the short run, their strategies while engaged in tasks, and their long-term goals and aspirations. Given that overall, mathematics achievement and persistence in the United States is moderate compared with that of our international counterparts (Provasnik, Gonzales, and Miller 2010), competence in mathematics is becoming even more pivotal for economic and intellectual competitiveness. So it is crucial that we ratchet up the challenge of our mathematics education programs. To do *that* implies that we need to rethink seriously how students interpret successes and nonsuccesses in their mathematics career so that they can begin to build healthy, efficacious attitudes and behaviors.

Able and Stable:
The Role of Attributions in Motivation

One of the strongest findings in all education research is that success and failure are not only influenced by the task, the curriculum, or the teacher per se, but also by the *learner* (Weiner 1972). This will seem obvious to veteran teachers, but it bears some discussion. All teaching is a kind of dance, where the partners are the teacher and the student. Each contributes to the mathematical experience's coherence. But like in traditional ballroom dance, one person must lead. The teacher has the responsibility and the broader knowledge to steer the student in a productive direction.

Some students, for example, show a high degree of tolerance for mistakes and continue blithely along, using information they gain from analyzing their mistakes to correct them, honing their skills in a process that we state not as *trial and error*, but perhaps as *conscious error analysis*. These students have become successful in part *because* they make mistakes. They have incorporated an appreciation for mistakes' role in their learning process and don't see mistakes as *failures*. Such students also tend to perceive difficulties in conceptualizing mathematical ideas as challenges to overcome. Psychologists would say that these students have attributed their *nonsuccesses* most likely to lack of effort. By expending a little bit more effort, they can ameliorate their errors and learn more in the process.

Other students tend to regard mathematical errors, poor test performance, or difficulty in conceptualizing mathematical concepts as actual *failures* in the sense that they see them as *bad*, in essence attributing these perceived negative outcomes to some personal flaw in their ability. Such an interpretation often leads to students disengaging from mathematics if at all possible. Why? In part, if students attribute poor performance to a lack of innate ability, they have a hard time seeing how they can do anything to fix the problem. "Some people are just good at math; others, like me, just aren't," they seem to say.

Still other students tend to see their mistakes as originating in the teacher or the text, believing that their lack of understanding stems from an external source. This interpretation can help maintain a sense of self-efficacy or self-esteem. If students' errors are minimal or random, this belief is not particularly harmful. If, however, it becomes a habit of blaming others instead of examining the root causes of nonsuccess, this attribution style can lead to a lack of motivation to change study habits, expend more effort, or engage in other strategies that could improve learning and performance.

The final group of students tends to attribute their failures to random chance (e.g., "the room was so cold, I couldn't concentrate" or "I never know which formula to pick"). In the absence of contingencies, or if contingencies don't seem to relate to the students' behavior, these students have little basis for winnowing through successful versus nonsuccessful strategies, and so they tend to disengage from mathematics tasks.

What is important here is that, for all intents and purposes, each of these four attributional styles exists at any one time in our classrooms. Each of the hypothetical groups of students described above might make the same mistakes and the same number of mistakes as the others. But their attributions of the *causes* of their mistakes will lead them to engage in very different learning behavior. Table 7.1 illustrates these four attributions of nonsuccess and their associated attributions of the causes of success.

Table 7.1
Attributions of Success and Nonsuccess in Academic Tasks

Stability of Cause	Source of Success or Nonsuccess			
	Internal		External	
	Success	**Nonsuccess**	**Success**	**Nonsuccess**
Stable	Ability +	Lack of ability	Teacher's positive bias	Teacher's negative bias
Unstable	Effort +	Lack of effort +	Good luck (random chance)	Bad luck (random chance)

+ indicates that the attribution is controllable. Ability attributions are a bit tricky, depending on whether or not the student sees ability as an innate, fixed quantity or as something that hard work can augment (Blackwell, Trzesniewski, and Dweck 2007).

Success Equals Ability + Effort

As we mentioned, ability attributions are somewhat tricky. Carol Dweck's crowning achievement in education has been establishing the fact that people hold two different kinds of beliefs about ability: (1) ability or intelligence is fixed for each individual; or (2) ability or intelligence is malleable and can be augmented through learning (Dweck 1996). Table 7.1 shows three cells, all internal, where these beliefs play out. For the first condition (*Internal Stable Success* attributions), when a person believes that they have at least a moderate ability in the domain *and* that this ability is a function of the effort they expend on a task, then it follows logically that effort expenditure will ultimately lead to success, and this will make the student feel more able. In the second condition (*Internal Unstable Success* attributions), clearly the more effort students put into a task, the more likely they will be successful. The third condition (*Internal Unstable Nonsuccess* attribution) implies that, when one experiences nonsuccess, the root cause is lack of effort. Again, this implies that, with improved effort, improved learning and success will result.

Taken together, these three conditions constitute a healthy attitude toward success, one that promotes hard work, encourages persistence in the face of frustration, and ultimately results in positive learning and achievement outcomes. Kristine's ability to persevere through her frustrations is a result of these internal, controllable factors.

In general, the body of research into people's beliefs about their success in academic tasks shows that attributing successes to a combination of the internal factors, namely ability and effort, and attributing nonsuccess to a lack of effort leads to highly productive academic behaviors and subsequent performance (Graham 1991). This is because effort and ability are controllable factors. If Kristine believes that she is basically capable (ability), then expending effort is worthwhile; she can apply her ability to resolving her frustrations with the class and continue to engage and persist. Moreover, because effort breeds success, her beliefs about her ability will tend to improve over time. In this manner, effort is a mediator of any innate differences in ability we may have. The old adage "Hard work pays off" is not just a cliché, but a fundamental principle of motivation and achievement.

Subject-specificity of ability and effort attributions

Bong (2004) found that ability attributions tend to be subject specific. Namely, when students believe themselves able or unable in mathematics, it does not generally reflect on their perceived ability in other academic subject matter. Effort attributions, like ability, associate with specific subject matter, but this association appears less strong. The most likely explanation for this finding is that the general, naïve consensus among pupils, that people differ in ability across domains, affects their personal beliefs about their own ability in each domain. Effort, however, is a generally recognized strategy for improving performance across domains. So, we must reiterate that for any given task in a particular class, a range of ability and effort attributional styles will play out across students. But more than this, a subtle interplay exists between students' beliefs about mathematics and those they hold about other domains, where ability tends to play a more dominant role, but where effort also plays a role in determining how they go about attributing the causes of their successes and nonsuccesses.

Failure Equals Lack of Ability

In contrast to this positive pattern of beliefs, attributing our nonsuccess to lack of ability yields counterproductive learning behaviors. Note that here we use the word *failure* to mean failure. Attributing nonsuccessful outcomes to lack of ability results in negative affect and a lower sense of self-efficacy, typical of feelings of failure. If Kristine had developed a belief that only some people were good at mathematics and that she had not inherited this math gene, wherein would be the benefit of her expending effort to learn? Instead, the most logical decision Kristine could make would be to engage only minimally in the mathematics to preserve her sense of self-worth, and to refocus her attention on aspects of her life where her "genetic" predisposition was stronger, say in socialization with her peers; in other subject matter, like reading; or in daydreaming or other "checking-out" behaviors.

Whereas the other three internal attributional styles initiate and maintain a positive cycle of hard work and success, attributing failure to lack of ability does quite the opposite. People who tend to believe themselves less able than others in mathematics, and who believe themselves incapable of augmenting their ability through effort, begin to "check out" of mathematics merely to preserve their sense of self-efficacy in school. Of course, this leads to lower performance, but not necessarily to a lower sense of self: students check out precisely to preserve a sense of self. If, after all, I don't engage in mathematics, I can't fail at it, can I? These self-preserving strategies are the reason that students in the United States tend to maintain good beliefs about themselves despite poor school performance (Dweck 2000).

Failure Due to Uncontrollable Circumstances

Attributing success and or failure to external factors like bad luck or teachers' bias leads students to develop really debilitating patterns of behavior, if these feelings persist and are not truly random, associated with isolated instances. In chapter 2 we briefly introduced these conditions as *learned helplessness* and *learned hopelessness*. We want to focus our current discussion on the more positive aspects of success attributions. A short digression down this more depressing path of learned negativity is worthwhile, however, because quite a number of students in the United States appear to have developed beliefs of helplessness concerning mathematical tasks, exhibiting such feelings as math anxiety (Tobias 1993) and even depression (Au et al. 2009).

It is a fact that people use their activity's outcomes as data by which they adjust their behavior to be more attuned to the tasks' requirements, social rules and obligations, and potentially transferrable strategies. When those outcomes seemingly have no bearing on the student's input strategies, when the student repeatedly fails despite their best attempts at success, they begin to believe that success is unattainable. When this happens, we say that the student has *learned helplessness*. "No matter what I do, the outcome will be a failure," they say to themselves. To preserve their sense of self-worth, they may blame others, like the teacher. Or, they may blame themselves—their ability. The difference does not matter, because students can control neither perceived source of difficulty.

In the absence of a sense of control, depression can creep in, and with it a lack of hope and a dread of the future (Au et al. 2009). Although such extreme outcomes are rare, mathematics is one area of education where they appear more often than in others, which bears some attention for teachers intent on helping students overcome their fear and loathing of mathematics.

Self-Efficacy: Anticipating Success

A synopsis of the research on how we use success as a factor in motivation would say that we tend to do things we think we can accomplish with a modest amount of expended effort. Some cognitive psychologists see this as a kind of cost-benefits analysis whereby we make quick judgments regarding what we will likely get out of a chosen course of action, given the amount of energy we willingly expend, factoring in the most salient of any potential negative consequences. If the positives (the benefits) outweigh the negatives (the costs), it only makes sense to choose to engage.

But it is not that simple. Most complex, social activities like mathematics learning have many potential benefits and costs. Evaluating each of the costs and benefits systematically would take too long to accomplish practically before the opportunity or necessity for actual engagement passes by. For this reason, humans tend to choose the *first* set of criteria that comes to mind, make a "good enough" decision, and get on with it (Simon 1990). This practical side to decision-making implies that we need to create some motivational memories—likes, dislikes, interests, and so on—for the purpose of identifying worthwhile opportunities efficiently in the future.

The rules by which we make success and failure attributions constitute these memories, as our implicit theories of intelligence do. Interests and noninterests constitute much of the remainder. Taking it all together, we must clearly reserve a significant amount of memory for monitoring motivational information, evaluating it, and making decisions about it and based on it. The focus of these memories—*each and every one of them*—associates with our success or nonsuccess. Over the course of a few years learning mathematics, children tend to develop a consistent system of beliefs around mathematics, called their *mathematical self-efficacy*—their personal judgments of their ability to learn mathematics successfully (Bandura and Schunk 1981; Pajares and Miller 1994; Zimmerman 2000). We introduced this concept in chapter 3; here, we want to move to what classroom factors enhance or inhibit mathematical self-efficacy.

Urdan and Schoenfelder (2006; see also Bandura [1986]) report that students develop self-efficacy in academic situations through a combination of factors. First, as we have established in discussing attributions, students evaluate their past successes and nonsuccesses, and the resulting causal attributions lead students to categorize themselves as successful or nonsuccessful. Second, students compare themselves with their peers who are successful or not, and make judgments about their own success relative to the social norm. They can emulate the strategies of others and coordinate their values with those of the class. Third, verbal persuasion from authorities and peers also can have an impact on students' judgments about their efficacy. Teachers can use a variety of strategies to convince students of their competence, including pointing out similar circumstances in the past where the student *has* been successful. In Kristine's instance, we went back to mathematics that she understood and carefully built the case that she had the ability to be successful and that her primary strategy was to go over previously learned and forgotten concepts and reintroduce herself to them. Armed with her refreshed memory, Kristine could engage successfully in the more difficult mathematics that we had originally planned. Moreover, her basic beliefs that she was capable in mathematics supported Kristine in choosing a difficult final project.

When students have a positive mathematical self-efficacy, they tend to value mathematics, have a sense of belonging at school, believe themselves autonomous and independent in completing tasks even if working in cooperative groups, and have a supportive teacher. These factors all intertwine, contributing to a positive sense of well-being and even a positive anticipation for engagement in mathematics. Feelings of control and autonomy foster risk-taking and develop competence. Competence, in turn, enables students to perceive themselves as capable of interacting at a high level with others. Competence also makes their interaction valuable to others working on the same task, thus contributing to relatedness (Deci and Ryan 1985).

Developing positive self-efficacy in the classroom does not just happen. The teacher plays a very important role in orchestrating the tasks, discussion, and feedback to promote optimal learning experiences and maintain the development of competence, relatedness, and self-efficacy (McCaslin 2009; Kunter, Baumert, and Koller 2007). Well-structured mathematics classroom environments, where students believe that the teacher monitors their learning and behavior closely and that the classroom rules are clear and transparent, yield students who are more interested in the mathematical subject matter. We do not intend to promote regimentation in classroom management technique, but establishing clear norms and rules, within which students can exercise their autonomy appropriately and pointedly, clearly contributes to optimal learning for both individual and collective.

Setting Goals for Success

It is probably becoming apparent to you that goal setting is one of the primary instructional strategies that affect each of the important factors contributing to mathematical motivation. In chapter 4, we saw that setting proximal goals provides control over task demands, increases the success probability in the task, orients the task's learning to transfer beyond the task, and contributes to the task's interest level.

In chapter 6, we talked about academic and social goals and how they sometimes agree and sometimes oppose one another. We now address goals as important features that connect motivation, self-efficacy, and problem-solving strategies in actual learning tasks.

Locke and Latham (2002, p. 709) define goals as "an object or outcome to aim for and a standard for judging satisfaction." If people have a goal, we can say that they will not be satisfied until they have attained that goal. In general, for tasks where students have established goals, the more they exceed the goal, the more satisfaction they tend to receive. Of course, goals can be unrealistic at times—unrealistically low, set at a bar so easy to overcome that success has little value, or unrealistically high, set to a difficulty that makes success unattainable. People who set the most difficult goals are often those least satisfied with their own performance. Locke and Latham call this a *seeming paradox*. "How can people who produce the most, those with difficult goals, be the least satisfied? The answer is implicit in the question. People with high goals produce more because they are dissatisfied with less" (p. 710). Helping students develop more challenging goals related to mathematics learning is a tricky dance. After all, challenge implies effort, and if a learning situation does not appeal to the student, they won't relish the challenge it affords. A short introduction to the types of achievement goals people tend to set will clarify the kinds of goals that are educationally healthy and that lead to increased efficacy, performance, and satisfaction.

Achievement goal orientations

Historically, motivation literature has distinguished between two types of goal orientations—*performance goal orientation* and *learning goal orientation*. The literature typically refers to these as *orientations*, meaning the same as *values* in this book—long-term, relatively stable approaches to mathematics motivation. We will drop the word *orientation* when we focus on goals-in-the-moment as opposed to general attitudes.

Learning goal orientation, also called *mastery goal orientation*, involves the desire to learn the content and incorporates the beliefs that hard work leads to success and a person's ability is malleable (Dweck and Leggett 1988; Nicholls et al. 1990). Students whose goals focus on learning tend to focus their attention on developing conceptual understanding and skill. They tend to work hard to meet their learning goals, and they often go beyond them, setting higher goals for themselves, if they achieve their original ones.

Performance goal orientation, also called *ego goal orientation*, involves the desire to compare favorably against the norm. Reading the word *performance* can confuse you here, because performance in mathematics is a good thing, right? In this context, however, the word *performance* takes on its other definition, that of being on stage. Students who hold primarily performance goal orientations believe that success hinges on social comparison—having a higher grade than others, or being more able in a particular area than others. As a result, their actual goal attainment is nominal; that is, they tend to only do enough to get by. Moreover, because their goals focus on the outward appearance of competence, they consider learning and remembering mathematics content for future use substantially less important, and their actual achievement is substantially less than that of their peers who hold learning goals.

We have seen in our classes what a huge difference learning goals versus performance goals can have on students' persistence in the face of nonsuccess, on their personal confidence and self-efficacy. But sometimes, a student who has performance goals may outperform students with learning goals. Or, a student with learning goals may appear too perfectionist at times. These tendencies can be explained by noting that, for any particular task, a person constructs goals designed to maximize their success. Researchers have classified these task-related goals as *approach* goals and *avoidance goals*. Taken together (see table 7.2), a student's goals in the moment can demonstrably contribute both to one of the two general orientations and to one of the two task orientations (Harackiewicz et al. 2002).

Table 7.2
Achievement Goal Orientations as a Function of Learning versus Performance Goals and Approach or Avoidance Task Orientations

	Task Orientation	
Goal Orientation	**Approach**	**Avoidance**
Learning (Mastery)	Develop skills and abilities, understand and apply mathematics	Avoid misunderstanding, prevent making mistakes
Performance (Ego)	Demonstrate high ability compared to others	Hide low ability compared to others

The punch line to all this is that when students develop learning goals, they tend to achieve more than students who develop performance goals. But even more telling is the fact that the learning-approach combination, when applied to specific mathematical tasks, yields deep cognitive processing, presumably because students are intent on improving their understanding and abilities: they are engaged deeply in learning the mathematics. On the other side of the coin, performance goals relate only tangentially to deep cognitive processing, and, in at least one study, related only remotely to shallow cognitive processing as well (Sins et al. 2008). Moreover, the learning-approach combination associates with positive mathematical self-efficacy. The achievement ramifications for these findings are obvious. If you want your students to think deeply, you should foster developing learning-approach goals. We conclude this chapter with some principles of classroom environments that promote learning-approach goals.

Classroom Environments

Ames and Archer (1988), in a now-classic study, examined the correlates of classroom climate on developing learning goals versus performance goals. Ames and Archer found that high-achieving students who had learning goals had better learning strategies, had a better attitude toward class, and embraced task challenge more than performance-oriented students. Students with learning goals attributed their causes of success to more internal factors—namely, ability and effort—and less on task ease. Interestingly, learning-oriented students considered the teacher more a major factor in their success than performance-oriented students did. Table 7.3 summarizes their perspective.

Table 7.3

Classroom Climate Variables and Goal Orientations (Adapted from Ames and Archer [1988])

Classroom Climate	Learning Goals	Performance Goals
Success defined as...	Improvement of knowledge and skill	High grades or recognition compared to others
Value placed on...	Challenge	Just enough to get by
Reasons for satisfaction	Learning challenging content	Doing better than others
View of nonsuccess	Data for improvement	Anxiety producing
Focus of attention	Process of learning	Performance comparison
Reason for expending effort	Overcome difficult challenge, learn something new	Receive recognition or external confirmation of success
Evaluation criteria	Progress, change in ability	Normative—do better or do no worse than others
Teacher's focus	Helping students learn	Evaluating students' performance

Generally speaking, the classroom's orientation toward learning versus performance goals are considered major contributing factors toward students' personal goal orientations (Meece, Anderman, and Anderman 2006: Maehr and Midgley 1996; Wolters 2004). But we must acknowledge that achievement, as measured by standardized tests, correlates only moderately with learning orientations (Wolters 2004). This may be because performance orientations can also induce some students to high achievement, but for the wrong reasons, or it may be because standardized tests are poor, incomplete indices of learning. More research is needed to determine what is behind this puzzling finding. Nevertheless, however you measure them, learning goals outperform performance goals on any and all sets of positive outcomes ever put to the test.

Summary

Teachers who are able to change their practices to engender the development of personal learning goals in their students have a major impact on their students' motivation, self-beliefs, and learning outcomes. This is because learning goals focus students' attention on the kinds of outcomes that, if realized, build autonomy, competence, and relatedness. It is also because students can attribute their successes to internal, stable factors—their ability and the hard work they put in. Thus they can take pride in their personal accomplishments. This maintains a cycle of positive accomplishment and self-efficacy.

Students with performance goals *can* achieve at a high level, but research indicates that, over the long haul, they tend to disengage early from challenging tasks, do only what is necessary to get by in order not to look bad compared to their peers, and feel bad doing it. Attributing their failures—and here, we really do mean *failures*—to internal, stable causes (i.e., lack of ability), or worse, to external unstable causes like random chance, leads students with performance goals to avoid mathematics if at all possible. The cycle that this engenders is debilitating, causing the students to perform poorly, evaluate their self-efficacy negatively, and ultimately choose life pathways that do not include mathematical sophistication, in essence eliminating many worthwhile jobs and pastimes for no good reason.

Success matters. It matters in school. It matters in life. How we handle our success and nonsuccess early on will determine, to a large extent, the possibilities we have available to us. Teachers can foster a positive attitude toward success by consciously changing their vocabulary and classroom norms to emphasize effort over ability, challenge over task ease, and learning over performance.

References

Ames, Carole. "Classrooms: Goals, Structures, and Student Motivation." *Journal of Educational Psychology* 84, no. 3 (September 1992): 261–71.

Ames, Carole, and Jennifer Archer. "Achievement Goals in the Classroom: Students' Learning Strategies and Motivation Process." *Journal of Educational Psychology* 80, no. 3 (1988): 260–67.

Au, Raymond C. P., David Watkins, John Hattie, and Patricia Alexander. "Reformulating the Depression Model of Learned Hopelessness for Academic Outcomes." *Educational Research Review* 4, no. 2 (2009): 103–17.

Bandura, Albert. *Social Foundations of Thought and Action: A Social Cognitive Theory.* Englewood Cliffs, N.J.: Prentice-Hall, 1986.

Bandura, Albert, and Dale H. Schunk. "Cultivating Competence, Self-Efficacy, and Intrinsic Interest through Proximal Self-Motivation." *Journal of Personality and Social Psychology* 41, no. 3 (September 1981): 586–98.

Blackwell, Lisa S., Kali H. Trzesniewski, and Carol S. Dweck. "Implicit Theories of Intelligence Predict Achievement across an Adolescent Transition: A Longitudinal Study and an Intervention." *Child Development* 78, no. 1 (January–February 2007): 246–63.

Bong, Mimi. "Academic Motivation in Self-Efficacy, Task Value, Achievement Goal Orientations, and Attributional Beliefs." *Journal of Education Research* 97, no.6 (July 2004): 287–97.

Deci, Edward L., and Richard M. Ryan. *Intrinsic Motivation and Self-Determination in Human Behavior.* New York: Springer, 1985.

Dweck, Carol S. "Implicit Theories as Organizers of Goals and Behavior." In *The Psychology of Action: Linking Cognition and Motivation to Behavior,* edited by Peter M. Gollwitzer and John A. Bargh, pp. 69–90. New York: Guilford Press, 1996.

———. *Self-Theories: Their Role in Motivation, Personality, and Development.* London: Psychology Press, 2000.

Dweck, Carol S., and Ellen L. Leggett. "A Social-Cognitive Approach to Motivation and Personality." *Psychological Review* 95, no. 2 (April 1998): 256–73.

Graham, Sandra. "A Review of Attribution Theory in Achievement Contexts." *Educational Psychology Review* 3, no. 1 (1991): 5–39.

Harackiewicz, Judith M., Kenneth E. Barron, Paul R. Pintrich, Andrew J. Elliot, and Todd M. Thrash. "Revision of Achievement Goal Theory: Necessary and Illuminating." *Journal of Educational Psychology* 94, no. 3 (September 2002): 638–45.

Kunter, Mareike, Jurgen Baumert, and Olaf Köller. "Effective Classroom Management and the Development of Subject-Related Interest." *Learning and Instruction* 17 (October 2007): 494–505.

Locke, Edwin A., and Gary P. Latham. "Building a Practically Useful Theory of Goal Setting and Task Motivation: A 35-Year Odyssey." *American Psychologist* 57, no. 9 (September 2002): 705–17.

Maehr, Martin L., and Carol Midgley. "Enhancing Student Motivation: A Schoolwide Approach." *Educational Psychologist* 26, nos. 3–4 (1991): 388–427.

Meece, Judith L., Eric M. Anderman, and Lynley H. Anderman. "Classroom Goal Structure, Student Motivation, and Academic Achievement." *Annual Review of Psychology* 57 (2006): 487–503.

McCaslin, Mary. "Coregulation of Student Motivation and Emergent Identity." *Educational Psychologist* 44, no. 2 (2009): 137–46.

Nicholls, John G., Paul Cobb, Terry Wood, Erna Yackel, and Michael Patashnick. "Assessing Students' Theories of Success in Mathematics: Individual and Classroom Differences." *Journal for Research in Mathematics Education* 21, no. 2 (March 1990): 109–22.

Nurmi, Jan-Erik, Kaisa Aunola, Katariina Salmela-Aro, and Maria Lindros. "The Role of Success Expectation and Task Avoidance in Academic Performance and Satisfaction: Three Studies on Antecedents, Consequences, and Correlates." *Contemporary Educational Psychology* 28, no. 1 (January 2003): 59–90.

Pajares, Frank, and M. David Miller. "Role of Self-Efficacy and Self-Concept Beliefs in Mathematical Problem Solving: A Path Analysis." *Journal of Educational Psychology* 86, no. 2 (June 1994): 193–203.

Provasnik, Stephen, Patrick Gonzales, and David Miller. "U.S. Performance across International Assessments of Student Achievement: Special Supplement to the Condition of Education 2009." Washington, D.C.: National Center for Education Statistics, 2010.

Schweinle, Amy, Julianne C. Turner, and Debra K. Meyer. "Striking the Right Balance: Students' Motivation and Affect in Elementary Mathematics." *Journal of Educational Research* 99, no. 5 (May–June 2006): 271–93.

Simon, Herbert A. "Invariants of Human Behavior." *Annual Review of Psychology* 41, no. 1 (February 1990): 1–19.

Sins, Patrick H. M., Wouter R. van Joolingen, Elvin R. Savelsbergh, and Bernadette van Hout-Wolters. "Motivation and Performance within a Collaborative Computer-Based Modeling Task: Relations between Students' Achievement Goal Orientation, Self-Efficacy, Cognitive Processing, and Achievement." *Contemporary Educational Psychology* 33, no. 1 (January 2008): 58–77.

Tobias, Sheila. *Overcoming Math Anxiety.* New York: W. W. Norton & Co., 1993.

Urdan, Tim, and Erin Schoenfelder. "Classroom Effects on Student Motivation." *Journal of School Psychology* 44, no. 5 (October 2006): 331–49.

Weiner, Bernard. "Attribution Theory, Achievement Motivation. and the Educational Process." *Review of Educational Research* 42, no. 2 (Spring 1972): 203–15.

Wolters, Christopher A. "Advancing Achievement Goal Theory: Using Goal Structures and Goal Motivation to Predict Students' Motivation, Cognition, and Achievement." *Journal of Educational Psychology* 96, no. 6 (June 2004): 236–50.

Zimmerman, Barry J. "Self-Efficacy: An Essential Motive to Learn." *Contemporary Educational Psychology* 25 (January 2000): 82–91.

PART 3

Teachers Matter: Strategies That Foster Motivation in Students

CHAPTER 8

Emphasizing Sense Making and Personal Investment: Using Contexts Judiciously

W e start this chapter with a story based on a classroom observation. At the time we wrote this book, Amanda Jansen (Mandy) and her colleague at the University of Delaware, Tonya Bartell, were in the midst of collaborating on a research project investigating how mathematics teachers build relationships with their students. As part of the project, Mandy observed a middle school mathematics teacher implementing a mathematics problem. The teacher was surprised that her students interacted with the problem's context differently from how she had envisioned. Some of the students had not had the prior experiences with the context that the teacher expected. This story provides inspiration for reflecting on the role contexts in mathematics tasks play in promoting understanding and motivating students.

Ms. Hartman wrote the following number sentence on the whiteboard for her seventh-grade class.

$$1.15 \times 49.64 = ?$$

Then she asked, "What would you say if I asked you to solve this?"

Bridget said, "I would say that it's a lot of multiplying."

"Okay, what else? Antonio?"

"Uh, yeah, I'm thinking that it's a long problem. I'd like to use my calculator, and I'm thinking that you won't let me. I guess we're going to do multiplying decimals today?"

Ms. Hartman replied, "Kind of. I'm just trying to gauge your reactions to this problem. Anyone else? Yes, Alicia."

Alicia said, "You want to know what I would really think? I would want to know the point of it. Why do we have to do that problem? It's kind of boring."

Some of the students laughed uncomfortably. They agreed that it was a boring problem, but they were surprised that Alicia admitted how she really felt about it.

"Okay, I can understand why you would think that this problem is boring," Ms. Hartman responded. "But I want us to think together about ways to solve problems like this. Sometimes you encounter a problem like this outside school. You probably won't have a calculator then, so I want you to feel like you can solve a problem like this."

"All right, let me take a quick poll," Ms. Hartman continued. "Raise your hand if you've eaten dinner at a restaurant recently with your family."

About half the class raised their hands.

"Great! Keep those hands in the air if you remember any of the adults paying the bill and leaving a tip."

At this point, most of the students put their hands down. Only three students kept their hands in the air. Ms. Hartman felt a bit unsure in that moment, because she planned the lesson with the assumption that students would have prior experience thinking about leaving a tip at a restaurant. She continued, "Thank you. Everyone can put their hands down now. I was thinking about a situation when I have to find fifteen hundredths of something. Fifteen hundredths is just like saying fifteen percent. Remember that?"

Ms. Hartman wrote on the board.

$$0.15 = 15\%$$

She went on to say, "When we leave a tip at a restaurant, we leave 15 percent of the amount on the bill. Sometimes, if the service and the food is really good, we might leave 20 percent."

Ms. Hartman then turned her back to the class to write on the board some more, partially to write the mathematical equivalences, but she also wanted to take a moment to think about explaining the idea of tipping to the students. She thought they would have had more experiences with tipping. She assumed that they would have been able to explain tipping to one another, but now she was unsure.

She wrote the following mathematical equivalences on the board:

$$1.15 \times 49.64 = (1.00 \times 49.64) + (0.15 \times 49.64)$$
$$115\% \text{ of } \$49.64 = (100\% \text{ of } \$49.64) + (15\% \text{ of } \$49.64)$$

"Let's see," Ms. Hartman thought aloud. "Where did you go out to eat with your families?"

Students mentioned several fast-food restaurants. Ms. Hartman felt more uneasy. She hadn't considered that many of her students' families could not afford taking their family to a restaurant with a menu and a server. She recognized that she could have made this connection if she had thought about it. After all, as a single adult without children, she could not regularly afford to eat at a restaurant on her own salary herself. It made sense that a family might hesitate to do so. When planning the lesson the day before, she assumed that tipping would be a somewhat universal experience that most students would find relevant. She quickly realized that it would not be, but she decided to continue to continue with the context, anyhow.

"So, as I was saying, about tipping, sometimes we go out to restaurants, and the server takes our order from a menu while we sit at a table or a booth. In those kinds of restaurants, we often leave a tip."

Kelsey raised her hand, and Ms. Hartman called on her.

"Sometimes in other places, you order at the counter, and they have a jar or a cup where you can put a tip."

"Yes. That's a good point, Kelsey. So sometimes when we want to leave a tip, we have to think about how much to leave. Maybe in a cup or jar, you put your extra change or an extra dollar, but in a restaurant, when you order from a waiter or waitress, there is a different expectation. As I said before, you usually leave a tip of something like 15 percent or even 20 percent if you were really impressed with the food or service."

"Whoa," Jason reacted. "These places are already expensive. I'm kind of not cool with having to pay money on top of already paying money. Why do I have to give the place more money?"

"Well, it's to pay the employees. People who work at a restaurant don't get paid much per hour for their base pay. They rely on tips to make money."

Jason responded, "That doesn't seem like a good system. Why doesn't the restaurant just pay them more?"

Ms. Hartman replied. "The system is not set up to pay the employees enough without tips. So, it's up to the customers to help add to their salaries. Often at the end of the night, everyone turns in their tips and the restaurant divides them up among the group."

"That doesn't seem right, either," Megan said. "You mean if I worked at a restaurant and was really good at it and got lots of tips, and Jason over there was a slacker as usual, he would benefit from my tips?" Jason rolled up a piece of paper, threw it across the room toward Megan, and Ms. Hartman intercepted it. The class clapped at her dexterity.

"Thank you. That was a rare example of physical coordination on my part. I rarely have any. Okay, okay. I hear you. Jason, you know it's not appropriate to throw things, so unless you want to see me in detention, keep it together. About these tips. Yes. I hear you that it's not an ideal working situation, but it's important to think about these things, because you may be at a restaurant yourself at some point and need to think about how much tip to leave and whether or not you want to leave a tip."

Marika raised her hand. Ms. Hartman called on her and she said, "At my mom's salon, she does hair, and she gets tipped."

"That's a great point, Marika. Tipping your stylist. That's another job where people earn tips. The tips for a job like your mom's job are usually right around 20 percent of the cost of the service."

"I don't really know," Marika said, "But I was just thinking that people leave tips in places other than restaurants."

"Excellent connection, Marika. Thanks. Okay, everyone, please take out a piece of paper."

As the students took out paper, Ms. Hartman wrote the following on the board.

Cost of food: $45.97
8% tax: $ 3.67
Total: $49.64

"Here is part of what you might see from the bill at a restaurant."

"That's not cheap, Ms. H!"

"You're right, Antonio. Let's say that it's either an expensive restaurant or more than two people went out to eat together. All right. As I was saying, a tip is either 15 percent or 20 percent or somewhere in between. Here's the information you have. How might you think about finding the tip? Let's think for a few minutes. Jot down some thoughts. Try to calculate a tip. We'll do think-pair-share, and I'll give you five minutes to think."

Students worked on their solutions, applying what they knew about decimals and percents to determine the tip that they might leave.

Bridget raised her hand and said, "Um, Ms. H? Do we calculate the tip on the subtotal before tax or the total after tax?"

"Oh, good point," Ms. Hartman said. "Let's go with the total after tax. Did everyone hear that?" She repeated Bridget's point for the group's benefit. "Now let's share our thinking with our partners. It's time for the pair in think-pair-share. After five more minutes, let's share with the whole class."

Ms. Hartman went around the room to listen to the pairs discuss their solutions and to ask the students questions to understand their reasoning.

Then, she sent four pairs of students to the whiteboard. She strategically chose students with different solutions. She anticipated that students would find 10 percent of the total and double it for 20 percent. She anticipated that students would find 10 percent of the total, take half of it for 5 percent, and add them both together for 15 percent. She found pairs that used these strategies, as they could easily find 10 percent of the total and scale up and down from that point.

She anticipated that at least one pair would double the tax for 8 percent to make 16 percent, which was close to 15 percent, and she found a pair that used that strategy.

She saw a pair of students say that they would leave a tip of $7.36, because then the total amount would be $57.00 ($49.64 + $7.36 = $57.00), which felt like a nice number for the total bill. They decided that $7.36 was enough, because they first estimated 10 percent of $49.64 to be about $5.00. Then they said that two groups of 10 percent would be 20 percent, or about $10.00, so 15 percent would probably be somewhere in between $5.00 and $10.00. They felt okay with $7.36.

Ms. Hartman was pleased with how the students could use their own solution paths and strategies to explore the mathematics of a context that wasn't as familiar to them as she thought it might have been.

She asked each pair of students to say how their approaches were similar to and different from one of the other approaches. She asked the students to say which other approaches they liked best and why. Finally, she assigned the students homework. She asked students to write explanations about why each method worked and how they were similar and different, and she also assigned 10 practice exercises.

We want students to believe that mathematics is useful and relevant to their lives. We want students to believe that mathematics can make sense and that they can make sense of mathematics. So, what can we do as teachers to promote the relevance of mathematics and create opportunities to make sense of it?

A common belief is that we should use mathematical tasks that involve real-world contexts to accomplish these goals. We often think that story problems involving contexts from life outside school promote connection to mathematics and opportunities to make sense of mathematics. Story-problem contexts can achieve these goals, but only under certain conditions. Sometimes contexts can interfere with understanding and lead to disengagement!

In this chapter, we explore using contexts in mathematics tasks. We credit many of the chapter's overarching ideas to Jo Boaler (1993). By *context*, we mean a situation in which a mathematical task is embedded. In some ways, contexts set outside mathematics or in situations outside school can support sense making and personal investment with mathematics. But such real-life contexts do not always help achieve these goals. Below, we reflect on the degree to which contexts *can* promote personal investment and sense making, and we also share why they might not. We provide some thoughts about strategies for teachers to consider that can lead to *judicious* use of contexts in mathematics classrooms.

The Role of Contexts in Mathematics Tasks: Supporting Personal Investment?

Contexts can help students see that mathematics is relevant to their lives outside school. Helping students see where and how mathematics can apply can help reduce the frequency of the dreaded question, "When are we ever going to have to use this stuff?" Depending on which contexts we use, the settings can help students become absorbed in exploring the mathematics. Their interest in the situation might help students become more engaged in doing mathematics.

However, just as some contexts may motivate some students, all contexts will not motivate all students. Just putting a mathematics problem in a real-life setting is not enough to promote personal investment in mathematics (Boaler 1993). In

Ms. Hartman's class, investigating percents through tipping at a restaurant could have connected with some students, but the context did not resonate with most of them. Ms. Hartman's context was not a part of her students' lived experiences; tipping was not a real-life context for them. *Contexts can promote personal investment in mathematics only if they are personally relevant and meaningful for students.* Remember back in chapter 4 how we discussed situational interest and how students' engagement can be seen as a relationship between the individual and the task. Contexts are critical situating features of mathematical tasks, so we are concerned for whom contexts may be relevant—or not—and whether the context actually aligns well with a teacher's mathematical learning goal for students.

Whose Contexts?

One challenge teachers face when using, choosing, or designing mathematics tasks set in real-world problem contexts is that a context that is relevant and meaningful for some of their students will not be so for all their students. A story problem may be no more real to students than an abstract situation, unless the context means something to students personally. Merely coating a mathematical task with a situation that we, as adults, have experienced is not sufficient to engage all students in a manner that helps them make sense of mathematics. Instead, the situation can become its own puzzle for students to comprehend in addition to the mathematics.

Story problems may be just that—stories. They may be fantasies in which students cannot recognize themselves. The problems are set in someone else's stories: urban students encounter mathematical tasks about fencing a farm, or rural students face a discrete math task about riding a subway. Paddling a canoe upstream and then down may be a common real-life context for some students, but the range of variables relevant to the actual event that may not be factored into the problem could oversimplify the situation to the point that it feels artificial. At times, the settings of mathematical tasks are not sufficiently real for anyone and perhaps seem fictional for most.

Story-problem contexts are culturally situated; in Ms. Hartman's class, the tip-calculating context was not personally meaningful to most of the students. A few had seen their parents calculate a tip at a restaurant and even helped calculate it. Most students had not eaten out recently other than in a fast-food restaurant, and most of those who had were not involved in paying the bill. Many students who thought about going out to eat had a fast-food restaurant in mind, so leaving a tip did not feel familiar to them.

A teacher may think of a situation like leaving a tip as a context relevant for a lesson about calculating percents of a number. This is a situation in life outside school where percents are relevant and regularly used. Yet, this is an adult's context. More specifically, it is a context for adults who have a certain amount of disposable income. It is not necessarily a meaningful context in the life of a young person.

However, in our experiences talking with adolescents similar in age to those in Ms. Hartman's class, we find that some students want the opportunity to work on mathematical tasks in adults' contexts, even if they are not yet the students' own contexts. Some students in the middle grades have expressed to us that they personally feel treated with greater respect as a young adult if they can work on mathematical tasks set in adult contexts (Jansen and Bartell 2011). An eighth grader told us that she preferred when a previous mathematics teacher set mathematical tasks about percents in contexts of buying a house (mortgage rates) or a car (interest rates on car loans), because she looked forward to making those purchases as an adult. She believed that her teacher respected her when her teacher gave her mathematics problems with grown-up contexts.

How Real Is "Real?"

Sometimes, when we have targeted mathematical goals for our students' learning, putting it into a context may be artificial. In the problem about calculating a tip, a customer at a restaurant may not be concerned with calculating exactly 15, 18, or 20 percent of the charge on the bill. A customer may be more interested in a general estimate of an approximately appropriate tip. A customer may use a tip calculation card or an application on his mobile phone to calculate a tip rather than thinking about the mathematics involved in the process.

In contrast, a mathematics teacher may want her students to demonstrate fluency with being able to calculate exact percents. With the tipping context, if a teacher pushes toward calculating exact percents (i.e., exactly 15% or exactly 18%), the problem context is not quite as real as a situation that uses appropriate estimates. Yet pedagogically we may have legitimate reasons for asking our students to demonstrate their skills with calculating exact percents of a number. Our desire as teachers to promote personal investment in mathematics among our students through using contexts may not always align with promoting targeted mathematical learning goals.

The Role of Contexts in Mathematics Tasks: Supporting Sense Making

We may choose story problems because their contexts can help students see and make sense of mathematical relationships. Contexts can support ways of entering into a mathematics problem by giving a way to think about the relationships in the problem. In Ms. Hartman's task about calculating a tip at a restaurant, students found numbers in the problem that helped them think about their solution strategy, such as thinking about the tax as half of the tip. Students could use the problem context to engage in making sense of how to find the tip amount.

However, contexts can be something to learn in themselves! Placing a problem in a story situation is not enough to promote mathematical sense making (Boaler 1993). Students in Ms. Hartman's class who did not know about leaving a tip had to be taught why tips are required and how much tip to leave. Students whose literacy skills are developing—English language learners or perhaps even special education students—may need additional support with some heavily verbal or textual mathematics problems (Campbell, Adams, and Davis 2007). Students who struggle mightily with making sense of the story problems' text may excel at solving tasks involving symbolic calculations. Students who appear to struggle with a mathematics task may be confused about the context, not the mathematics embedded in it.

Judicious Use of Contexts

We have demonstrated why we think that using contexts in mathematics classrooms can be complicated, but that does not mean that we oppose using them. On the contrary, we believe that contexts can promote sense making and personal investment. We wanted to acknowledge challenges for using contexts, and below we share strategies teachers could consider to address these challenges. Teachers can provide scaffolding to help students learn about the story problem's context as well as its mathematical relationships. Students could generate their own contexts. Teachers could give students choices of which contexts to use for a task. Teachers could learn about students' communities and neighborhoods to design problem contexts that include locally valuable and relevant situations.

Providing scaffolding to help students learn about the context

As we mentioned, we may need to teach students some contexts alongside the mathematics. Students whose experiences outside school diverge from the problem context would benefit from learning about the context so that they can engage in the task's mathematical goals. Rather than serve as an access point to help students explore mathematics, the context becomes something additional to learn. Teachers aware of this possibility—that their students might benefit from learning more about the task's situation—can prepare appropriate scaffolding. The time that Ms. Hartman spent talking with her students about what a tip is, why a customer might leave a tip, and how much tip to calculate is an example of this sort of scaffolding. *Allocate time to talk about and explore the problem's context.*

If students' experiences diverge from the problem's context, they would benefit from opportunities for experiences with the situation. Another example of scaffolding students' understanding about contexts would be in a problem about proportional reasoning. We have seen a problem in which teachers ask students about mixtures, either of orange punch mix and water or chocolate cocoa mix and water. The teacher asks whether a mixture becomes more or less orange- or chocolate-tasting as one adds more or less powder or water to initial mixtures. The class explores various combinations consider proportional relationships. This context assumes that students have had some experiences making and tasting mixtures like this. To support engagement with these problem contexts, some teachers spend time with their students making the drinks, allowing students to see the mixture become more and less diluted with water and to taste the differences. Giving a class of students experience with a problem context can help equalize experiences across the class, which will support more students' engagement with the context's mathematical relationships.

Students can generate contexts or teachers can provide choices of contexts

Choice matters in promoting students' motivation and engagement (Cordova and Lepper 1996; Urdan and Schoenfelder 2006). One way to provide opportunities for personally meaningful contexts in mathematics tasks is to give students a choice about which contexts to use. Not all students need to use the same context in their mathematical tasks. We can make choice available in multiple ways. Teachers could ask students about their interests and design problems aligned with those interests. Teachers could offer a range of contexts for students to reach the same mathematical goal and allow students to choose which context they prefer.

Locally relevant problem contexts

If we need knowledge of cultural or life experiences to help students engage in a problem context (Campbell, Adams, and Davis 2007), then why not highlight activities in students' communities and neighborhoods when designing problem contexts? Teachers could spend time in neighborhood community centers, churches, parks, workplaces, and even visit students at home to see what mathematical practices happen at home with their families. Mathematics problems could be created that incorporate situations that feel familiar to students. Getting to know families and students' lives outside school can help inspire mathematics contexts that students can find more personally relevant.

For example, a student teacher at a high school in New England realized that half of his Algebra 1 students had fathers who were lobstermen. (We would like to credit this example to Tim Fukawa-Connelly, a mathematics educator at the University of New Hampshire.) The student teacher decided to have students solve word problems that involved lobstering. In this instance, the teacher wanted the students to think about the intersection point between two lines—one representing the selling price per pound of lobsters, and the other, the expenses—and then consider how many pounds of lobster they needed to sell to make a profit. The teacher's task, however, presented incorrect, noncurrent prices per pound and fuel costs. This lobster-fishing context felt real to the students, so they could correct the task's original, unrealistic facts and help the teacher improve the task's realism. The students could thus own the process of making the mathematical tasks feel more real. Opening up problems' contexts, making them relevant to local students' lives, can make the tasks more useful and accessible.

Alternative Ways to Think about Contexts

We think it worth saying that real-world contexts are not the only ways to think about what can be personally relevant and promote sense making. Contexts can be motivating and support learning not because they are in a particular context, but because a problem-solving context can open the task to a range of solution strategies. Also, the mathematical task's aesthetic aspects can offer personal relevance and promote engagement and sense making. Finally, we believe that mathematics is a valuable context in its own sake, independent from story problems, and that occasionally engaging in a "pure" mathematical task is an important pedagogical choice.

Openness to a range of solution strategies

Personal meaning and sense making can happen when students have the opportunity to construct their own solution strategies. Another way to think about choice in mathematics classrooms is about not so much the choice of the problems' context, but the choice of solution strategy. We believe that students should have the chance to follow solution paths that make sense to them. Then, classroom discourse can make these solution paths explicit, making connections among them. We could then extend the solution paths to move students toward more efficient or conventional strategies over time. This approach to choice is often more realistic in terms of planning and curriculum for the teacher, and moreover, it allows the students to personalize their own learning.

In the instance of the problem about computing a tip, Ms. Hartman invited her students to pursue and discuss their own solution strategies. It appears to us that what engaged students in thinking about calculating percentages, and what made a difference in engaging more students, was not the context alone, but the opportunity for students to follow solution paths that made sense to them. The classroom seemed to buzz with interest more around comparing and contrasting different solutions than it did around the context of tipping one's server at a restaurant. The teacher structured the context to be open enough to allow students to pursue their own strategies. Contexts are valuable when they give students a way to develop personal meaning by creating strategies that they understand.

The aesthetic is relevant

By exploring mathematical relationships to see how and why mathematical structures unfold and relate, students may develop personal meaning for mathematics through aesthetic responses (Sinclair 2001). This can occur when students see relationships among various representations for similar concepts or ideas. For example, students might explore patterns through varying sizes and shapes of polygons in interactive geometry software. They may be drawn into thinking about mathematical relationships by thinking about the beauty of the dynamic variations in lines and angles. In the tipping context, students might see connections as they move between decimals and percents. When students start to make connections among graphical, tabular, symbolic, and story-problem contexts for functional relationships— all representations of the same relationship—they may feel inspired and engaged by seeing structure and beauty among these representations.

Mathematics as a context for its own sake

Mathematics is worth appreciating for its own sake, as its own context. Not all mathematics maps neatly onto story-problem contexts. For instance, creating contexts for integer operations can be challenging. Some story-problem contexts, such as those used to illustrate why a negative integer multiplied by a negative integer results in a positive integer, require so much head spinning to understand that we conjecture that exploring such operations in the mathematics domain itself could be more useful. (As it turns out, this concept is an arbitrary decision made by mathematicians in order for the set of integers to be closed over the operation of multiplication. There is no *real* context that can illustrate this case outside of consistency in the abstract rules for number systems). In such instances, setting mathematics in a context outside itself would involve just as much, if not more, learning about how the context maps onto the mathematics as it would about the relationship we wanted to teach in the first place.

Teachers play a role in helping students see the value in mathematics as a context for its own sake. We can model appreciation for beautiful relationships and structures in mathematics. We can demonstrate genuine interest in mathematics by pursuing our own mathematical questions during and outside class. We can expect and assume our students will value mathematics for its own sake, too, because students may engage with content in the ways that we expect of them.

Seeking Balance in Our Use of Contexts in the Mathematics Classroom

We do not mean to suggest that the answer is avoiding using story problems or problems in context, because we see the potential for such problems to support students' motivation and learning. However, we think it important not to assume a general familiarity with a problem's context among our students. We value opportunities to explore solution strategies, and we recognize that setting a problem in a story problem context can afford students opportunities to develop their own solution strategies. We also see that mathematics can be a context worth pursuing for its own sake. We hope that this chapter has offered ways of thinking about mathematics tasks that support teachers' judicious use of problem contexts.

References

Boaler, Jo. "The Role of Contexts in the Mathematics Classroom: Do They Make Mathematics More 'Real?'" *For the Learning of Mathematics* 13, no. 2 (June 1993): 12–17.

Campbell, Anne E., Verna M. Adams, and Gary E. Davis. "Cognitive Demands and Second-Language Learners: A Framework for Analyzing Mathematics Instructional Contexts." *Mathematical Thinking and Learning: An International Journal* 9, no. 1 (2007): 3–30.

Cordova, Diana I., and Mark R. Lepper. "Intrinsic Motivation and the Process of Learning: Beneficial Effects of Contextualization, Personalization, and Choice." *Journal of Educational Psychology* 88, no. 4 (December 1996): 715–30.

Jansen, Amanda, and Tonya Bartell. "Enacting Care for Mathematics Learners: Middle School Students' and Teachers' Perspectives." Paper presented at the ninety-first Annual Meeting of the American Educational Research Association, New Orleans, La., 2011.

Sinclair, Nathalie. "The Aesthetic 'Is' Relevant." *For the Learning of Mathematics* 21, no. 1 (March 2001): 25–32.

Urdan, Tim, and Erin Schoenfelder. "Classroom Effects on Student Motivation: Goal Structures, Social Relationships, and Competence Beliefs." *Journal of School Psychology* 44, no. 5 (October 2006): 331–49.

CHAPTER 9

Providing Challenge: Start Where Students Are, Not Where They Are Not

In 1996, Amanda Jansen, the second author of this book, began her career as a middle school mathematics teacher. She experienced a journey toward learning to support her students as they engaged in challenging mathematical tasks. She has wondered, "If I knew then what I know now, what would I have done differently?" This chapter is her effort to process and preserve some of what she has learned about scaffolding students' mathematical thinking.

When I was a first-year mathematics teacher, I sometimes defeated my own goals in my desire to help more students be successful at mathematics. I struggled to be the kind of teacher I wanted to become. In some ways, I could improve gradually over time. In others, I knew that becoming a better teacher would be a career-long process.

As part of my effort to improve as a teacher, I reflected on what I thought it meant to be a good teacher. I realized that I thought I was successful as a teacher when my students performed well on our district-level assessments, even though these assessments then mostly measured students' proficiency at executing procedures. Unfortunately, I do not think that I provided my students with enough opportunities to develop meaning for the procedures. I did not offer my students many opportunities to engage in problem solving. I thought that more challenging mathematical tasks would take too much time. I thought that my goal was to be focused and efficient as a teacher toward helping my students succeed on their exams in the spring.

I felt pressure to raise my students' scores on those exams, because my principal would compare teachers on the basis of their students' performances on them. When I'm honest with myself, I realize that I focused on raising students' test scores out of self-preservation and self-protection. It's understandable why I responded that way. But, looking back, I do not think that I gave my students enough challenge. I am glad that I gave my students experiences that helped them feel successful on those exams. Yet, I started to realize that learning mathematics is more than learning to perform well on assessments.

Looking back on myself as a first-year teacher, I realized that I was the person who talked the most during class. Usually the person doing more of the talking is the one doing more of the thinking. I assumed that I could teach efficiently by working examples for students to imitate. I talked by narrating what I did, and I sometimes tried to explain why I did it. I assumed that modeling solutions allowed all students access to strategies for solving similar tasks. I assumed that students thought about mathematics the same way I did.

Although my students performed well on tests, I started to want to offer them more enriching opportunities. I wanted my students not only to be successful, but also to have opportunities to be interested, engaged, and curious about mathematics. I wanted math to come alive for them. My classroom lacked life and energy at times. This hit home for me most directly when my most successful student wrote a letter to me at the semester's end. Being humorous, he told me that he sought to identify a pattern: When would I decide to change overhead pens and use a pen of another color? He made me laugh, but he pointed something out to me subtly. My marker choices were more interesting that the mathematics in the classroom.

I realized that my students did not enthusiastically approach mathematics because I did not give them opportunities to do so. I worried that I did not have time for more challenging and interesting tasks, because I thought that what mattered was their success on the district test. Then I decided that I wanted both students' success on achievement tests and a lively classroom with engaged students. After all, other teachers could do so (e.g., Hiebert and Wearne [1993]). Why not me? Over the next few years, I decided to seek out and create my own professional development experiences by observing colleagues and inviting the district mathematics specialist to my classroom.

Uncovering My Misconceptions about Teaching Mathematics through Observing Others

I asked my colleagues if I could observe their classes during my planning period. I would take my students' papers, grade them in a colleague's classroom, and observe her or his class. I am fortunate that so many of my colleagues opened up their doors to me. As I observed their teaching, I started to recognize my own conceptions, or perhaps misconceptions, about teaching. As I noticed that their lessons looked different from mine, I recognized that my conception of effective teaching was about promoting students' success on exams that emphasized procedural fluency. Once I recognized that conception, I started to question it, which put me in a position to learn more about my own conceptions of mathematics teaching. Observing my colleagues gave me an opportunity to learn about how I thought about teaching as I learned from them.

During my observations, I started to think that I had a misconception about mathematics teaching related to teaching through problem solving. My misconception was that teachers who teach with problem-based, investigatory lessons do not spend much time talking. I thought that the students were supposed to do all the talking during these sorts of lessons. I realized that although colleagues' students talked often and shared their thinking, my colleagues talked quite a bit, too. The teachers clarified and highlighted significant mathematics at strategic moments. They summarized important ideas at a lesson's end. They asked students to elaborate on students' own explanations. They restated students' thinking and focused students' attention on connections among students' solutions. I didn't realize that I had this misconception—about teachers not telling their students much when teaching with problem-solving techniques—until I observed and saw something different from what I expected to see. I learned that teachers have an important role to play when teaching through problem solving, and that that role looked different from how I enacted my role when teaching students to develop procedural fluency.

I found myself wanting to engage my students in more interesting, challenging mathematical tasks, but I believed I needed some help to change my teaching practice. Although my colleagues were willing to help, they were busy teaching their own students. They referred me to our district's mathematics specialist. She came to my classroom and worked with my students and me directly. I had three class periods in a row of seventh-grade general mathematics, and she worked with them and me. For the first class period, she would teach and I would work on the mathematical tasks with the students as a learner. During the next period, I would observe as a teacher. By the third class period, I was ready to try teaching the lesson; she would observe me and provide feedback after the lesson.

As I observed the mathematics specialist working with my students, I confronted some additional misconceptions that I did not know that I had. I realized one misconception was that my students could not do more challenging tasks. When I saw how successful—and interested—my students were in the tasks that the mathematics specialist implemented, I realized that my expectations for my students had been too low. My students were capable of more challenge. Indeed, they *wanted* more challenge!

Also, I observed that the mathematics specialist spoke with my students more explicitly than I usually did. I didn't realize that explaining to the students how you wanted them to interact with one another would be so helpful. The mathematics specialist would say things like, "I really like how Ashley explained her strategy. She gave enough information to help us understand what she did, and she explained why she did it that way. I hope other people will give explanations like that, too, because they help all of us learn." I hadn't thought much about the importance of highlighting how students talked and encouraging more students to talk similarly.

Through seeking support, I started to develop a vision of the kind of teacher I wanted to become. I made progress in the next few years toward enacting that vision. I became a teacher who developed some tools for scaffolding students' learning and engagement in problem solving. But then I left full-time teaching to go to graduate school and eventually start my current job as a university professor teaching future teachers.

I often think to myself, "If I only knew then what I know now, I would have been a better mathematics teacher." So, I decided to write a letter to myself, reproduced below, about what I have learned about supporting students' learning and engagement through scaffolding. I wrote this letter thinking about myself as an early-career middle school teacher, keeping in mind that I would need some conceptual anchors and tools for thinking about students' learning and engagement. Those anchors and tools would be inspiration and opportunities for reflection as I attempt to improve my teaching incrementally over time to learn from my own practice (Hiebert et al. 2007).

Dear Mandy,

I'm writing this letter to you to help you think about how to support your students. I know that you want more of your students to have opportunities to succeed in mathematics. You hope that your students will be able to develop a strong sense of confidence and competence from experiencing success. You want your students to feel as if mathematics makes sense to them. You want your students to enjoy doing and learning mathematics. So far, you've only been able to achieve some of those goals. Although you have seen your students become more successful with mathematics and feel more confident in themselves while they are in your classroom, you are less sure whether they enjoy doing mathematics. Also, you wonder if they are going to take that sense of confidence with them after they leave your classroom.

Here's some tough love: Look at how you've been trying to support your students. In your attempts to make mathematics accessible to them, you may have made the intellectual demands on them easier than they need to be. Your students are capable of doing more challenging tasks. You're doing a lot of the challenging mathematical thinking for them. Sure, more of the students have been successful, but are they learning what you hope for them to learn? Are they truly interested and intellectually engaged during class? Your efforts to help your students haven't been doing them any favors.

What do I mean? Okay, they're able to express a fraction in lowest terms successfully when they see a familiar problem on a quiz or test, but can they apply what they know to solve a more challenging task? Perhaps not. They're attentive during class and well behaved, but are they curious? Not so much. I think you want more for them. And you've been feeling that your students depend on you too much when mathematics tasks become difficult. I think one reason why they are not as curious as you would hope is that you do not do enough to inspire that sort of curiosity. I think one reason why you feel like they depend on you so much is that you might be creating that kind of dependence, however subtly. I know at this point you that you can do more to support your students, but thinking about where to begin is difficult.

I have some ideas for you! Below, I want to share some ways of thinking about connecting to your students and supporting their learning. The ideas came from a combination of my experiences as a teacher and my own reading about what researchers have learned about scaffolding students' learning. I think that the ideas could help you enact your vision for mathematics teaching. If you want to support your students' engagement with challenging mathematical tasks, scaffolding will help you meet your students where they currently are and help them move toward where you want them to be.

Scaffolding: Connecting to Students Where They Are and Helping Them Grow

One way to think about supporting students is through a process of *scaffolding*. Scaffolding means that a teacher gives students an opportunity to work on a challenging task, and a teacher or peer offers *just enough* assistance for a student to complete the task on his or her own, but not so much that the task becomes less challenging or too easy (Henningsen and Stein 1997). It is a delicate balance. This kind of balanced support enables students to take over their own learning gradually over time (Schoenfeld 1985). When scaffolding students' learning, teachers *build bridges between where students are currently and where teachers want students to be,* providing the optimal level of arousal and control that we discussed earlier as crucial for the development of interest. An important aspect of scaffolding, however, is that for any set of concepts and skills, the teacher eventually *phases out all forms of it over time*, as students internalize ways of thinking and behaving and become more mathematically autonomous.

Three Goals for Scaffolding: Developing Mathematical Understanding, Classroom Community, and Autonomy

Debra Meyer and Julianne Turner (2002) describe three different ways of thinking about scaffolding, as follows.

1. Scaffolding students' developing *mathematical understanding*
2. Scaffolding the developing *classroom community*
3. Scaffolding individual students' developing *autonomy and self-regulation*

These three approaches support different but interrelated goals.

The first approach supports students with opportunities to access and understand challenging mathematics, which is what concerns us, as mathematics teachers, the most. As teachers, we want to help students understand important mathematical concepts and related procedures and skills so that mathematics makes sense to them (Meyer and Turner 2002). Because this type of support is primarily concerned with helping students understand content, some scholars have given it the name *analytic scaffolding* (Baxter and Williams 2010).

Yet, for more students to have access to opportunities to learn challenging mathematics, we must create classroom communities where students feel supported in taking mathematical risks together. In these classrooms, students have clear ideas for how to interact with one another about mathematics. Students in these classrooms feel comfortable and accepted for who they are as people. This type of scaffolding involves creating an engaging classroom context where it is socially desirable to learn and where each student is recognized as having gifts to add to the class. These high expectations, coupled with strong support, will likely motivate students to learn mathematics. Again, researchers have given a special name for this, labeling it *social scaffolding* (Baxter and Williams 2010).

Individual students benefit from opportunities to develop autonomy and self-regulate. We can give students support in developing a sense of ownership to monitor their own learning and engagement while learning and doing mathematics. Achieving these goals is a delicate balance between supporting students enough and not supporting them too much. Scaffolding's purpose is to connect with your students, to try to understand how they think, and to support them in moving toward how you would like for them to think mathematically.

Scaffolding: Enacting Instructional Practices

So, how do you scaffold? Maybe you would like to promote students' mathematics learning in a way that increases its challenge level. Perhaps you want to create a supportive community where students develop ownership for their own learning. Some researchers have identified instructional practices that appear promising for achieving these goals. Findings have accumulated across a number of different, independent research studies to point to the productivity of scaffolding strategies, as shown in figure 9.1.

Analytic scaffolding: Scaffolding mathematical understanding's development	Social scaffolding: Scaffolding the classroom community's development	Scaffolding to promote developing autonomy, self-regulation, and ownership
1. Select optimally challenging tasks—a good match between the tasks' demands and students' prior knowledge.	1. Talk about talking. Explicitly clarify expectations for working together and talking about mathematics.	1. Model self-monitoring.
2. Don't avoid "telling." Use telling judiciously. Be explicit at times.	2. Reinforce desired behavior through modeling, including asking clarifying questions and giving elaborated, meaningful explanations.	2. Explicitly communicate how tasks build on students' prior knowledge and experience.
3. Give students representational tools to make sense of mathematics.	3. Create a nonthreatening environment where students feel safe taking intellectual risks.	3. Give learners choices. Allow students to choose strategies that make sense to them.
4. Ask focusing questions to direct students' attention.	4. Provide emotional support by mediating frustration and offering encouragement.	4. Transfer to students the responsibility for making sense of mathematics.
5. Press students to make elaborated, meaningful explanations of their thinking.		5. Provide meaningful rationales for activities.
6. Give students an appropriate amount of time to work on tasks.		6. Give students descriptive feedback and comment on their progress.
7. View and treat students' errors constructively.		

Fig. 9.1

Although these are long lists, their goals interrelate. So, choosing to enact one of the instructional strategies can help you address multiple goals. If teachers scaffold the classroom community and students' autonomy, complementary conditions will be in place as well that can support students' opportunities to learn mathematics. Perhaps a place to begin is to try enacting scaffolding practices that complement one another or that can potentially achieve multiple goals.

Before we reflect on scaffolding strategies that can achieve multiple goals, we want to share a bit about each type of goal—why and to what end a teacher might scaffold in the classroom.

Scaffolding Students' Development of *Mathematical Understanding*: Analytic Scaffolding

John Dewey (1902) described building a bridge from how students currently think—and what students are currently interested in doing—to ways of thinking and knowing that represent the mathematics discipline more. He referred to this process as *psychologizing the curriculum*. This process involves connecting the child's personal experiences with potentially less personal subject matter. A teacher works to make connections between the school subject matter's abstract nature and a student's prior experiences. Dewey considered the child and the curriculum to be endpoints on a continuum, and he said that the teacher could provide the student with experiences to help her move along that continuum. Psychologizing the subject matter involves translating abstract ideas into the learner's experiences. The teacher constructs experiences so that learning grows from engaging in an activity. The experience engages students' interests and creates a palpable need to engage in the activity, which in turn leads to learning.

Okay, that sounds great, but *how* to do that is not instantly clear. As teachers, we want to have high standards and expectations for our students. But students need support to reach these expectations; reaching high standards is a journey that teachers take along with their students. Research over the past couple of decades provides insights into how teachers can psychologize the curriculum and help students negotiate the meaning of pivotal concepts and related procedures and skills by engaging in challenging mathematical activities.

Various researchers have highlighted the following teaching practices as types of analytic scaffolding that support students' mathematical thinking and learning.

1. When selecting challenging tasks appropriately, consider whether alignment exists between the task's demands and students' prior knowledge, so that the task is neither too easy nor too difficult (Henningsen and Stein 1997; Turner et al. 1998).

2. You may want to avoid telling, but you can use telling judiciously to support students' understanding (Chazan and Ball 1999; Smith 1996). Students will benefit if you are strategically explicit at times that connect with and extend students' thinking (Baxter and Williams 2010; Goos 2004).

3. You can have students interact with representational tools to help them make sense of mathematics (Anghileri 2006).

4. You can direct students' attention by asking focusing questions (Anghileri 2006; Baxter and Williams 2010).

5. Students will benefit if you press them to provide elaborated, meaningful explanations of their thinking (Henningsen and Stein 1997; Hiebert and Wearne 1993; Kazemi and Stipek 2001).

6. The amount of time students have to work on a task, such as that for working in groups, is another delicate balance (Webel 2010). You can monitor students and consider whether they have worked on the task long enough to have listened to one another's thinking, but not so long that they've diverged away from the task (Anghileri 2006; Henningsen and Stein 1997).

7. You can consider ways to view and treat students' errors constructively as learning opportunities (Turner et al. 1998). (We would like to thank Laura Cline, a former elementary school teacher and a Ph.D. student at the University of Delaware at the time we wrote this book, for directing our attention to this instructional practice's importance.)

Each of these strategies is important in its own right, but an underlying truth connects them all into a coherent perspective on pedagogy. Jerome Bruner, generally credited with developing the idea of scaffolding as a developmental theory, based his work in part on Vygotsky's (1978) description of the *zone of proximal development*, that psychological and social space just beyond the student's current ability. According to Bruner, the teacher consistently must strive to engage the student, through designing tasks, questioning, introducing instructional tools, and reflecting productively on strategy and errors, in thinking about and doing things the student has never thought about or done before. This means that the teacher must develop an implicit theory of instruction by which the teacher's understanding of the task to be undertaken—and of the learner and his or her abilities, knowledge, and interests— merge in the instruction's moment into a specific strategy to move the student to a new level of understanding and doing (Wood, Bruner, and Ross 1976). These seven strategies are excellent choices to help you accomplish this under the real constraints of teaching.

So, what is the opposite of analytic scaffolding? Sometimes teachers control and direct to the point that they do not connect with students' thinking or that they reduce the task's challenge so it becomes easier (too easy?). Perhaps teachers pose questions that are too narrow, like asking for the next step, rather than more open ones that focus students' attention. Perhaps teachers move too quickly, without giving students enough time to think about the problem, or too slowly, so that students' engagement drops off. This can happen unintentionally or out of the intention to help students. Attending to analytic scaffolding can give teachers a role in supporting their students' learning that is not overly directive but still makes mathematical ideas and relationships explicit.

Scaffolding the Classroom Community's Development: Social Scaffolding

Have you ever put students in groups or pairs without spending much time talking with them about your expectations for how they should work together? By the time students arrive in your middle school classroom, they have had experience working together in mathematics. So, not talking with students about how to work together could seem reasonable. Also, in a class period's limited time, choosing not to spend a lot of time talking about how to work together could be reasonable. Maybe once you've covered your expectations once, you don't necessarily believe you should have to reinforce them.

However, students do benefit from scaffolding the classroom community's development, both at the beginning of the school year or semester and throughout the year as reinforcement. Social scaffolding includes explicitly setting expectations for how to work together—in pairs, in small groups, or during whole-class discussions. Sometimes this sort of scaffolding is relatively nuanced, such as in pointing out what counts as a valuable and helpful contribution during classroom discussion.

Various researchers, as shown below, have highlighted the following instructional strategies as types of social scaffolding that support the classroom community's development.

1. Talk about talking (Cobb, Yackel, and Wood 1993). Explicitly clarify expectations for working together and talking about mathematics (Baxter and Williams 2010; Wentzel et al. 2010).
2. Reinforce desired behavior through modeling, including asking clarifying questions and providing elaborated, meaningful explanations (Baxter and Williams 2010; Goos 2004).
3. Create a nonthreatening environment where students feel safe taking intellectual risks (Ciani et al. 2010; Turner et al. 1998; Urdan and Schoenfelder 2006; Wentzel et al. 2010).
4. Provide emotional support by mediating frustration and giving encouragement (Ciani et al. 2010; Urdan and Schoenfelder 2006).

These ways of enacting social scaffolding have in common a concern for helping students make progress on challenging tasks by using explicit instructions, modeling, and emotional support for working through challenge. What these descriptions make less clear is precisely how to enact these strategies effectively.

What is the opposite of social scaffolding? When we forget to use social scaffolding, we pay less attention to students' emotional and social needs. We forget to talk about talking. We are not explicit about expectations for working together, for providing elaborated solution strategies, or for listening to one another and connecting to one another's thinking. If we forget to use social scaffolding, students are left on their own to decide on appropriate ways to interact. If we do use social scaffolding, we can support more students with opportunities to interact with one another productively and respectfully.

Scaffolding Individual Students' Development of *Autonomy and Self-Regulation*: Supporting Students' Ownership

One thing you've probably been thinking about, or even struggling with, is how to ensure that students depend on you, the teacher, a bit less. You would like your students to feel more responsible for their own learning and sense making, and you would like them to feel more capable at doing mathematics. The following scaffolding strategies are worth considering to promote students' autonomy in the mathematics classroom.

1. Encourage self-monitoring and model it yourself (Goos 2004; Henningsen and Stein 1997).
2. Explicitly communicate how tasks build on students' prior knowledge and experience (Urdan and Schoenfelder 2006).
3. Offer learners choices. Allow students to choose strategies that make sense to them (Ciani et al. 2010; Urdan and Schoenfelder 2006).
4. Transfer responsibility to students for making sense of mathematics (Turner et al. 1998).
5. Provide meaningful rationales for activities (Ciani et al. 2010).
6. Give students descriptive feedback, and comment on their progress (Turner et al. 1998).

To start where students are, we need them to be able to think in ways that make sense to them. Encouraging them and giving them opportunities to use their own, invented strategies is a way to promote autonomy. Then we can build on their invented strategies to promote seeing connections among them and perhaps move students toward using more efficient ones.

We want students to be able to assess themselves and take responsibility for their understanding and progress, but they might not know that. They might be willing, but unsure about how to do so. We can model what it might look like to assess oneself and monitor one's own mathematical thinking. We can comment on students' progress rather than only on their products or outcomes, so that students see their progress as valuable and start to monitor it on their own. Perhaps students will start internalizing the questions we ask them when we monitor their progress.

Students would more likely develop ownership if they understood our intentions as teachers. We can tell them why we think the learning activity and mathematical task are valuable, which could potentially give them a reason to value it personally. We could communicate why we chose this particular task for them and elicit the prior knowledge that they could draw on to solve it.

Scaffolding Strategies That Achieve Multiple Goals

One reaction to Mandy's letter might be feeling overwhelmed. The list may seem so extensive that you don't know where to begin. First, we'd like to recommend starting by describing the instructional strategies that can help you achieve multiple goals. Scaffolding practices exist that support students' engagement and learning concurrently. Below, we will direct your attention to a few of these strategies, because they are worth trying.

Selecting Challenging Tasks That Build on and Extend Students' Prior Knowledge

If we want to challenge our students mathematically, we begin with choosing mathematical tasks carefully. To start where our students are, and not where they are not, we can choose tasks aligned with their prior knowledge. Then, if the tasks truly challenge students, engaging with the tasks will be a formative experience for them. The tasks will prompt students' thinking and move their ideas forward. Tasks that overlap students' prior knowledge too much will be practice, not ones in which they will learn new concepts and skills. If tasks do not overlap at least somewhat with students' prior knowledge, students won't be able to make progress on them. Also, talking with students about why you selected the task for them to solve—why is it worth solving, what prior knowledge could they draw on while solving it—is worthwhile. Tasks aligned with students' prior knowledge can motivate students because the challenge piques their interest, and the tasks are neither too easy, and thus boring, nor too difficult, and thus overwhelming.

Pressing Students for Elaborated, Meaningful Explanations

To build on students' thinking, we can use teaching strategies that make students' thinking more visible. When we ask students to talk about their mathematical thinking, we can support their effort to make conceptual connections for the meanings behind procedures by modeling what an elaborate, meaningful explanation might look like. Additionally, we can hold them accountable for providing more elaborated explanations by pressing them to explain further. We can encourage their peers to ask one another for elaborations and explanations. We have seen effective classrooms where young students ask each other questions like "I don't understand what you mean by that. Can you tell me more? Why did you do it that way?" When we explicitly press for elaborated explanations, students can learn to self-regulate and push themselves for similar explanations. If students become aware of our expectations, they can internalize them.

Judicious Telling

When scaffolding students' mathematical thinking, considering when and how much to tell students explicitly is a delicate balance. On the one hand, you want to build on students' mathematical thinking, which involves making the students' thinking visible by having students talk about mathematics. But this does not mean that the teacher has no room to talk. Indeed, teachers play an important role in the process of making mathematical ideas and connections explicit. Opportunities to tell your students something explicitly must be chosen judiciously. You can time these instances for when students can most readily hear and make sense of what you say. You can talk with students about mathematics in a manner that connects closely to their current thinking.

Juliet Baxter and Steven Williams (2010) have identified some specific instances when teachers used analytic scaffolding that looked like judiciously selected opportunities to tell students about mathematics. The middle school teachers they observed chose to "tell" or explain mathematics explicitly to their students in these sorts of situations: when the students think of only one solution strategy, when the whole-class discussions are not making progress on the mathematics, to summarize lengthy discussions, to help students see connections among alternative solution strategies, to repair solution strategies that do not yield valid results, and to model elaborated explanations when students' solution methods are brief. Classroom discussions can center on students' thinking and still have a place for the teacher's voice. Teachers who engage in judicious telling support not only students' mathematical understanding, but also students' motivation, by focusing and directing their attention and engagement.

Foster a Nonthreatening Environment

When engaging in challenging mathematical tasks, students benefit from a nonthreatening learning environment. In nonthreatening classrooms, students feel comfortable and accepted socially (Ciani et al. 2010). This leaves individual students feeling less concerned about social consequences associated with how competent they might or might not be. Students can instead focus on learning and taking intellectual risks, because they feel like valued members of a community.

Another way that a learning environment can be less threatening is by treating errors and mistakes productively, as part of everyone's learning process. Treating the error as a learning opportunity is more productive than treating it as a sign that someone is not good at mathematics. If tasks truly are challenging, everyone should struggle when working them. Struggle is an essential part of learning anything new.

If someone thinks about mathematical competence or ability as fixed—either you have it or you don't—then error analysis, particularly of one's own errors, is scary, because that then outs you as someone who doesn't know how to solve the problem.

Error analysis is dangerous when it pins the errors on an individual, because that student gets positioned as someone who errs.

But if we think of mathematical competence as evolving and constantly shifting and reject the notion of fixed ability, and if we think of learning as necessarily involving struggle, then error analysis can elevate the struggle to the forefront. We can validate struggle as productive, because then everyone has an opportunity to learn from the struggle. We can highlight that everyone will struggle at times. That's how one makes sense of anything new. Indeed, someone can help the group by asking a question and admitting that they do not know the answer. Someone might say, "I am confused and wondering about…" and pose a question. By giving the group an opportunity to wonder together, we can all learn together. So, being good at mathematics could mean that we can admit what we do not know and ask questions that can help the class learn together.

Two Lingering Thoughts about Scaffolding: Flexibility and Meeting Every Student's Needs

We have two final points to make regarding scaffolding. One is that when you scaffold, being somewhat flexible in response to your students is ideal. The other is that different, viable scaffolding strategies may exist that meet the needs of every student in your classroom. Scaffolding is not a formulaic process.

Flexibility

Planning your scaffolding strategies ahead of time is not always easy. If you want to scaffold students in a way that responds to individual learners, you may need to be flexible (Anghileri 2006). For instance, time—too much or not enough—seems to be an essential factor in scaffolding students' learning from, and engagement with, mathematical tasks (Henningsen and Stein 1997). Although we may become effective over time at estimating just how much time is enough, predicting precisely how much time any particular student will need can be difficult. Monitoring your students can help, to see whether they have had enough time to share and listen to one another's thinking, but not so much time that they have stopped working on mathematics. The choice of how much time you schedule for your students to spend on a task could be a flexible estimate. You would base the estimate on experience, but, depending on your students' response, you could end the activity sooner or later than you planned. Implementing other scaffolding strategies could also vary according to your students' needs.

Meeting Every Student's Needs

When thinking about how to reach all learners, particularly when teaching English language learners and those with other special needs, considering the role of contextual story problems is important. Different students may need different kinds of scaffolding to engage with a contextual story problem's task. If the problem's context lies outside the students' experience, they may need some support with making sense of the context before they engage with the mathematics (Campbell, Adams, and Davis 2007). For instance, if a proportional-reasoning problem is about mixtures, have students spend time making the mixtures in class. If the problem asks students whether the mixtures of milk and cocoa powder are more and less chocolatey, then having students make mixtures and taste them could offer more students ways to enter into making sense of the context.

English language learners

The language level in mathematical tasks may not correspond to that of English language learners (Campbell, Adams, and Davis 2007). Teachers in multilingual classrooms may encounter dilemmas. Some of the dilemmas relate to teachers in all mathematics classrooms, such as how explicit to be with students. We may want to provide access to all learners, but we may also want to support students as active, capable meaning makers. Navigating this dilemma in multilingual classrooms has unique aspects, including whether and when to "code switch," or move back and forth between languages (Adler 1998). As a useful general principle, teachers could prioritize strategies that help more students have access to mathematical ideas in a manner that connects with where students currently are.

Learners with special needs

We would like to credit Dina Neyman, a former secondary school teacher and elementary school administrator, and a Ph.D. student at the University of Delaware when this book was written, with directing our attention to supporting students with special needs.

Recommendations for reaching students with special needs align with the principle that instruction should not present content above or below students' frustration level (Deshler and Schumaker 2006). Scaffolding is essential to help students with special needs have full access to the same educational experiences as their peers. Deshler and Schumaker (2006) highlight reading demand as one curriculum aspect that often needs mediation for special-needs students mainstreamed into content-area classrooms. A contextual story problem's reading level may not align with the student's. Students with special needs may need support in order to access the story problem's ideas. One strategy that the first author, Jim, has seen used effectively is for the teacher to audio record the textual presentation of the problems and allow poorer readers access to a playback machine with headphones. Simple and effective, this strategy allowed smart students with a particular learning difficulty to overcome that difficulty and engage with the rest of their peers. This was one of the most powerful examples of efficacy-raising teaching practices he has ever seen.

Moving Forward: Now What?

We recognize that Mandy's letter has not articulated these instructional practices—analytic scaffolding, social scaffolding, and scaffolding the students' developing autonomy—in great detail for you. We hope that these ideas can be tools for you to think with as you teach. You can hold them up as lenses to view your instructional decisions. They can help you think about ways to engage every student in challenging mathematics, offer your students a supportive classroom community, and promote each student's sense of owning mathematical thinking and learning. Keep in mind the overarching idea that students think about mathematics differently from adults (Ambrose et al. 2004), but with the right support, they *can* engage in challenging mathematics.

Integrating all these practices into your instructional repertoire at once is not realistic. This is a long list! But considering the strategies as possibilities and cycling them gradually into your teaching can help scaffold students' learning. You could videotape yourself teaching and use the list of practices as a lens through which to view your instruction. You could ask another colleague to view the video with you to see if they think you are enacting any of these practices. You both could consider together whether you missed any opportunities to enact the practices.

A Final Reflection from Mandy

I first started teaching middle school mathematics about 15 years ago. I wonder how I would think and what I would be doing in 2011 if I had received a letter like this in 1996. Would I be a different kind of thinker and teacher today if I knew then what I knew now?

References

Adler, Jill. "A Language of Teaching Dilemmas: Unlocking the Complex Multilingual Secondary Mathematics Classroom." *For the Learning of Mathematics* 18, no. 1 (February 1998): 24–33.

Ambrose, Rebecca, Lisa Clement, Randolph Philipp, and Jennifer Chauvot. "Assessing Preservice Teachers' Beliefs about Mathematics and Mathematics Learning: Rationale and Development of a Constructed-Response-Format Beliefs Survey." *School Science and Mathematics* 104, no. 2 (February 2004): 56–69.

Anghileri, Julia. "Scaffolding Practices That Enhance Mathematics Learning." *Journal of Mathematics Teacher Education* 9, no. 1 (February 2006): 33–52.

Baxter, Juliet A., and Steven Williams. "Social and Analytic Scaffolding in Middle School Mathematics: Managing the Dilemma of Telling." *Journal of Mathematics Teacher Education* 13, no. 1 (February 2010): 7–26.

Campbell, Anne E., Verna M. Adams, and Gary E. Davis. "Cognitive Demands and Second-Language Learners: A Framework for Analyzing Mathematics Instructional Contexts." *Mathematical Thinking and Learning* 9, no. 1 (2007): 3–30.

Chazan, Daniel, and Debra Loewenberg Ball. "Beyond Being Told Not to Tell." *For the Learning of Mathematics* 19, no. 2 (July 1999): 2–10.

Ciani, Keith D., Michael J. Middleton, Jessica J. Summers, and Kennon M. Sheldon. "Buffering against Performance Classroom Goal Structures: The Importance of Autonomy Support and Classroom Community." *Contemporary Educational Psychology* 35, no. 1 (January 2010): 88–99.

Cobb, Paul, Erna Yackel, and Terry Wood. "Theoretical Orientation." In *Rethinking Elementary School Mathematics: Insights and Issues, Journal for Research in Mathematics Education* Monograph No. 6, edited by Paul Cobb, Erna Yackel, and Terry Wood, pp. 21–122. Reston, Va.: National Council of Teachers of Mathematics, 1993.

Deshler, Don D., and Jean B. Schumaker. *Teaching Adolescents with Disabilities: Accessing the General Education Curriculum.* Thousand Oaks, Calif.: Corwin Press, 2006.

Dewey, John. *The Child and the Curriculum.* Chicago: University of Chicago Press, 1902.

Goos, Merrilyn. "Learning Mathematics in a Classroom Community of Inquiry." *Journal for Research in Mathematics Education* 35, no. 4 (July 2004): 258–91.

Henningsen, Marjorie, and Mary Kay Stein. "Mathematical Tasks and Student Cognition: Classroom-Based Factors That Support and Inhibit High-Level Mathematical Thinking and Reasoning." *Journal for Research in Mathematics Education* 28, no. 5 (November 1997): 524–49.

Hiebert, James, and Diana Wearne. "Instructional Tasks, Classroom Discourse, and Students' Learning in Second-Grade Arithmetic." *American Educational Research Journal* 30, no. 2 (Summer 1993): 393–425.

Hiebert, James, Anne K. Morris, Dawn Berk, and Amanda Jansen. "Preparing Teachers to Learn from Teaching." *Journal of Teacher Education* 58, no. 1 (2007): 47–61.

Kazemi, Elham, and Deborah Stipek. "Promoting Conceptual Thinking in Four Upper-Elementary Mathematics Classrooms." *Elementary School Journal* 102, no. 1 (September 2001): 59–80.

Meyer, Debra K., and Julianne C. Turner. "Using Instructional Discourse Analysis to Study the Scaffolding of Student Self-Regulation." *Educational Psychologist* 37, no. 1 (March 2002): 17–25.

Schoenfeld, Alan H. "Metacognitive and Epistemological Issues in Mathematical Understanding." In *Teaching and Learning Mathematical Problem Solving: Multiple Research Perspectives,* edited by Edward A. Silver, pp. 361–79. Hillsdale, N.J.: Lawrence Erlbaum Associates, 1985.

Smith, John P., III. "Efficacy and Teaching Mathematics by Telling: A Challenge for Reform." *Journal for Research in Mathematics Education* 27, no. 4 (July 1996): 387–402.

Turner, Julianne C., Debra K. Meyer, Kathleen E. Cox, Candace Logan, Matthew DiCintio, and Cynthia T. Thomas. "Creating Contexts for Involvement in Mathematics." *Journal of Educational Psychology* 90, no. 4 (December 1998): 730–45.

Urdan, Tim, and Erin Schoenfelder. "Classroom Effects on Student Motivation: Goal Structures, Social Relationships, and Competence Beliefs." *Journal of School Psychology* 44, no. 5 (October 2006): 331–49.

Vygotsky, Lev. "Interaction between Learning and Development." *Mind and Society.* Cambridge, Mass.: Harvard University Press, 1979.

Webel, Corey. "Shifting Mathematical Authority from Teacher to Community." *Mathematics Teacher* 104, no. 4 (November 2010): 315–18.

Wentzel, Kathryn R., Ann Battle, Shannon L. Russell, and Lisa B. Looney. "Social Supports from Teachers and Peers as Predictors of Academic and Social Motivation." *Contemporary Educational Psychology* 35, no. 3 (July 2010): 193–202.

Wood, David, Jerome S. Bruner, and Gail Ross. "The Role of Tutoring in Problem Solving." *Journal of Child Psychology and Psychiatry* 17, no. 2 (April 1976): 89–100.

CHAPTER 10

Limiting the Use of Rewards and Other Reinforcers: The Hidden Costs of Rewards

The story of Emma's sixth graders illustrates that extrinsic rewards, often used by teachers to motivate students, have limitations. If we use extrinsic rewards excessively to motivate our students, we may imply that we don't expect our students to be interested in doing mathematics. But rewards are not necessarily problematic in themselves; what matters is how students interpret the rewards. Rewards can reduce intrinsic motivation, but under certain conditions, they can activate or maintain students' interests meaningfully.

Emma was puzzled. She had just moved from teaching fourth grade to teaching sixth grade. Her fourth graders had been wonderful in mathematics. They had learned all the Standards for her grade, and performed at an "exceeding the standard" level on the state assessments each year. To keep them motivated, she reinforced hard work with lavish praise, stickers, and even the occasional pizza party if they did well on the test. Her fourth graders would work for her willingly, and she rewarded them accordingly.

But her sixth graders were different. Nothing she did seemed to work. She tried stickers, but the students thought that too babyish for them now that they were in middle school. She used praise, but students didn't believe her when she said, "Good work!"

"What's so good about it?" asked Stephen. Emma wasn't sure. Stephen had gotten the correct answer, but his strategy was pretty much like everybody else's, and the work wasn't too hard.

"Well, you got it right," said Emma.

"Of course I got it right," Stephen mumbled. "You would have to be a monkey to get it wrong."

The final straw occurred when she went all-out to plan a pizza party as a reward if the class scored above the district average on the prealgebra assessment. She announced the incentive about a month prior to the test. Students were excited at first. "If the class average is higher than the district average, you get a reward. We will knock off math for the day, and we'll have pizza!"

The students immediately began planning for the party. Now *this* was something! She thought she had finally found a means to make the students focus and get to work on ratios, proportions, equations, and formulas. After a few days, however, the excitement for the party began to wane as the mundane, everyday tasks of completing exercises took over. Students' attention began to wane. Some complained that the tasks were too hard, and that they would need soda at the pizza party to make it worthwhile. Emma capitulated. After all, soda wasn't so expensive, and if it motivated the students to work, that was all that mattered.

Stephen immediately sized up the situation. "How about we get a movie if we score above the sixtieth percentile?" he asked.

Again, Emma thought, "That isn't a bad idea. If the class averages above the sixtieth percentile, that will reflect well on me, and they will have learned the mathematics even better!" So she agreed.

"What will you give me if I get a perfect score?" Stephen pushed.

"Stephen, you are pushing it," warned Emma. "Isn't a pizza party enough?"

"Not for me it isn't," remarked Stephen. "I will get a high score anyway."

A few weeks later, after the test was taken and scored, Emma was shocked to find out that her class scored just *below* the district average. Individual variation was certainly present, but overall the students performed less well than she had hoped. Even Stephen, who normally performed exceptionally well, only scored in the seventy-fifth percentile.

"I don't know what I could have done to improve their motivation," lamented Emma. "I thought the pizza was enough, but it seemed that nothing was ever enough."

Rethinking Rewards: Pressures and Prizes

A great controversy exists over using rewards to induce children to engage in mathematics. The colloquial wisdom is to praise children for doing well, provide neutral feedback for performing poorly, use incentives to get students to expend more effort, and never, ever use punishment or aversive behavior as a motivational strategy. Some of this is hard to dispute. Research (Skiba and Peterson 1999, 2000) has consistently shown punishment and other forms of negative contingencies for poor performance to be detrimental to both performance overall and students' psychological well-being. But some reinforcements, like praise for good work, are so engrained in teachers' psyche that we rarely examine them to see if, by trying to do good, we may in fact harm our students' desire to learn mathematics.

Part of the controversy behind using rewards depends on what our true, as opposed to illusory, expectations are regarding students' motivations in mathematics.

Let us be frank about this. As a society, we really do not expect students to like mathematics much. We expect them, as a whole, to do minimal work because we require it, not because mathematics has any intrinsic value or any utility beyond simple shopkeeper applications. We certainly do not expect students to engage voluntarily in advanced mathematics beyond what their chosen occupations need.

We may believe that our expectations are justified. It is a fact that students, on average, tend to do minimal work in mathematics, take only what is necessary, and dislike doing even this (Gottfried et al. 2007; Simpkins, Davis-Keane, and Eccles 2006; Eccles et al. 1993). The preponderance of data supports our expectations. We see students, even very mathematically able ones, disengaging from mathematics courses, and this happening may often seem like a sad but necessary fact of life. In such circumstances, we must to do whatever is within our means to induce students to study mathematics, so that they will be better prepared for future coursework and life in general. What other inducement do we have other than reward and punishment?

Moreover, the educational psychology courses we took in our teacher preparation programs tell us that actively manipulating the contingencies for successful task completion, what psychology often calls *behavior modification,* is an effective practice for getting students to do something they are not naturally inclined to do. So, like Emma, we offer small tokens to students to reinforce the behaviors we believe are productive. Unfortunately, a sizeable body of research indicates that these practices are in fact counterproductive. Generally, we can say that using extrinsic rewards undermines existing intrinsic motivation, in essence making students *less* inclined to expend effort in mathematics in the future when no extrinsic rewards are available (Deci 1971; Lepper, Greene, and Nisbett 1973; Lepper, Corpus, and Iyengar 2005).

Like Emma in our opening story, we find that when we give students the same rewards to induce them to engage in academic tasks, they tend to become jaded over time and begin to demand more for their efforts. This effect is most salient for those students who find mathematics motivating intrinsically: what the students once considered enjoyable, free activity becomes an economy, where the social contract implies obligations both from the students, to produce work, and from the teacher, to "pay" a fair wage for that work.

We have already discussed in chapters 2 and 3 how important fostering intrinsic motivation is for developing perseverance, cognitive depth, interest, and task enjoyment. Anything that would undermine developing these clearly positive outcomes, we should eliminate or use with extreme caution (Middleton and Spanias 1999).

But it is also clear that any real pursuit in life, even those we love the most, has associated with it costs and benefits, natural contingencies that serve as reinforcements, rewards and punishments for our actions. So we must account for these natural contingencies at the very least, if we try to enhance intrinsic motivation and minimize the costs associated with extrinsic motivation. Examples of the kinds of naturally occurring extrinsic motivators students have to negotiate include good grades, praise and recognition, and tokens like gold stars or candy on the positive side, and poor grades, ostracism (e.g., timeouts), negative comments, and other sanctions. These are part of the educational landscape and are unlikely to be eliminated. So, we must become aware of our actions and those of others in students' lives to help them negotiate the pressures better on the one hand, and the prizes better on the other.

Martin Covington (2000) likens the classroom rules that govern how we dole out rewards and levy sanctions to a set of games that revolve around (1) rewards' availability and (2) how individuals can maximize prize-getting while minimizing pressure (see also Alschuler [1973]). Interestingly, despite our ultimate goals at building students' success, Covington suggests that most games are failure-oriented in that they encourage performance goals (see chapters 5 and 7) that have the express intent of obtaining the rewards available in the classroom, primarily recognition, praise, and grades. Because these rewards are typically scarce, they amount to a zero-sum game whereby when we reward one student with a high grade, for example, we diminish the probability of another student receiving such a grade. Such games have clear winners and losers, and furthermore, because they have a winner, by implication they *must* also have a loser. The best a struggling student can do is avoid failure and thus not appear the loser. The whole emphasis of the class's contingencies becomes either to appear better than others or avoid appearing worse.

If you think back on your own mathematics experiences in school, we suspect that, like us, you will easily see that the *norm* for mathematics instruction is this kind of performance-goal-oriented atmosphere. Students are often afraid to present their work in class, particularly if they are unsure or if they have made mistakes. They use this self-preserving strategy to avoid appearing incompetent. How many times have we exhibited this behavior ourselves? Most students, in fact, engage in this kind of behavior. The primary point here is that the contingencies, *the rewards and sanctions* of the classroom, have engendered these norms—have caused us to feel that success depends on social comparison instead of on content learning and mastery.

Functionality of Rewards: Feedback and Motivation

Until about 2000, the prevailing advice that we would give teachers regarding using rewards to motivate mathematical engagement was, "*No!* Don't do it! It will undermine their intrinsic motivation!" The evidence appeared overwhelming. But now evidence suggests that rewards in and of themselves are neither good nor bad. Like in the discussion of most mathematics classrooms' rules of the game, we can see here that how students interpret rewards is what really matters. In fact, we can even think of personal satisfaction and pride in a well-accomplished task to be rewards.

We see these natural rewards as integral to performing a task and, no surprise, that they enhance intrinsic motivation.

We see other rewards as superfluous to the task. Obtaining a pizza party for completing a task, for example, is not integral to mathematics learning. We can, in fact, consider it a coercion put in place to get us to do something that we did not want to do. In such circumstances, the reward *will* often get us to do the task, but the reward actually reinforces recognizing that the task *isn't worth doing on its own*. So, in subsequent tasks, without the pizza party or some other reward of similar or greater value, we are less likely to engage than we were before!

Rewards as Feedback

One of the salient, as opposed to superfluous, aspects that some rewards can offer is feedback to the student. By providing a "good job, Stephen!" Emma may let Stephen know that he has performed well on some particular activity. But it doesn't go far enough to tell Stephen exactly what it was that defined the "good" in "good job." For this reason, paying close attention to the class's goal structures can augment the use of rewards. Schunk (1984) showed that when students' extrinsic reward couples with clear, coherent goals for learning, they tend to achieve more than students who receive rewards but do not have explicitly presented goals. Brown and Walberg (1993) show us that, in instances like mathematics, where students likely have little intrinsic motivation, developing explicit learning goals with the students, coupled with social pressure to achieve, gives them a mechanism to be successful and an inducement to work harder to be successful. Once students taste success, their negative cycles of ego goals and low self-efficacy begin to erode.

So, if Stephen, knowing what the goals for success are, receives a "good job, Stephen!" he knows exactly what he has done to warrant the reward, and he can store that information away so that he can behave similarly in future situations that have a similar set of goals. Transferring knowledge and skill from the situation that teaches them to situations to which they are required to apply it is one of mathematics education's elusive goals. Learning goals, coupled with social rewards (i.e., social pressure) yield a situation where transfer will more likely occur, because the goals serve as informational feedback.

But one crucial aspect needs to be present for rewards to induce positive motivation and learning rather than undermine them. That is, *the student should not expect the rewards* (Deci 1972; Lepper, Greene, and Nisbett 1973; Lepper, Keavney, and Drake 1996). Going back to our pizza-party example, expecting the pizza party as just compensation for engagement caused Emma's students to lose enthusiasm over time. If she had, for example, developed learning goals with the students, using positive remarks and other occasional reinforcements, and then sprung the pizza party as an *unexpected* surprise, the students would have received the party's reward value but would have not have had their motivation undermined, because they did not expect pizza as a necessary condition for their engagement!

Cameron, Banko, and Pierce (2001) performed a meta-analysis of 145 independent studies, representing the body of research on the effects of extrinsic rewards on intrinsic motivation. Table 10.1 summarizes their results.

Table 10.1
Summary of Meta-Analysis of Studies of the Impact of Extrinsic Reward on Intrinsic Motivation and Task Interest

	Free Choice Intrinsically Motivated Tasks	Tasks in Which Students Express Task Interest
Low Task Interest	+	0
High Task Interest		
Verbal Reward	+	+
Tangible Reward		
Reward Expected	Mixed	Mixed
Noncontingent	0	0
For Doing Well	−	0
For Engaging in Task	−	−
For Finishing Task	0	+
For Surpassing a Score	0	+
For Exceeding Others (ego)	+	+
For Each Unit Solved	−	+
More Than Maximum Reward	−	Too Little Information to Classify
Less Than Maximum Reward	0	Too Little Information to Classify
Reward Unexpected	0	0

0 = Reward has no reliable effect.
+ = Reward has a statistically significant, positive effect.
− = Reward has a statistically significant, negative effect.

Essentially, we now know that verbal rewards appear to be useful tools for helping students engage in tasks where they have low task interest. Used judiciously, rewards can induce students to engage enough in tasks so that they have the opportunity to begin building success, exploring challenge, controlling conditions, and developing intrinsic motivation. Where students already have expressed high task interest, verbal rewards appear to have a positive effect, given that the situation meets the feedback conditions we discussed earlier. For rewards other than verbal praise (e.g., tangible rewards like treats, pizza parties, and the like), we can see some obvious pitfalls, including rewarding people for just engaging in a task, which was Emma's mistake. When you have to pay people just to begin a task, it reduces their subsequent intrinsic motivation and interest. This is also true when we split rewards up by each unit solved or when students know the reward structure and perceive that they haven't received the maximum reward.

One of the most interesting findings in the field to date is that, if a student has developed interest in the task, offering tangible rewards doesn't appear to detract from their interest, except where they receive rewards just for engaging. In particular, rewarding students for achievement appears to enhance their developing intrinsic motivation, because the feedback issues we discussed previously contribute to students' sense of increased competence. The damaging results are for the pursuit's long-term valuation, not for the task itself. Cameron and colleagues (2005) show that rewards for achievement improve students' sense of competency, but they also tend to affect external attributions of success, undermining students' sense of autonomy. So, while rewards may actually increase task interest, they are likely to undermine long-term valuation of mathematics as a pursuit.

Summary

Overall, the evidence shows that using rewards as a strategy for managing engagement in mathematics tasks decreases the intrinsic motivation students display, particularly for tasks that the students have chosen freely.

We *can* use rewards meaningfully to help jump-start students' interest (Cameron, Banko, and Pierce 2001; Cameron et al. 2005). We can use them to induce students to begin an activity and, using proper behavior modification principles, to shape students' performance over time (Schunk 1984). Moreover, when students' interest wanes, we can use rewards to maintain engagement and performance. Rewards are most innocuous and most effective when the students do not expect them, and they present the most problems when we use them just to get students to agree to engage in a task.

The take-away we promote in this discussion is that, if you choose to use rewards as a strategy, you must be very careful regarding to whom you give them, why you give them, and how the students interpret them. We cannot overemphasize intrinsic motivation's importance as the mechanism by which students develop persistence in mathematics beyond the school day and school years. The research on this is clear. Everything we know points to misusing rewards contributing to a steady, downward trend in students' interest in mathematics, their intrinsic motivation, and the subsequent benefits of intrinsic motivation to cognitive processing, effort, and enjoyment (Middleton and Spanias 1999; Lepper et al. 2005).

Over time, when students lose commitment to learning goals and substitute these with more ego and performance goals (Anderman and Midgley 1997), they tend to value school—and, consequently, effort—less (Gottfried et al. 2007; Covington 2000). Intrinsic motivation is the key to turning this trend around. Rewards *can* be an important tool at times for us, but, because the peril of their use is so high, we suggest using them sparingly, and with understanding.

References

Alschuler, Alfred S. *Developing Achievement Motivation in Adolescents: Education for Human Growth.* Englewood Cliffs, N.J.: Educational Technology, 1973.

Anderman, Eric M., and Carol Midgley. "Changes in Achievement Goal Orientations, Perceived Academic Competence, and Grades across the Transition to Middle-Level School." *Contemporary Educational Psychology* 22 (1997): 269–98.

Brown, Steven M., and Herbert J. Walberg. "Motivational Effects on Test Scores of Elementary Students." *Journal of Educational Research* 86 (January–February 1993): 133–36.

Cameron, Judy, Katherine M. Banko, and W. David Pierce. "Pervasive Negative Effects of Rewards on Intrinsic Motivation: The Myth Continues." *Behavior Analyst* 24, no. 1 (Spring 2001): 1–44.

Cameron, Judy, W. David Pierce, Katherine M. Banko, and Amber Gear. "Achievement-Based Rewards and Intrinsic Motivation: A Test of Cognitive Mediators." *Journal of Educational Psychology* 97, no. 4 (November 2005): 641–55.

Covington, Martin V. "Goal Theory, Motivation, and School Achievement: An Integrative Review." *Annual Review of Psychology* 51 (February 2000): 171–200.

Deci, Edward L. "Effects of Externally Mediated Rewards on Intrinsic Motivation." *Journal of Personality and Social Psychology* 18, no. 1 (April 1971): 101–15.

Eccles, Jacquellyn S., Allan Wigfield, Carol Midgley, David Reuman, Douglas MacIver, and Harriet Feldlaufer. "Negative Effects of Traditional Middle Schools on Students' Motivation." *Elementary School Journal* 93, no. 5 (May 1993): 553–74.

Gottfried, Adele Eskeles, George A. Marcoulides, Allen W. Gottfried, Pamella H. Oliver, and Diana Wright Guerin. "Multivariate Latent Change Modeling of Developmental Decline in Academic Intrinsic Math Motivation and Achievement: Childhood through Adolescence." *International Journal of Behavioral Development* 31, no. 4 (2007): 317–27.

Lepper, Mark R., David Greene, and Richard E. Nisbett. "Undermining Children's Interest with Extrinsic Reward: A Test of the 'Overjustification' Hypothesis." *Journal of Personality and Social Psychology* 28, no. 1 (1973): 129–37.

Lepper, Mark R., Jennifer Henderlong Corpus, and Sheena S. Iyengar. "Intrinsic and Extrinsic Motivational Orientations in the Classroom: Age Differences and Academic Correlates." *Journal of Educational Psychology* 97, no. 2 (2005): 184–96.

Lepper, Mark R., Mark Keavney, and Michael Drake. "Intrinsic Motivation and Extrinsic Rewards: A Commentary on Cameron and Pierce's Meta-Analysis." *Review of Educational Research* 66, no. 1 (Spring 1996): 5–32.

Middleton, James A., and Photini A. Spanias. "Motivation for Achievement in Mathematics: Findings, Generalizations, and Criticisms of the Recent Research." *Journal for Research in Mathematics Education* 30, no. 1 (January 1999): 65–88.

Schunk, Dale H. "Self-Efficacy Perspectives on Achievement Behavior." *Educational Psychologist* 19 (1984): 48–58.

Simpkins, Sandra D., Pamela E. Davis-Kean, and Jacquellyn S. Eccles. "Math and Science Motivation: A Longitudinal Examination of the Links between Choices and Beliefs." *Developmental Psychology* 42, no. 1 (January 2006): 70–83.

Skiba, Russell J., and Reece L. Peterson. "School Discipline at a Crossroads: From Zero Tolerance to Early Response." *Exceptional Children* 66, no. 3 (Spring 2000): 335–46.

———. "The Dark Side of Zero Tolerance: Can Punishment Lead to Safe Schools?" *Phi Delta Kappan* 80 (March 1999): 1–11.

CHAPTER 11

Exploiting Interests: Building Intrinsic Motivation

*I*n this chapter, we reflect on how to catch and hold students' interest to promote their motivation to learn mathematics. We also explore instructional strategies that can foster students' longer-term, intrinsic interest in mathematics. Below, we share a story about a sixth-grade classroom. The story originated in Mandy's experience teaching preservice elementary school teachers. She taught a similar lesson in her college classroom at the University of Delaware. We moved the story into the setting of a sixth-grade classroom because the instructional practices are relevant for grades K–12 teachers as well as university instructors working with preservice teachers. The story in this chapter illustrates some pedagogical principles that can promote students' interest in mathematics.

Mr. Towson turned to his group of sixth-grade students as they got settled after coming back from their physical education class. He asked them to get out a piece of paper, and he wrote the following number sentence on the whiteboard.

$$6 \div \frac{1}{2} = ?$$

"Here's a division problem for you. We've been working with multiplication of fractions for a while. We've been getting better at not only finding the correct answers, but also at drawing diagrams to explain the problem. We're also improving how we talk about our strategies with each other. Now we want to use those skills and strategies when we divide fractions. You may remember some kind of rule for dividing fractions from last year. If you've seen some sort of rule before, I don't want us to use it yet. We want to think about how division works, and then we can use our ideas about how division works and create our own diagrams to figure out the answer.

"So, I put this number sentence on the board." He drew a rectangle around the problem. "Write it down on your papers. I want everyone to think about a story problem for this division problem and write it down. If you finish your story problem, then draw a diagram that can help you solve the problem. See how far you get. Let's go with independent work for now. I haven't decided yet if I will collect this from you or not, all right? Okay. Go for it." After Mr. Towson explained what he wanted from the students, most students started writing quietly, but Michelle immediately raised her hand.

Mr. Towson walked over to Michelle to touch base with her one-on-one.

"Um, Mr. T?" Michelle said. "I don't know what you mean. You said to think about how division works. I'm not sure how division works."

"Well, do you think that you can try to write a story problem that's about dividing?" Mr. Towson asked her.

"I don't know. I think so."

"You could try using whole numbers instead of fractions. You could think of it like six divided by three, write a story problem for that, and then change the three to one-half."

Michelle looked up and nodded at Mr. Towson. He then walked to the center of the classroom and spoke to the entire class, asking, "I hope that Michelle doesn't mind if I share her question with the group." Michelle put up both hands to cover her face and looked embarrassed. "I want to share the question because she was brave enough to ask it. I appreciated her question, because she helped me see that I could give you a little more help with this problem. If she's not sure about this problem, then she's not the only one." Michelle took her hands off of her face, but she continued to look down at her paper.

Mr. Towson continued, "So, I'm curious. Was anyone confused when I said to think about how division works when writing your story problem or drawing your picture?" Students nodded.

Jason shouted from the back of the class, "Yeah! Michelle's not the only one who's confused."

"Okay. So, here's what I think you could try. If you're having trouble writing a division story problem that includes a fraction, think about it with whole numbers. Go with something like six divided by three, think about that kind of problem, then try it with six divided by one-half." Mr. Towson glanced at Michelle, who was working busily, and then over at Jason, who nodded at him.

Jason said, "I'll try it." Mr. Towson smiled, and he started circulating the room to look at his students' work.

As he anticipated, he observed two different answers among his students: three and twelve. Many students wrote story problems and diagrams that appeared to model

$$\frac{1}{2} \times 6 = ?$$

rather than

$$6 \div \frac{1}{2} = ?$$

Mr. Towson expected and hoped for these responses so that he could compare and contrast them during whole-class discussion. He assumed that the students who thought the answer would be three would be convinced about their solution and not recognize initially that they had thought about the problem as "half of six" rather than something like "how many groups of one-half fit into six?" He hoped to compare and contrast the sets of two different story problems and diagrams, to elicit surprise from students and engage them in thinking about meanings of division, so that they would understand fractions division conceptually.

After Mr. Towson noticed most students getting to the point where they started to draw their diagrams to represent their solutions, he brought the class back together as a group. He walked to the whiteboard, pointed to the number sentence, and said, "I've had the chance to look at what you've come up with so far, and I'd like for you to see and hear what your classmates have found. Why don't we take some volunteers?"

Although Mr. Towson knew that he wanted to hear certain solutions, he didn't want to call on students directly. He wanted them to have a chance to volunteer themselves. He then would solicit solutions among the volunteers. He wanted the misconception to be shared, but he didn't want to single out students purposefully who held the misconception. Enough students had a story problem that represented "half of six" that he was comfortable leaving it up to the students to volunteer. The students would probably offer the answers he hoped to see.

Several hands went up. "Okay, Sergio, let's hear from you," said Mr. Towson.

"Twelve. The answer is 12!" Sergio grinned.

"Wait, what?!" Jennifer exclaimed. "That's totally not what I have. It's three."

Murmurs spread throughout the room. Some students craned their necks to look at their peers' papers. Other students turned around to look at papers behind them or next to them. They wanted to know if their answer matched their peers' answers.

Beth-Ann looked back and forth slowly between Sergio and Jennifer. She raised her hand and said, "Normally I agree with Jenny, but right now I think Sergio is right."

Jason shot his hand in the air.

Mr. Towson said, "Jason, you look like you want to add something?"

"Sure do. Jenny is right."

Michelle said, "Now I'm really confused."

Mr. Towson replied, "Whether or not the answer is 12 or 3 remains to be seen. Let's back up, I know that I pointed at this number sentence and asked for us to talk about it, but what did you write on your papers? Story problems. And many of you have diagrams, too. Let's share those." He drew a vertical line on the board to divide the whiteboard in half. "If your answer agrees with Sergio, 12, raise your hand." About two-thirds of the students raised their hands. "Okay, I need volunteers. I'd like for volunteers to write story problems over on the board up here. I need other people to draw pictures—diagrams that illustrate the solutions."

Mr. Towson walked around to look briefly at the students' papers. He handed out dry-erase markers to some students who had representations for a measurement model of division, where they repeatedly subtracted copies of one-half away from six. He also gave dry-erase markers to additional students whose representations showed the partitioning meaning of division, where six represented a quantity that made up one-half of a group and the problem asked for how much was needed for one whole group. The students began to write their problems on the board.

"Thank you for volunteering," Mr. Towson continued. "Now, just because more people have an answer of 12 doesn't mean that we know that they're right. Math isn't decided by 'majority rules.' We need to see why the answer works or why it doesn't work. Who would like to share their story problem or diagram for an answer of 3?" He then passed dry-erase markers to two more students, who reproduced their answers on the board.

Here are the different problems invented by the students:

> Kevin is the basketball team's manager. He wants to fill a large 6-gallon bucket with water so the team can drink water during the game. He will use a pitcher to fill the bucket. The pitcher holds a 1/2-gallon of water. How many times does Kevin have to dump the pitcher into the bucket to fill it?

> A half-full pizza box had six slices of pizza left in it. How many slices of pizza were originally in the box?

> I started with 6 cookies in my cookie jar. Next, I divided the cookies in half. I kept half for myself and gave the rest to my best friend. How many cookies did I keep?

Mr. Towson asked, "So, what do we think about the story problems?"

Jason said, "The problem I wrote is kind of like the cookie problem. It's right, because it's about dividing in half."

"Because it's about dividing in half? Okay. What do other people think? Beth-Ann?"

Beth-Ann said, "I'm not sure about the pizza problem, but I like the one about the water and the bucket and pitcher. It's kind of like mine."

"How is it like yours?"

"It's kind of like mine because mine is like…. Can I just read mine?"

"Sure."

Beth-Ann read, "Kelsey has six cups of sugar. She needs half a cup of sugar to make a recipe of cookies. How many recipes can she make?"

Mr. Towson said, "A recipe of cookies? Do you mean a batch? Like a recipe of cookies makes a batch of cookies?"

"Uh, yeah. Whatever. You know what I mean."

"I think I do. Okay. How is your problem like the one about Kevin and the water?"

Beth-Ann explained, "Yeah, so… in mine, it's like, you have to see… one-half, one-half, one-half, how many one-halves are in six? 12. Twelve one-halves makes six. How many times do I count one half until I get to six? I could make six recipes, I mean 12 recipes, 12 batches! Ugh! I can make 12 batches of cookies with six cups because that's 12 one-half cups. The water problem is like that. Twelve times filling up a pitcher of one-half of a gallon to get six gallons."

Mr. Towson pointed at the diagram that illustrated the quantity of six divided into 12 copies of size one-half and said, "That's like this picture? Twelve copies of one-half in six?"

Beth-Ann said, "Oh. Yeah, I see the picture. Yeah. I didn't get to draw one yet, but that is like mine. Yeah."

Mr. Towson looked at the class and said, "Now I know that Beth-Ann has a similar problem to the one about Kevin managing the basketball team, and I know that Jason has a problem like the one about the cookies, but I still don't know which one represents the number sentence on the board. Let's do this. For all three story problems on the board, let's write number sentences for each story problem. Work with your partners. Talk about a number sentence for each story problem, and discuss why you think it's the right number sentence. Make sure you talk about why."

The students talked intensely with each other for longer than Mr. Towson anticipated. Some students were amazed that the first two story problems were so different, even though both problems had an answer of 12. Other students didn't know whether the cookie problem involved subtraction, division. multiplication, or some combination of operations. Mr. Towson let them keep working in partners, and rather than end the mathematics class period with a whole-class discussion, he decided to let the students continue thinking about this idea overnight. He planned to start the next mathematics class period with a whole-class discussion about meanings of fraction division and why "dividing it in half" was like finding "half of six," which involved multiplying one-half and six.

What Can We Learn about Promoting Interest in Mathematics from Mr. Towson's Classroom?

We want students to *want* to learn and do mathematics. In our experience as teachers, we find that sometimes our students disengage during math class for good reasons. We may have looked at our students and thought, "They're not interested." Instead, we should try to ask ourselves, "Is my mathematics lesson interesting?" Although a negative answer to that question may be difficult to accept, it is quite often the truth (and the truth hurts sometimes) that if our students have checked out, we may have given them a (good) reason to check out. Our classes aren't always as interesting as we hope! Some people talk about interest as a trait, but we have found that it is also situational (Harackiewicz and Hulleman 2010), and it can be cultivated.

Although Mr. Towson's classroom doesn't describe uninterested students becoming more interested, it does describe a scenario when students *were* engaged and interested. Thinking about what happened in Mr. Towson's class is worthwhile. What did he do to keep his students interested when working on fraction division, a topic in mathematics that typically mystifies students in the middle grades?

Just like Mr. Towson, when we teach, we look for more than good behavior from our students. We hope to inspire students to be interested in learning and doing mathematics. We hope for genuine curiosity. However, students who seem to be engaged in doing mathematics may be merely cooperating with our expectations, not necessarily engaging because they are personally interested (Cobb, Gresalfi, and Hodge 2009). We want to give students the opportunity to care sincerely about what they are doing in school and give them something to do that is worth caring about and learning about. How can teachers create mathematics classrooms that inspire students to be more interested?

One step involves recognizing when our students are interested. How can we tell if students are interested or just cooperating with us? Interested students are engaged, engrossed, or entirely taken up with an activity, object, or topic (Dewey 1913). We recognize interest in action when someone freely chooses to spend time on something. In deep engagement, our actions appear and feel effortless. Yet interest does not exist only within the student. Interest is an interaction between the person being interested and the environment that is interesting (Dewey 1899, as cited in Long et al. [2007]), so we want to think about how to foster that sort of deep engagement.

A great deal of evidence suggests that students' interest in mathematics, and their motivation to learn in general, declines as they go through school (e.g., Pajares and Graham [1999]; Wigfield and Eccles [1994]; Wigfield et al. [1991]). What can we do to break this cycle? We can evoke situational interest by creating interesting mathematical experiences for our students in hopes of fostering longer-term, intrinsic, personal interest in mathematics. We know that we have done our jobs well as mathematics teachers if we create interest in mathematics where there might not be much interest otherwise. We try to catch students' interest and hold it. We also want to take care that we don't turn off students' interest when teaching. If teachers create more opportunities for students to be interested in mathematics during mathematics class, then more students may develop longer-term, intrinsic interest in mathematics.

For the remainder of this chapter, we reflect on strategies teachers can use to evoke interest in the classroom (i.e., create situational interest) and potentially move students to become more personally interested in mathematics beyond the classroom (i.e., foster intrinsic interest). We learned about these strategies through reading about what strategies others have found effective in promoting students' interest, and we highlight the strategies that we thought would be most useful in mathematics classrooms.

Creating Situational Interest: Catching and Holding Students' Interest

To evoke situational interest in students during mathematics class, teachers must first *catch* students' interest and then *hold* it. The instructional strategies described below have the potential to catch and hold students' interest during mathematics class.

Catching Interest

We are familiar with the importance of using some sort of "hook" to capture students' attention during a lesson, usually near the lesson's beginning, when we launch the activity or task. We can hook students' attention through a number of effective strategies—using personally relevant and meaningful tasks; helping students see how the content is potentially surprising or incongruous with what they currently believe; and giving rationales for why we believe that the task is important, delivered in a way that supports students' autonomy.

Use tasks that students find personally relevant or meaningful

To capture students' interest, mathematical tasks should be meaningful and have some relevance to their lives. Mathematics can give students the power to make sense of the world around them. Although us wanting to use tasks that our students find relevant and meaningful makes sense, putting this into practice can be complicated. One challenge with selecting relevant tasks is that what is useful, relevant, or meaningful to one student is not necessarily so for another. Students' interests can be idiosyncratic. Catering to the personal interests of all the individual students in a classroom seems overwhelming. It may not even be possible.

Another challenge with situating mathematics in possibly relevant contexts is that mathematical relationships do not always map nicely and meaningfully onto contexts (Boaler 1993). For example, as we discussed earlier, if the context is too artificial, it can turn students off. So, if we want mathematics to seem relevant and personally interesting, we want to take care to make sure that our contexts are not pseudocontexts (Boaler 2008). What makes an activity authentic, in general, to the discipline and to students' lives?

In spite of these challenges, teachers can help more students see meaning and relevance in school tasks. Mr. Towson navigated this challenge by asking the students to design story problems themselves. If students had to create the context, they would likely think about situations that interested them. As an added bonus, students had to wrestle with the mathematical relationships to write a story problem that mapped onto the number sentence. So, Mr. Towson asked students to write story problems to both appeal to a range of students' interests and help them think about mathematics.

Additionally, teachers can talk explicitly about why and how they see mathematical tasks as meaningful and relevant, to help students see the value in potential learning opportunities that they have not yet come to appreciate on their own (Brophy 1999). Students become more interested when their teachers model enthusiasm and interest in the task (Covington 1999). This could involve helping students see the beauty in the mathematics they are exploring. Developing or encouraging an aesthetic appreciation for mathematics (Sinclair 2001, 2009) can help mathematics have a personal meaning in a way different from that of needing mathematics to be useful in other settings.

Point out incongruous or surprising information

Beyond relevance, we can hook students by eliciting and confronting their misconceptions. When we do this, we help students see that what they might think is true may actually not be. Of course, students think about a lot of things that are actually true, too. Creating cognitive conflict or dissonance, however, can evoke students' curiosity (Hidi and Renninger 2006). In Mr. Towson's classroom, students encountered dissonance when they entertained story problems that all appeared to be correct, but actually led to different answers. This dissonance experience motivated them through the need to understand whether these problems were all accurate or not, and why. Students will likely want to resolve the conflict or dissonance and learn about why their thinking may not be quite accurate. Mr. Towson skillfully and seamlessly illuminated students' misconceptions, demonstrating one of the primary methods of promoting interest in his classroom. He used this method to develop conceptual understanding, as he purposefully tried to bring misconceptions to the surface during the lesson.

Provide rationales and support autonomy

Providing explicit rationales to students can help catch their interest (Jang 2008). Meaningful rationales describe an activity's importance and usefulness, as well its long-term relevance, such as in opportunities for personal growth and opportunities to contribute to the world around them (Vansteenkiste, Lens, and Deci 2006). Rationales are more effective for hooking students' interest when they are delivered in an autonomy-supportive manner. Small changes can make a big difference, such as using noncontrolling language ("you can…" "we suggest that you…") rather than controlling language ("you have to …" "you should …") (Vansteenkiste, Lens, and Deci 2006), provided the students do legitimately have choices.

Mr. Towson used autonomy-supportive language during his lesson's launch when he tried to use purposefully the pronoun *we* to emphasize that they were working *together* to figure something out. He also tried to be supportive by encouraging the progress that the students had made and showing how the current experience related to their prior knowledge. In this way, he tried to articulate that he expected students would continue to be mathematically successful. He tried to support their autonomy most specifically when he said that he suggested that they do not use their rule for dividing fractions. He acknowledged that they may know a rule, but he asked them to avoid it because he knew their remaining misconceptions and fragile conceptual understanding of fraction division would surface. Therefore, he wanted them to focus on how division works and the operation's relationship to a diagram.

Additionally, teachers can support students' autonomy by pointing out what students can do well already and directing students to tap into that knowledge or skill to succeed on their own when working on a new task. Mr. Towson directed the students to use what they already knew by sharing how they could do so to work on the division problem, thus supporting students' autonomy to make sense of the division problem for themselves.

Holding Interest

Once we've caught students' interest, we want to strive purposefully to hold their interest. We can sustain students' interest by continuing to use personally relevant and meaningful tasks and continuing to support students' autonomy; by giving students tasks at an appropriate degree of challenge, with the opportunity to engage socially with one another around the content; and by providing instructional support and scaffolding. These strategies keep students' interest and maintain their engagement, which is important because we do not want students to start to disengage after they have been initially hooked.

Continue providing opportunities to engage in personally relevant and meaningful tasks

As we evoke students' interest, they may start to wonder more about mathematics. They may develop their own questions and conjectures about relationships they observe. How can we offer more opportunities for students to pose questions about mathematics (Brown and Walter 2005)? Students' own wonderments are, indeed, personally meaningful to them. We could turn students' own questions about mathematics into longer-term, project-based experiences for them as they pursue answers. We could turn students' own mathematical questions into shorter-term tasks, such as problems of the week, as well. Freedom to choose to study topics that already interest students can help them develop interest (Bergin 1999). Mr. Towson hoped that his students would develop their own questions and wonderments through his effort to elicit contrasting solutions (see when Jennifer asked, "Wait, what?").

Continue supporting students' autonomy

Students' interest will more likely thrive in classrooms where teachers support their students' autonomy. Teachers can support students' autonomy by empathizing with the learner's perspective, allowing opportunities for legitimate self-initiation and choice, giving a meaningful rationale if choice is constrained, refraining from pressure or contingencies to motivate behavior, and providing timely and positive feedback (Vansteenkiste, Lens, and Deci 2006).

Mr. Towson valued empathizing with his students' perspective. When a student was confused, such as when Michelle was stuck on his suggestion to think about how division works, he thought about how he might have contributed to the confusion and could help resolve it. Also, when his class became restless when they shared two different answers, rather than assume that they were off task, he realized their interest had been piqued and he took their perspective. When learners become interested, you may feel a sudden burst of energy throughout the room. What may appear to be off-task behavior could be the restlessness of curiosity. Murmurs of discussion throughout a classroom could be a good event!

Provide tasks at an appropriate degree of challenge

School tasks become boring when they are too easy. Learning activities evoke interest when they are optimally challenging—not too difficult and not too easy (Brophy 1999). However, what challenges one student optimally may not do so for another.

One way to design tasks at an appropriate challenge level is to align them effectively with students' prior knowledge, so the students can move from their prior knowledge to new knowledge by using what they already know. Mr. Towson tried to help his students see that their thinking about division with whole numbers could help them create story problems to divide fractions. He also wanted them to see how drawing diagrams to make sense of division could help them interpret the problem.

Provide opportunities for social engagement around mathematics content

We can sustain some students' interest through opportunities for personal involvement in a task through interaction with peers. By talking about ideas and sharing their own thinking, students can explore and connect with the task in ways that make sense to them. So, another benefit of collaborative learning could be holding students' interest (Hidi and Renninger 2006). Mr. Towson hoped to promote social engagement by having his students work with partners. They ended up talking about mathematics for even longer than he predicted.

Provide support and scaffolding

A teacher's support for his or her students can help hold students' interest. For instance, when teachers shift from their own perspective and to the students', which is also called *cognitive decentering*, teachers show they care for and support students (Hackenberg 2010). This kind of mathematical care helps students develop renewed interest in the activity and experience an increased energy level. Cognitive decentering can also help teachers find renewed energy and interest by fostering an experience of relatedness. If students feel supported by their teachers, they will more likely be interested in school tasks (Wentzel et al. 2010). Mr. Towson hoped to be supportive as he attempted to take students' perspectives and connect their current thinking with prior knowledge.

Once we have caught and held students' interest in the classroom situation, we hope to use strategies to develop longer-term, or intrinsic, interest in mathematics. Although getting students interested in a classroom situation is a good start, ideally students will want to do mathematics beyond our classrooms. Below, we discuss instructional strategies that promote intrinsic motivation to learn and do mathematics.

Fostering Intrinsic Interest in Mathematics

We want to promote students' interest during mathematics class because we hope that they will develop intrinsic motivation to do mathematics on their own in the future, beyond our classrooms. When students are intrinsically motivated, they complete a task for its own sake rather than for some external reward, like a grade (Urdan and Schoenfelder 2006, p. 337). In other words, students are intrinsically motivated when they undertake an activity for its inherent interest and enjoyment, and they are extrinsically motivated when they engage in a school task to attain an outcome separable from the learning itself (Vansteenkiste, Lens, and Deci 2006).

Intrinsic motivation is personal. Expecting all students to become intrinsically interested in all subjects in school is not realistic. An important part of teaching to support the development of interests is acknowledging that students can exercise the freedom to choose not to be interested in a longer-term connection with mathematics. After all, "… the key to acquiring values is feeling free enough to accept them as one's own" (Deci et al. 1991, p. 338). We care about our students enough not to coerce them, so we accept that they have their own free will to choose to appreciate mathematics as a valuable aspect of their lives or not.

Teachers Can Model Interest in Mathematics for Their Students

However, teachers can have a positive influence in some ways on the development of a longer-term, personal, and intrinsic interest in mathematics. Teachers can serve as models of someone who truly appreciates and loves doing mathematics and learning more about it. Such a model gives students a vicarious experience, one that can support their development of intrinsic interest (Hidi and Renninger 2006). Models provide stronger vicarious experiences when an extended relationship exists over time, such as a student's relationship with her or his teacher.

Teachers Can Offer Support in the Face of Difficulty

If students engage in a challenging activity, they will likely run into difficulty once in a while. If teachers offer support and encouragement in the face of the difficulties, in ways that allow students to persist and see themselves overcoming the hurdle through effort, students will more likely develop intrinsic interest (Hidi and Renninger 2006). The satisfaction of overcoming a challenge helps us take pride in what we have accomplished and, as a result, believe that we can overcome future difficulties. Mr. Towson tried to support students in the face of challenge by turning their difficulties into learning opportunities for the entire class.

Learning More about Mathematics Content Can Support Developing Interest

When students know more about a school subject, they can appreciate and value it more. This helps build their interest in it (Hidi and Renninger 2006). Some researchers have found that adolescent students in grades 7 through 10 who were high achievers expressed more interest in math than low achievers (Köller, Baumert, and Schnabel 2001). However, interest in a subject without deeply understanding it is still possible, and interest in a subject can inspire effort to learn more about it.

Expecting students to be interested can be a self-fulfilling prophecy

Students may be as interested as we expect them to be, if we treat them as though they are interested. If we think that students are intrinsically motivated, we might more strongly support their autonomy, because we may expect that they will manage themselves in ways that promote learning (Pelletier and Vallerand 1989). Conversely, if we teachers think some students are extrinsically motivated, we may be more controlling with those students because we may believe that we have to coerce them to do what we want them to do. If students do not appear interested, perhaps we are not treating them as if we expect them to be.

Promote Learning and Interest Simultaneously!

Our final point about fostering intrinsic motivation is that promoting students' interest and their conceptual understanding can go hand in hand. When Mr. Towson confronted his students' misconceptions, he not only promoted situational interest, but also provided opportunities for his students to develop their conceptual understanding about fractions division. We hope that promoting interest in mathematics can be a learning outcome that mathematics teachers strive to attain. However, because some pedagogical strategies useful for promoting students' interest, such as scaffolding students' learning, promoting students' autonomy, and providing personally meaningful, appropriately challenging tasks, can simultaneously support students' development of understanding, we believe that promoting intrinsic interest in mathematics does not mean adding to a long list of additional pedagogical strategies. We envision that when teachers help students become more interested in mathematics, they can also help their students learn more mathematics content.

References

Bergin, David A. "Influences on Classroom Interest." *Educational Psychologist* 34, no. 2 (1999): 87–98.

Boaler, Jo. "The Role of Contexts in the Mathematics Classroom: Do They Make Mathematics More 'Real?'" *For the Learning of Mathematics* 13, no. 2 (June 1993): 12–17.

Brophy, Jere. "Toward a Model of the Value Aspects of Motivation in Education: Developing Appreciation for Particular Learning Domains and Activities." *Educational Psychologist* 34, no. 2 (1999): 75–85.

Brown, Stephen I., and Marion I. Walter. *The Art of Problem Posing.* Mahwah, N.J.: Lawrence Erlbaum Associates, 2005.

Cobb, Paul, Melissa Gresalfi, and Lynn Liao Hodge. "An Interpretive Scheme for Analyzing the Identities That Students Develop in Mathematics Classrooms." *Journal for Research in Mathematics Education* 40, no. 1 (January 2009): 40–68.

Covington, Martin V. "Caring about Learning: The Nature and Nurturing of Subject-Matter Appreciation." *Educational Psychologist* 34, no. 2 (March 1999): 127–36.

Deci, Edward L., Robert J. Vallerand, Luc G. Pelletier, and Richard M. Ryan. "Motivation and Education: The Self-Determination Perspective." *Educational Psychologist* 26, nos. 3–4 (1991): 325–46.

Dewey, John. *Interest as Related to Will.* Chicago: University of Chicago, 1899.

———. *Interest and Effort in Education.* Cambridge, Mass.: Riverside Press, 1913.

Hackenberg, Amy J. "Mathematical Caring Relations in Action." *Journal for Research in Mathematics Education* 41, no. 3 (May 2010): 236–73.

Harackiewicz, Judith M., and Chris S. Hulleman. "The Importance of Interest: The Role of Achievement Goals and Task Values in Promoting the Development of Interest." *Social and Personality Psychology Compass* 4, no. 1 (February 2010): 42–52.

Hidi, Suzanne, and K. Ann Renninger. "The Four-Phase Model of Interest Development." *Educational Psychologist* 41, no. 2 (2006): 111–27.

Jang, Hyungshim. "Supporting Students' Motivation, Engagement, and Learning during an Uninteresting Activity." *Journal of Educational Psychology* 100, no. 4 (2008): 798–811.

Köller, Olaf, Jurgen Baumert, and Kai Schnabel. "Does Interest Matter? The Relationship between Academic Interest and Achievement in Mathematics." *Journal for Research in Mathematics Education* 32, no. 5 (November 2001): 448–70.

Long, Joyce F., Shinichi Monoi, Brian Harper, Dee Knoblauch, and P. Karen Murphy. "Academic Motivation and Achievement among Urban Adolescents." *Urban Education* 42, no. 3 (2007): 196–222.

Pajares, Frank, and Laura Graham. "Self-Efficacy, Motivation Constructs, and Mathematics Performance of Entering Middle School Students." *Contemporary Educational Psychology* 24, no. 2 (April 1999): 124–39.

Pelletier, Luc G., and Robert J. Vallerand. "Behavioral Confirmation in Social Interaction: Effects of Teachers' Expectancies on Students' Intrinsic Motivation." *Canadian Psychology* 30, no. 2a (1989): 404 (abstract).

Sinclair, Nathalie. "The Aesthetic 'Is' Relevant." *For the Learning of Mathematics* 21, no. 1 (March 2001): 25–32.

———. "Aesthetics as a Liberating Force in Mathematics Education?" *ZDM* 41, nos. 1–2 (2009): 45–60.

Urdan, Timothy C., and Erin Schoenfelder. "Classroom Effects on Student Motivation: Goal Structures, Social Relationships, and Competence Beliefs." *Journal of School Psychology* 44, no. 5 (2006): 331–49.

Vansteenkiste, Maarten, Willy Lens, and Edward L. Deci. "Intrinsic versus Extrinsic Goal Contents in Self-Determination Theory: Another Look at the Quality of Academic Motivation." *Educational Psychologist* 41, no. 1 (2006): 19–31.

Wentzel, Kathryn R., Ann Battle, Shannon L. Russell, and Lisa B. Looney. "Social Supports from Teachers and Peers as Predictors of Academic and Social Motivation." *Contemporary Educational Psychology* 35, no. 3 (July 2010): 193–202.

Wigfield, Allan, and Jacquellyn S. Eccles. "Children's Competence Beliefs, Achievement Values, and General Self-Esteem Change across Elementary and Middle School." *Journal of Early Adolescence* 14, no. 2 (May 1994): 107–38.

Wigfield, Allan, Jacquellyn S. Eccles, Douglas MacIver, David A. Reuman, and Carol Midgley. "Transitions during Early Adolescence: Changes in Children's Domain-Specific Self-Perceptions and General Self-Esteem across the Transition to Junior High School." *Developmental Psychology* 27, no. 4 (July 1991): 552–65.

CHAPTER 12

Building Relationships: Characteristics of Knowledge-Building Communities

We last read about Mrs. Targett's seventh-grade mathematics classroom in chapter 6. The students in Mrs. Targett's classroom were working together on the mathematics problem written below. Students compared and contrasted pledge plans for a walkathon. We wrote the story to highlight how teachers can create collaborative classroom communities; we based the story on a seventh-grade class that Mandy observed when conducting a study about students' participation during mathematics classroom discourse (Jansen 2008). Mrs. Targett's classroom illustrates that we can motivate and engage students more when we furnish them opportunities to work together collaboratively, which helps them build relationships with one another and mathematics.

Mathematics Problem in Mrs. Targett's Classroom

Ms. Chang says that some sponsors might ask the students to suggest a pledge amount. The class wants to agree on how much they ask for. Leanne says that each sponsor should pay $10 regardless of how far a person walks. Gilberto says that $2 per kilometer would be better because it would bring in more money. Alana points out that if they ask for too much money, not as many people will want to be sponsors. She suggests that they ask each sponsor for $5 plus 50 cents per kilometer. (This problem was modified from a Connected Mathematics unit, "Moving Straight Ahead" [Lappan et al. 2002].)

For each pledge plan:
1. Make a table showing the amount of money a sponsor would owe if a student walked distances from 1 to 6 kilometers.
2. Graph the three pledge plans on the same coordinate axis. Use a different color for each plan.

3. Write an equation that can be used to calculate the amount of money a sponsor owes, given the total distance the student walks.

As Alejandro and Maritza walked back to their seats near Jasmine, Mrs. Targett said, "Thanks to Maritza and Alejandro's group, we were able to see the graphs and think about how the graphs show us which plans make more money. How is this going to help us choose a walkathon plan? Yes? Jacob, what do you think?"

"My group didn't agree about which plan we preferred," Jacob said.

Mrs. Targett asked, "Well, which plans were you trying to decide between?"

Jacob replied, "We weren't done talking about it, but I can try to share some of the stuff we talked about."

"That would be fine," Mrs. Targett said. "We don't have to be finished with our ideas to share them with the group. Share how you've been thinking so far, or how your group's been thinking, if you can, and then hopefully your colleagues can join you and think about this with you." Mrs. Targett wanted a group that hadn't resolved their thinking to share, to promote the idea that sharing in-progress work was productive, and she thought that the particular ways that Jacob's group had been puzzling through their selection of pledge plan would benefit the class.

Jacob said, "Okay. Um, you know how Gilberto said that his plan, for $2 each kilometer, that plan would bring in more money? Well, we did not agree with him, because what if someone got tired, you know? Sometimes the races, the walkathons, they are only 5 K, five kilometers, so …."

"Yeah," Kelly said, interrupting. "When my group was talking about that, we noticed that, too. Gilberto, in the problem, he isn't always right. Sometimes $2 for each kilometer doesn't bring in more money. If you go for only a couple of kilometers, $2 for each kilometer is less than both of the other plans."

Mrs. Targett noted, "So, we're saying that one way to decide which plan is better is to think about how far we're going to walk or run?"

"I guess, yeah. You could say it like that," Jacob reflected.

Mrs. Targett looked around the room at the other students in the class. "I'm not sure that everyone is with us. Let me check in with the other groups. Did anyone notice what Jacob's group and Kelly's group noticed?"

Maritza said, "They're thinking about—yeah, my group thought about this, too— we're thinking about how sometimes Gilberto's plan doesn't make any more than the other plans."

"Okay. How can we show that sometimes Gilberto's plan doesn't make more than the other plans? What representation do we want to use to compare when Gilberto's plan makes more and when it doesn't?" Mrs. Targett asked.

"We can talk about it with our graphs up there, but the book starts with tables. We could make tables, too," Maritza suggested.

Enthusiastically, Mrs. Targett said, "Great! Let's do that. Tables for each plan. Could I have tables from the groups that I haven't heard from yet? A table representing each plan? Please put the tables on the board for us." Mrs. Targett would have suggested using a tabular representation to complement the graphical one if the students hadn't suggested using tables.

Students from the three other groups that hadn't presented their thinking about the pledge plans yet came to the board and wrote the following information for the three pledge plans:

All Three Pledge Plans

Leanne			Gilberto			Alana	
Km	**$**		**Km**	**$**		**Km**	**$**
1	10		1	2		1	$5.50
2	10		2	4		2	$6.00
3	10		3	6		3	$6.50
4	10		4	8		4	$7.00
5	10		5	10		5	$7.50
6	10		6	12		6	$8.00

Mrs. Targett looked at the board and said, "Okay, so, now we can see these tables. What do we think? Yes, Kelly?"

Kelly responded, "Mrs. Targett? My group's table looks different for Alana's plan."

Mrs. Targett inquired, "What did your group write?"

"Could I come up?" Kelly asked.

"Sure."

Next to the dollar amounts for Alana's plan, Kelly created an additional column where she wrote her dollar amounts. Then she pointed at each number in the table and said, "Okay, for one kilometer, we got five dollars. For two kilometers, then we had $5.50, and, yeah, like that."

Kelly's Group, Alana's Pledge Plan

Alana	
Km	**$**
1	$5.00
2	$5.50
3	$6.00
4	$6.50
5	$7.00
6	$7.50

Mrs. Targett looked at the board, nodded, and turned to the class, shrugging. "So, which is it?" she asked. "Two kilometers for $6 or two kilometers for $5.50?" When circulating the room previously, while students were working in groups, Mrs.

Targett observed that students had been unsure about how to incorporate the initial amount of five dollars into the representations for the pledge plans. So she wanted an opportunity to compare and contrast representations for Alana's pledge plan.

"For Alana's plan, you need 50 cents for every kilometer," Eliza called out from the back of the room. "You also need $5 to start, so I think it's 50 cents plus 50 cents, for each of the two kilometers, and then the $5 to start, so $6 for 2 kilometers."

As Kelly walked back to her seat, she shook her head in disagreement.

"No," she said, "it's $5 to start, so $5 for one kilometer, and then 50 cents for each of the next kilometers, so $5 for one kilometer and then when you get to 2 kilometers, 50 cents more. $5.50 for 2 kilometers."

Mrs. Targett asked the class, "How are we going to resolve this? Thank you, Jasmine, you're going to help us out?"

"I understand what Kelly is thinking," Jasmine explained, "but in our group we thought about it more like Eliza did. The $5 is like if you just showed up and didn't walk anything. You got there, decided not to walk, so you went zero kilometers. In that case, you'd collect $5 for showing up. Then, if you even went one more kilometer, you would add in 50 cents each time. Show up, $5. Go one kilometer, 50 cents. Then another kilometer for two kilometers, another 50 cents. So, one dollar plus five dollars is six dollars for two kilometers."

Kelly replied, "Ooooh … not $5 for the first kilometer, but $5 for *no* kilometers?"

"That's what we thought," Jasmine said.

"Yeah, me, too," Eliza chimed in.

Mrs. Targett picked up her copy of the textbook. "Let's look back at the book. On page 8, it says that Alana wants to ask each sponsor for $5 plus 50 cents for each kilometer. So, you could collect the $5 before you even walk or run. Then, after the run, you would go back to your friend who pledged money. You could say, all right, I went 1 kilometer, or I went 8 kilometers, however far you went. And you could ask for 50 cents for each of those kilometers. What do you think about that, Kelly?"

Kelly looked up from her textbook and stared at the tables, pausing for a moment. Then she said, "Okay, so even if I went 1 kilometer, I would still have to ask for 50 cents more than $5.00. I think I get it."

Mrs. Targett called on Ben, who had been raising his hand. "Yes, Ben, what would you like to add?"

"You know, this is why I liked Leanne's plan. It wasn't as confusing. It's just $10 all the way. See?" Ben gestured side to side to demonstrate that the graph was $10 no matter how many kilometers that someone ran or walked. "There's no way to get that graph or that table wrong."

Jacob said, "Now we're back to why my group disagreed, because, yeah, Ben liked Leanne's plan because you don't have to solve for anything. I wanted to like Gilberto's, because he said you'd make more money, but when you look at his table, his plan isn't always making more money. Because, like, maybe it's just a 5 K walkathon. Then it doesn't matter which plan you pick; either Leanne's and Gilberto's make the same amount. So it doesn't really matter if you like Leanne's or Gilberto's. Ben is right. I am right. Both plans work for making more money."

Ben replied, "Only kind of, though. Both plans wouldn't always make more money, even if it was a 5 K. What if you get tired? You might stop at four kilometers. Then Leanne's plan brings in more money than Gilberto's."

"Okay, let's step back for a minute," Mrs. Targett said, jumping into the conversation. "Let's notice what Ben and Jacob are pointing out when they compare the two plans. What is similar and what is different between these two plans?"

"They're similar because they both have 10 dollars for 5 kilometers," Jacob observed.

"Right," said Mrs. Targett. "That's what you just said. Good. What do you think, Kelly?"

"They're different because they have different amounts for all of the other kilometers."

Eliza raised her hand and said, "Another difference is that Gilberto's table is going up by twos and Leanne's table isn't going up by anything."

Maritza agreed, "Yeah, Gilberto's table is linear, but Leanne's table isn't linear."

"Wait, what?" Ben asked.

Mrs. Targett looked over at him. "What's wrong, Ben?"

"Maritza said that Leanne's table isn't linear, but when you draw the graph for Leanne's plan, it's a straight line."

Mrs. Targett turned to Maritza. "What do you think about that?"

Maritza replied, "I agree that Leanne's plan has a straight line for a graph, yeah. I mean, that's what we had when we put the graphs up. Leanne's plan was flat, but it was straight."

"So, is her plan linear?" Mrs. Targett asked. "You said that it wasn't. Can you explain what you mean?"

"It doesn't go up by anything, like Eliza said. How can it be linear if it doesn't go up by anything?" Maritza looked over at her group mates for help.

Mrs. Targett said, "Doesn't go up by anything. Okay. What do others think about that?"

Alejandro responded, "Now I'm confused, because I thought all of these plans were linear."

"All right, so here's a question for everyone." Mrs. Targett said, deciding that it was time for the groups to think about this issue. "What makes one of these plans linear, anyhow? Are they all linear? How do we know? Take two minutes and talk with your groups." Mrs. Targett wanted to orient the students to the larger conceptual question about criteria for linear relationships. She hoped that her choice to move the students back into groups would allow the students more time to process this bigger idea together.

The groups turned to one another and talked about the problem. Some students gestured to the tables and graphs. Others looked in their notebooks for more information about linear relationships, because they wanted to see how they talked about linearity on previous class days.

Mrs. Targett stood in the back of the room and asked, "So, Jasmine, I observed your group's discussion, and I think you should talk with the class about what your group discussed. Please share."

Jasmine said, "Okay, um, ... So, we thought about our definition in our notebooks. We looked back at the definition that we wrote. For a plan to be linear, it has to go up by the same amount each time, in the table. Maritza noticed that Leanne's plan didn't go up by anything, but when I talked with my group, I saw that it went up by zero each time in the table. When it goes up by zero all of the time, every time, it's still going up by the same amount every time. Zero, zero, zero."

Alejandro said, "Should we add that stuff to our definition in our notebooks?"

"That's a great idea." Mrs. Targett affirmed Alejandro for noting that the class could record this advance in thinking about linear relationships. "Could everyone please open their math notebooks to your definition section?" She waited while the students turned pages in their notebooks to find their section with definitions. "I appreciate that Jasmine's group referred back to their definitions in their notebooks, and I really like that Alejandro suggested that we preserve and record what we're noticing about linear plans. We need to keep track of our thinking and write down when we come to new understandings. What do we have in our notebooks so far?"

Jasmine replied, "We wrote that linear tables go up by the same amount in the y column when the x column is changing by the same amount."

"And your group wanted to add something to the definition?"

"Yeah," Alejandro said. "We want to say that even when the y column isn't going up by anything, that's still going up by zero, so even problems when the y amount doesn't look like it's going up by anything, it's still got an equal change every time. It's just zero."

Mrs. Targett said, "Okay, so what we had was a general definition, and you want to provide additional information about a specific case. That can extend our definition. We can describe how the general definition applies to special cases. How do we want to phrase it?"

"Going up by zero is still linear," Maritza said, "because the y column is going up by zero every time, for every time x is going up by one."

Mrs. Targett replied, "Okay. Let's write down a version of what Maritza said in our notebooks." On the board, she wrote, "When linear relationships go up by the same amount every time, that amount can be zero (Leanne's plan)."

A few moments of silence passed while students wrote in their notebooks. Then, Mrs. Targett provided some directions to regroup the class.

"We still haven't finished our work on this problem," she said, "and I need to see where you're at. We have about 10 minutes left in class today. I would like to have each group, on one piece of paper, choose one of the plans and write about why it is or is not the best plan of the three to choose. You need to justify your decision using more than one of the representations from the problem—tables, graphs, equations—use two of the three representations, or use or all three. The most important part is that you support your reasons for why you want to choose the plan using mathematical information from the representations. I will collect only one piece of paper from each group at the end of class, so you need to work together and make sure that each of you have your thinking represented on your group's paper. We'll start class tomorrow by talking about what your groups decided."

We want students to push themselves further and give elaborated explanations of their solutions to one another when working in their small groups and during whole-class discussions. We think that students would learn more from one another if they would not only show *that* their solutions lead to a correct answer, but if they would also explain *why* they think their solutions work. We think that students would benefit if they considered why their peers' solutions could also be effective or potentially more elegant, so we may want students to compare and contrast their thinking and seek mathematical connections.

Getting students to cooperate with one another during mathematics class, let alone collaborate on a problem, can seem challenging. Students may resist contributing their ideas, waiting to hear from someone who already figured out how to solve the problem. Once students have a correct answer, they may not think they need to discuss anything more with their group members. We can get frustrated when students focus on just getting their work done as opposed to trying to extend their or their group's thinking. We get even more frustrated when students appear to rely much on us or on peers, and because this allows them to arrive at correct answers, they fool themselves into thinking they think are more knowledgeable than they are.

If students do not engage with mathematics in ways that we think are beneficial, it's likely that we did not create a classroom culture that encourages that kind of engagement. How can we structure our mathematics classrooms so that our students truly collaborate with one another? How can we structure our mathematics classrooms so that our students develop powerful mathematical understandings through their collaboration? In this chapter, we explore these questions to understand how learners can build stronger relationships with mathematics, their peers, and their teacher in mathematics classrooms.

Collaboration Happens in Knowledge-Building Communities

Truly collaborative mathematics classrooms are *knowledge-building communities*. Knowledge-building communities emphasize *growth in understanding* over time and *interdependence* among students (Hewitt and Scardamalia 1998; Lee, Chan, and van

Aalst 2006; Moss and Beatty 2006; Scardamalia 2002; Zhang et al. 2007; Zhang et al. 2009). Teachers promote collaboration by fostering opportunities for learners to become personally curious about mathematical tasks and to become increasingly invested in understanding and learning from their peers' thinking.

Knowledge Building = Ideas Can Be Improved

A key to creating a collaborative classroom—a knowledge-building community—is promoting the belief that ideas can be *improved*. If we believe that our solutions, ideas, and justifications are continuously improvable and revisable, then we have more to discuss once we have achieved a correct answer. The conversation about mathematics does not end. Instead, we encourage students to look across solutions and representations, make connections and generalizations, and justify their thinking to one another. When we treat mathematics as an evolving body of knowledge that can develop in the classroom, students will likely develop a sense of owning the ideas and build a positive relationship with mathematics as a field of study. This attitude aligns closely with the belief that intelligence is malleable, which, as we reviewed in chapter 7 leads to expenditure of effort, persistence, and ultimately, success (e.g., Dweck [1996]). Knowledge is built. Understanding grows. Relationships with mathematics and with classroom community members develop.

Students built knowledge about linearity through their discussion of the walkathon problem. A pivotal moment in Mrs. Targett's classroom was when they refined the class's definition for *linear*. Through engaging in mathematical tasks that incorporate multiple representations and a range of task constraints, students could stretch their thinking for what counted as a linear relationship. They had a recording of their group's knowledge about linearity in their mathematics notebooks that they could revisit and revise. Students appeared to have ownership in the knowledge-building process, given that they prompted their definition's revision. Students' relationship with mathematics grew through the opportunity to engage in building knowledge about mathematics together.

Communities = Interdependence

When a mathematics classroom functions as a community, its members are interdependent. Students depend on one another: the mathematics problems are so challenging and meaningful to the community's members that they need to hear from one another. Students depend on one another because they want to improve continually on what they know. They engage by sharing their own mathematical thinking and truly listening to others' thinking (Blumenfeld et al. 1996). Students wonder about, analyze, and evaluate others' thinking. They take responsibility for their understanding *and their groups' and class's evolving knowledge*. Positive relationships among students, and with their teacher, support this interdependence and grow from being interdependent.

In Mrs. Targett's class, we could see students' interdependence in and across groups. In groups, the disagreement about which pledge plan students preferred prompted dialogue and discussion about the different plans' characteristics. Across groups, comparing graphical and tabular representations that different groups created elicited ways of viewing the different pledge plans that helped the students think about linearity. Groups worked together to discuss whether a problem with a zero slope could be linear, and they discussed how to make sense of a situation when the "starting point" was not zero. Groups worked together to understand one another's thinking, whether or not they were correct, which suggests that the students took responsibility for their own understanding and that of their peers. At the end of class, Mrs. Targett put a structure on the task—collect one piece of paper—to inspire continued interdependence.

Encouraging Knowledge Building and Interdependence

Researchers have documented that knowledge-building communities can be created in classrooms with children as young as nine or ten years old, in both mathematics (Moss and Beatty 2006) and science classrooms (Zhang et al. 2007; Zhang et al. 2009). So, if this is possible, how do we do it?

Deliberately working together to improve ideas does not come easily. We need strategies, tools, and structures to support students with a continuing push for generalizations and stronger justifications (Moss and Beatty 2006). To promote knowledge building and treat ideas as improvable, mathematical tasks must be challenging and meaningful to students, students' thinking must be made visible and preserved, and evaluations should reflect improvement over time. We can foster interdependence through challenging tasks, explicitly talking about how we expect students to talk with one another and transferring responsibility so that students are accountable to themselves and one another.

Encourage Knowledge Building

When we treat ideas as improvable, classroom interactions go beyond sharing answers or factual responses, and we use errors as opportunities for learning. One way that we can treat knowledge as improvable is by discussing why a solution did not result in a correct answer. Exploring errors to find where the strategy went wrong can help learning. Treating errors as learning opportunities reduces risks associated with participating (Turner et al. 1998). The group learns more when students share thinking in progress or when they explore processes that led to incorrect answers (Stipek et al. 1998).

Mrs. Targett's students had opportunities to learn from incorrect or imprecise thinking. Consider when Kelly shared her discrepancy with the table for Alana's pledge plan. Alana's pledge plan had both a slope—50 cents per kilometer—and *y*-intercept—an initial pledge of $5.00. This plan provided an opportunity to discuss how to create a table for these types of contexts. If Kelly's confusion were not an object of discussion, other students who may have been similarly unsure about such a pledge plan would not have had the chance to learn.

We treat knowledge as improvable when our conversation does not end once it achieves correct answers; instead, the class could continue to discuss why the solution is correct, whether alternative solutions are possible, whether certain solutions are more efficient or elegant, and especially whether we can find generalizations. During these conversations, teachers and eventually peers press for understanding, requesting elaborations, rationales, and justifications. Questions are asked. This process of negotiating meaning gives more students opportunities to be involved (Turner et al. 1998; Turner et al. 2002) and helps adjust instruction to adapt to and guide students' thinking.

The conversation about the walkathon problem could have ended with the students sharing accurate representations—graphs, tables, and equations—and using those representations to observe when each plan would make more or less money compared to the others. In Mrs. Targett's class, however, the conversation went a bit further to discuss what they could learn about characteristics of linear functions through these pledge plans. Discussing the concept of linearity afforded the opportunity to treat knowledge as improvable, because the students could refine their understanding of a concept through their work on specific tasks.

Select challenging and personally meaningful mathematical tasks

If we want students to make connections, generalize, and justify, we need to give them problems sophisticated enough to require this sort of higher-order mathematical activity. To support students in engaging in knowledge building, mathematical tasks should be challenging enough to elicit multiple solutions, possibilities for generalizations, and a need for justifications. The majority of tasks should not be narrow exercises in which students repetitively practice a skill. Students will engage more when tasks involve more cognitive effort.

The walkathon problem involves cognitive effort because it asks students to compare and contrast pledge plans using multiple representations, and it expects them to create their own criteria for why they would select one plan over another. Using tables, graphs, and equations allows the students to view the linear relationship's features, such as the slope or the *y*-intercept, and determine the underlying regularities of linear functions through comparing their different representations. Asking students to develop their own criteria gives them opportunities to analyze the representations, particularly by encouraging them to notice intersection points in tables and graphs. In Mrs. Targett's class, students considered the intersection points when they thought about the distances at which they made the same dollar amount with more than one pledge plan.

If we want students to engage with mathematics, we need to provide them with mathematical tasks that they find personally meaningful, authentic, and relevant to their lives (Zhang et al. 2007). Students want to work on tasks when they are curious about them, but designing problems meaningful to all students in a classroom is difficult. Teachers can help students see what is interesting or valuable about a task by explicitly talking about why the task is worthwhile. We can model enthusiasm and interest in the problems. Additionally, we can give students the opportunity to redefine the problem, amending it so that it means more to them (Engle and Conant 2002), as long as the teacher monitors the changes so they do not reduce the problem's mathematical challenge.

The walkathon problem expects students not only to generate multiple representations, but also to compare and contrast them in choosing a pledge plan. They imagine themselves as the students in the problem who need to pick a plan. Although ideally students will include some mathematical elements in their criteria for selecting a pledge plan, such as the point of intersection on related graphs or tables, they may also incorporate personally meaningful criteria, such as wanting to make it easier to ask for pledges (e.g., $10 no matter what) or to raise money even without walking far. In chapter 6, when the students initially encountered the walkathon task, the teacher mediated students' interest in the problem by talking with them about the charity for the walkathon and thinking together with them about charities that mattered to them.

Mathematical tasks need to be appropriately aligned with students' skill level. If the problems are too easy, students will quickly become bored and avoid their work (Turner et al. 1998). Ideally, the tasks align with students' skill levels so that students can build on and extend their understanding as they work on the tasks. Teachers can mediate the potential frustration that students can face when working on challenging tasks. They can offer social support and encouragement (Stipek et al. 1998; Turner et al. 1998; Turner et al. 2002) as well as access to resources (Engle and Conant 2002) and scaffolding to help students enter into the problem without reducing the task's challenge.

Mrs. Targett's students were ready to think about linear relationships that involved a "starting point" (i.e., a y-intercept) and linear relationships that did not have a constantly increasing slope; the pledge plans' designs allowed students to stretch their thinking about linear relationships. If all the pledge plans raised only a certain amount of money for each kilometer, the task would have been less interesting because of the similarity among plans and because such a task would have been too easy for these students. Although these sorts of linear relationships were relatively new to these students, the classroom's social structure offered opportunities to learn from them and build knowledge about linearity as a result.

Make students' thinking visible and preserve it

Students' thinking is the focus of discussions in knowledge-building communities. To build on their classmates' thinking, students need to be aware of what their peers are thinking. To have *others* build on *their* thinking, they need to share their thoughts. Community members have a responsibility to share their thinking and to try to make sense of and improve that of others.

Promoting courage and modesty can foster a culture of publicly sharing mathematical thinking to advance the class's knowledge (Lampert 1990). Even though we reduce some risk when we treat incorrect answers as learning opportunities, some degree of risk will always associate with publicly sharing ideas. Not everyone will be comfortable putting their ideas into a public forum for revision and constant improvement. To share thinking routinely, even when they are not sure it is correct, students need courage. Sharing in-progress thinking can help the class advance their mathematical understanding. It takes modesty for students to accept suggestions that improve their ideas for the benefit of advancing the class's knowledge. In Mrs. Targett's class, Jacob demonstrated courage when he willingly shared his group's in-progress thinking about their preferred pledge plan, and Kelly demonstrated modesty when she was open to having her thinking about Alana's pledge plan revised.

For a group to build knowledge over time, members need to preserve and record students' thinking and the group's evolving knowledge, so they can revisit, expand, and revise them over time (Scardamalia 2002). Students could record their thinking on chalkboards or dry-erase boards, but they should take care to preserve the work so that they can revisit it later (they can take photographs of the boards, perhaps). Alternatively, we can use other media to record and save students' solutions, such as SMART Board screen captures or other documents where students preserve their thinking to share with others (e.g., flip charts, overhead transparencies, or paper shared over a document projector). Public, visual representations of students' work discussed in class can promote greater awareness of what others are thinking, because the visual representations can be viewed and reviewed. The teacher or students can reference prior ideas and build on them more readily if they can reference them visually and revisit them after time has passed.

Mrs. Targett's class preserved knowledge and made it public in a variety of ways beyond verbal discourse. Students shared their representations (e.g., tables, graphs) so that they could become objects of discussion. Their mathematics notebooks served to record the class's evolving knowledge about linearity. Since they had preserved their knowledge, they could revisit their thinking about linearity, review it, and decide whether they needed to add to their recorded knowledge base as a result of that day's mathematical exploration.

Base evaluations on improvement over time

Knowledge-building communities view themselves as successful based on improvement, on advances in their understanding and growth in their learning over time. Teachers can model this value for improvement by making comments on the group's progress periodically, summarizing where they have been and providing direction for where they can go. Students may start to adopt this practice as well and publicly comment on, and suggest direction for, the group's progress. Mrs. Targett commented explicitly on how the class was building knowledge when she said that they had a general definition for *linear,* and they were refining it on the basis of the special cases they encountered. This talk about their progress as a group emphasized the value for growth in knowledge over time.

Formal evaluations can emphasize improvement over time as well. Teachers can provide written feedback on students' work, quizzes, or tests (Stipek et al. 1998) that describes how students' thinking has improved and suggests how their thinking can continue to improve. Year-end or quarter assessments can be broken down by growth in understanding of various mathematical topics. Portfolio assessments (Lee, Chan, and van Aalst 2006) can give students the opportunity to assess their own improvement over time.

Knowledge-building communities do not define successes solely by high scores on performance measures, such as chapter tests. They value improvement over time, effort, and the development of understandings. When students perceive that their effort and improvement in their understanding matters in their classrooms, they feel more supported and cared for (Roeser, Midgley, and Urdan 1996). Additionally, in knowledge-building communities, improving an individual student's understanding is not enough. The *group's* understanding must improve as well.

Encourage Interdependence

In knowledge-building communities, the advances in knowledge belong to, and are distributed among, the *group* of students (Hewitt and Scardamalia 1998). Challenging, meaningful mathematical tasks can create a felt need to share one's thinking and listen to others', because the tasks are so challenging that a single person working alone cannot complete them. The mathematics problems create a climate where students need one another. Additionally, teachers foster interdependence when they talk explicitly about their expectations for how students should talk with one another and transfer responsibility for making progress to the students.

Talk about talking

Social scaffolding, when teachers talk about the kind of talking they expect in their classroom, makes a difference for supporting students' engagement (Baxter and Williams 2010). Providing clear expectations for social and behavioral, as well as academic, outcomes is a form of social support for students (Wentzel et al.

2010). Students need some "pretraining" to move from cooperation to collaboration (Blumenfeld et al. 1996). We can tell students that, for those who tend to talk, listening to others' thinking is important for learning, and, for those who tend to listen, depriving others of your voice limits the group's learning. Some of the pretraining for collaboration involves teaching specific strategies for productive interaction, such as questioning, clarifying, summarizing, predicting, or facilitating (Cohen 1994).

Mrs. Targett explicitly talked about talking during this lesson. For instance, she encouraged Jacob to share his group's thinking and commented, "… we don't have to be finished with our ideas to share them with the group." This talk promoted the value of sharing in-progress thinking, because the rest of the class could think about what Jacob's group had been thinking. They could make progress on the work as a group, picking up where Jacob's group left off. Additionally, when Alejandro made the move to suggest that they add to their definition of linearity, Mrs. Targett took the opportunity to talk about the importance of recording advances in understanding.

Students benefit from explicit discussions about what counts as an acceptable and valuable contribution during classroom interactions (Gresalfi et al. 2009; Yackel and Cobb 1996). To involve more students, teachers work to convince them that many types of contributions will help advance the class's knowledge—questions, alternative solutions, possible false starts, connections among strategies or ideas, generalizations, conjectures, and justifications, to name a few. If the problems are challenging enough and if the goal is to advance the group's knowledge continuously, a wide range of methods of participating would be valuable (Boaler and Staples 2008). If more ways exist to participate acceptably and valuably, then more students can feel comfortable and courageous enough to contribute.

Norms appear to be in place, presumably developed through Mrs. Targett's efforts to talk about talking, such that students feel comfortable participating in class in a variety of ways. For instance, they made connections when one group had thinking similar to or different from another's. So, one type of valuable contribution in this class was connections with other students' thinking. This type of contribution allows more students to engage with talking about mathematics, in contrast to classes where the discussion's goal is to elicit a correct answer efficiently.

Transfer responsibility to students

Teachers can work toward helping students feel responsible for their own progress and for the group's improvement and growth over time. When the teacher is not the sole mathematical authority in the classroom, students feel more autonomous; they have greater feelings of control and enjoyment (Stipek et al. 1998). When we transfer to students responsibility for their own progress, they become accountable to themselves and one another (Gresalfi et al. 2009; Kelly and Turner 2009; Turner et al. 1998; Turner et al. 2002).

We can see instances of the students in Mrs. Targett's class evaluating each other's thinking. Kelly noticed that her table was different from her classmate's table, so she took responsibility to make this contrast a topic of discussion rather than hiding this difference from others. When Kelly made the choice to make her thinking public, she took responsibility for her own learning, and, in turn, provided her classmates with the opportunity to learn from the contrast between tables.

To take over responsibility for knowledge building, students must recognize that they can continually improve both their own ideas and ideas in general (Zhang et al. 2009). If their work builds on their classmates', they come to depend on one another to advance the discourse, share ideas in a timely way, and check one another. When knowledge building occurs in a classroom community, a system of social pressure develops, and the teacher is no longer the primary taskmaster. Students begin to push one another so that the group's knowledge builds as they pose questions to one another, request elaboration, analyze one another's thinking, and make new connections and generalizations.

Students in Mrs. Targett's class appeared to take responsibility for knowledge building. Jacob redirected the class back to discussing comparisons among pledge plans, which was the goal of the mathematical task, after they had diverged to discuss how to complete the table accurately. Directing the group toward the problem's goal is an example of accepting responsibility for knowledge building. Alejandro was the community member who determined that the group had made enough progress to add to their definition for *linear*. If a student initiates the process of recording advances in understanding, this suggests that the students have taken over responsibility for knowledge building.

Students evaluate the group's progress in a knowledge-building community. When students monitor their class's understanding, they determine what is known and what needs to be known. Ideally, the students' assessment of their own work would exceed the other, external assessors' expectations (Scardamalia 2002). To engage in this progress, students need to learn ways of evaluating and judging their peers' thinking (Yackel and Cobb 1996). Group products, such as presentations, could aid in supporting students with assessing the classroom community's progress.

The teacher is also a member of the community, however. Even when students have taken some of the responsibility for advancing knowledge, the teacher has a role to play. For instance, as students make their thinking visible, a teacher can offer analytic scaffolding by filtering students' attention toward certain ideas or strategies to support growth in the group's understanding (Sherin 2002).

During the discussion, although students engaged actively in dialogue with one another, Mrs. Targett also played an important role. She engaged in judicious telling when she interpreted Alana's plan, to help the class understand how to complete the table. She gave a just-in-time explanation to address a student's confusion in a manner that connected to her thinking. Mrs. Targett filtered the discussion to highlight the concept of linearity, directing the students to attend to Maritza's comment about linearity that could have been treated as an aside. Filtering the discussion to highlight Maritza's contribution afforded the opportunity to build knowledge about the concept of linearity.

Summary

Collaborative classrooms are knowledge-building communities. Knowledge-building communities consider ideas and solution strategies continually improvable and revisable. They value advances in knowledge over task completion. The classroom's learners are interdependent. They believe that the group's knowledge as a whole needs to advance, not just individuals'. Group members value sharing their thinking with one another and feel a need to hear the others' thinking to make progress. Knowledge-building communities offer students opportunities to develop stronger relationships with mathematics, their peers, and their teacher.

Deliberately creating knowledge-building communities takes work. Students benefit from appropriately challenging, personally meaningful mathematical tasks, so we must put time into task selection. Additionally, structuring expectations for classroom interaction takes effort. We should encourage students to contribute to the class discussion in a variety of ways beyond correct answers, because we need to make a wide range of thinking visible to build the group's knowledge. Explicit talk about how to talk with one another makes a difference in supporting students' engagement in knowledge-building activity. Finally, we should evaluate students' mathematical thinking by growth and improvement over time, and we should transfer some of the responsibility for evaluating their progress to the students.

References

Baxter, Juliet A., and Steven Williams. "Social and Analytic Scaffolding in Middle School Mathematics: Managing the Dilemma of Telling." *Journal of Mathematics Teacher Education* 13, no. 1 (February 2010): 7–26.

Blumenfeld, Phyllis C., Ronald W. Marx, Elliot Soloway, and Joseph Krajcik. "Learning with Peers: From Small Group Cooperation to Collaborative Communities." *Educational Researcher* 25, no. 8 (November 1996): 37–40.

Boaler, Jo, and Megan Staples. "Creating Mathematical Futures through an Equitable Teaching Approach: The Case of Railside School." *Teachers College Record* 110, no. 3 (2008): 608–45.

Cohen, Elizabeth G. "Restructuring the Classroom: Conditions for Productive Small Groups." *Review of Educational Research* 64, no. 1 (Spring 1994): 1–35.

Dweck, Carol S. "Implicit Theories as Organizers of Goals and Behavior." In *The Psychology of Action: Linking Cognition and Motivation to Behavior,* edited by Peter M. Gollwitzer and John A. Bargh, pp. 69–90. New York: Guilford Press, 1996.

Engle, Randi A., and Faith R. Conant. "Guiding Principles for Fostering Productive Disciplinary Engagement: Explaining an Emergent Argument in a Community of Learners Classroom." *Cognition and Instruction* 20, no. 4 (2002): 399–483.

Gresalfi, Melissa, Taylor Martin, Victoria Hand, and James Greeno. "Constructing Competence: An Analysis of Student Participation in the Activity Systems of Mathematics Classrooms." *Educational Studies in Mathematics* 70, no. 1 (January 2009): 49–70.

Hewitt, Jim, and Marlene Scardamalia. "Design Principles for Distributed Knowledge Building Processes." *Educational Psychology Review* 10, no. 1 (1998): 75–96.

Jansen, Amanda. "An Investigation of Relationships between Seventh-Grade Students' Beliefs and Their Participation during Mathematics Discussions in Two Classrooms." *Mathematical Thinking and Learning* 10, no. 1 (January 2008): 68–100.

Kelly, Sean, and Julianne Turner. "Rethinking the Effects of Classroom Activity Structure on the Engagement of Low-Achieving Students." *Teachers College Record* 111, no. 7 (2009): 1665–92.

Lampert, Magdalene. "When the Problem Is Not the Question and the Solution Is Not the Answer: Mathematical Knowing and Teaching." *American Educational Research Journal* 27, no. 1 (Spring 1990): 29–63.

Lappan, Glenda, James T. Fey, William M. Fitzgerald, Susan N. Friel, and Elizabeth Phillips. *Moving Straight Ahead: Connected Mathematics, Teacher's Guide, Grade 7, Algebra.* Upper Saddle River, N.J.: Prentice Hall School Division, 2002.

Lee, Eddy Y. C., Carol K. K. Chan, and Jan van Aalst. "Students Assessing Their Own Collaborative Knowledge Building." *International Journal of Computer-Supported Collaborative Learning* 1, no. 2 (June 2006): 277–307.

Moss, Joan, and Ruth Beatty. "Knowledge Building in Mathematics: Supporting Collaborative Learning in Pattern Problems." *International Journal of Computer-Supported Collaborative Learning* 1, no. 4 (December 2006): 441–65.

Roeser, Robert W., Carol Midgley, and Timothy C. Urdan. "Perceptions of the School Psychological Environment and Early Adolescents' Psychological and Behavioral Functioning in School: The Mediating Role of Goals and Belonging." *Journal of Educational Psychology* 88, no. 3 (1996): 408–22.

Scardamalia, Marlene. "Collective Cognitive Responsibility for the Advancement of Knowledge." In *Liberal Education in a Knowledge Society,* edited by Barry Smith, pp. 67–98. Chicago: Open Court, 2002.

Sherin, Miriam Gamoran. "A Balancing Act: Developing a Discourse Community in a Mathematics Classroom." *Journal of Mathematics Teacher Education* 5, no. 3 (2002): 205–33.

Stipek, Deborah, Julie M. Salmon, Karen B. Givvin, Elham Kazemi, Geoffrey Saxe, and Valanne L. MacGyvers. "The Value (and Convergence) of Practices Suggested by Motivation Research and Promoted by Mathematics Education Reformers." *Journal for Research in Mathematics Education* 29, no. 4 (July 1998): 465–88.

Turner, Julianne C., Debra K. Meyer, Kathleen E. Cox, Candice Logan, Matthew DiCintio, and Cynthia T. Thomas. "Creating Contexts for Involvement in Mathematics." *Journal of Educational Psychology* 90, no. 4 (December 1998): 730–45.

Turner, Julianne C., Carol Midgley, Debra K. Meyer, Margaret Gheen, Eric M. Anderman, Yongjin Kang, and Helen Patrick. "The Classroom Environment and Students' Reports of Avoidance Strategies in Mathematics: A Multimethod Study." *Journal of Educational Psychology* 94, no. 1 (March 2002): 88–106.

Wentzel, Kathryn R., Ann Battle, Shannon L. Russell, and Lisa B. Looney. "Social Supports from Teachers and Peers as Predictors of Academic and Social Motivation." *Contemporary Educational Psychology* 35, no. 3 (July 2010): 193–202.

Yackel, Erna, and Paul Cobb. "Sociomathematical Norms, Argumentation, and Autonomy in Mathematics." *Journal for Research in Mathematics Education* 27, no. 4 (July 1996): 458–77.

Zhang, Jianwei, Marlene Scardamalia, Mary Lamon, Richard Messina, and Richard Reeve. "Socio-Cognitive Dynamics of Knowledge Building in the Work of 9- and 10-Year-Olds." *Educational Technology Research and Development* 55, no. 2 (April 2007): 117–45.

Zhang, Jianwei, Marlene Scardamalia, Richard Reeve, and Richard Messina. "Designs for Collective Cognitive Responsibility in Knowledge-Building Communities." *Journal of the Learning Sciences* 18, no. 1 (January 2009): 7–44.

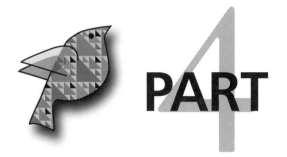

PART 4

Change Is Hard: Motivating Ourselves

CHAPTER 13

Choices We Must Make: Implications for Action

*T*hrough the process of writing this book, we have found ourselves inspired to try some new practices—some stolen from each other, some invented in our conversations, and some taken directly from one or more of the studies we have reviewed. We thought that we could do even more to push ourselves in our college classrooms so that our students, who are typically mathematics teachers, could become even more motivated and intellectually engaged. We share a few examples of things we have implemented that illustrate our own change in practice. After all, we would not ask you to do something that we would not try ourselves.

Pushing Ourselves to Be Better: Jim and Mandy Try It Out

Field trips are one of the strategies Jim uses to build a sense of trust, teamwork, and social sense of motivation for his classes. An avid lover of the mountains (and when the temperature is above 100°F, who in Phoenix is not?), he takes his students to historical sites, camps, and hidden places of beauty where they can find mathematics hidden but waiting to be uncovered. A few years ago, he and his colleagues arranged for about one hundred of his preservice mathematics and science education students to travel up to a camp owned by Arizona State University. There, the students took microscopes to the stream to look at the microbes living there, drew timelines to show the area's geologic layering in logarithmic time, and took core samples of trees and compared them to dendrochronology data to show how archeologists date ancient sites to within a single year, up to 10,000 years ago with certainty or up to 26,000 years ago when combined with data from marine sediments. A group of fifth graders from an inner-city school in Phoenix, most of whom had never been out of town or seen the mountains up close, then joined them. Jim's preservice teachers introduced the fifth graders to many of the activities they had done themselves. The experience motivated both the soon-to-be teachers and their students.

The primary take-away from the field trip for the preservice teachers was connecting their own emotional experience—their intrinsic motivation— to that of the fifth graders. For the fifth graders, it was (1) seeing mathematics and science as useful tools for helping them learn about the fascinating new environment they were exploring, and (2) creating a positive motivational bond between mathematics as a living, interesting subject in the camp and the more mundane mathematics in their textbooks, of which Jim was an author. Many of the preservice teachers, now veteran teachers of mathematics, have reported that this field trip was the most important experience, outside student teaching, that they had in their entire undergraduate career at Arizona State University. They also reported using the same activities they did at the camp with their own students. They made friends during the field trip, and they saw how powerful the trip was for their own learning and how mathematics could enhance an already great experience.

One last strategy Jim always uses on field trips, whether a three-day affair in the mountains or an afternoon at the Arizona Science Museum, is to design activities that require students to collect data so that participants can bring the experience back to the classroom. Doing so allows the class to dive in deeper, use computers and spreadsheets to crunch the numbers, and get one or two weeks of focused learning out of one to two days of less structured activity. The learning always is the ultimate goal; the motivation makes it possible.

After hearing about Jim's experience taking his students on field trips and considering how the excursions could support students' motivation and engagement, Mandy took her own students on field trips during the following semester. She thought that a field trip scheduled at a time near the beginning of the semester could build community among her students and support their intellectual engagement. Mandy and her students examined and critiqued educational research together. As a part of this course, she took her graduate students to Philadelphia (about 45 minutes away from campus) to watch a recently released documentary, *Waiting for Superman*. She and her students examined rhetoric in educational research—how authors use evidence to support their claims and how authors structure their arguments. She met with her students after the movie to discuss not only its content, but also how the filmmakers presented their argument. Spending time together outside the boundaries of the classroom allowed the group to get to know one another better, and the content of the activity supported students' intellectual engagement in her course's goals.

Providing Choice and Supporting Autonomy through Projects

In her Shadow a Student project, Mandy assigned her preservice middle school teachers, undergraduates at her university, an opportunity to choose and shadow a middle school student over a period of time. (Mandy would like to credit her colleague at the University of Delaware, Tonya Bartell, for helping her develop this project.) This assignment had future teachers challenge any assumptions they might hold about adolescent learners and get to know a single student very well so that they could design instruction that built on that student's strengths and competencies. Secondary benefits of this assignment were that the future teachers could see what being a middle school student is like from a student's perspective (i.e., hectic between-class activity, trying to meet social and academic needs simultaneously), and that they could see the instructional practices and classroom structures of a range of middle grades teachers across content areas.

The preservice teachers had several opportunities to make decisions and choices to tailor this assignment to their own interests and professional goals. They could set criteria for how they would choose the focus student and decide how they wanted to represent their final product for the project. In selecting which student to shadow, the future teachers had to consider what they wanted to learn from the project. Some preservice teachers wanted to understand the experiences of English language learners. Others wanted to learn about gifted students. Still others wanted to learn about a student whose teachers said had problems with misbehavior; these undergraduates wondered if the misbehavior was about the student or about situations or interactions in the mathematics classroom that could drive a student to misbehave. In common across their selection of focus students, the preservice teachers desired to understand how to support learners better, but each preservice teacher had to set his or her own goal about what he or she wanted to learn about students through the project. They also had choices for how to construct and present their final projects. Some preservice teachers wrote papers, whereas others created posters or PowerPoint representations. Options for how to represent the product allowed them to either align with their preferences (i.e., preferring to write a paper or create an alternative representation) or choose to stretch themselves beyond that, which some who chose an alternative representation spoke about not usually doing. Mandy hoped that, if the preservice teachers had opportunities to make decisions, they would feel more autonomous about their own professional learning and enjoy the project more.

We know that money and time are tight, and that classroom teachers working with young children are not as free to experiment with such experiences as college professors. But think back on your own experiences in school. What do you remember? We suspect a field trip or two features prominently. How can you build such powerful memories with your students? As you take your students on field trips, how do you integrate connections to various content areas as you build relationships and community among your students? As you implement projects in your classroom, how do you incorporate opportunities for students to have choices and develop autonomy? More broadly, how might the ideas in this book affect your own instructional design and decision-making? We believe that our own stories provide examples of how the chapters in this book inspired at least two readers, who also happened to be the book's authors. We assume that our own stories are only minor examples compared to the efforts of you, the motivated teachers who read this book.

Research-Based Strategies Revisited

In the preface, we credited this book as part of the NCTM strategic initiative Linking Research and Practice. Each principle and instructional strategy that this book discusses represents the best, most consistent research on students' motivation and self-regulation existing at this time. We have confidence that if you consider these principles and strategies useful lenses through which to think about your students and teaching practices, and if you increase your own level of challenge a bit, you can fundamentally change many of your students' mathematical experiences. We have tried to portray these principles and strategies as stemming from real dilemmas teachers face every day. Do you identify with Emma, trying to encourage your students just to engage, or with Tanisha, trying to maintain her personal identity while her peers want to work together? Are you Ms. Targett, working on the social norms that would encourage Alejandro's participation, or are you Kristine, trying to persevere against challenging content? Whether your own experience mirrors one, some, or none of these experiences, we hope that you can relate to the dilemmas facing these illustrations' teachers and students, and that the principles and strategies this book describes align with some of the ways you already think about students' motivation.

We also hope that you encounter some new ideas and directions for your own practice, because this book is not about motivation for its own sake. Its fundamental premise is that, knowing a bit more about students' motivation in mathematics and armed with a few strategies to try out, you can, *through hard work*, turn around your students' mathematical lives. We believe that the key to helping children succeed in mathematics is for *students'* motivations to become *teachers'* motivating factors. You chose to read this book because you have committed to motivating your students: *you are already a motivated teacher!* Use the reviewed strategies to optimize what you know about students' motivation, learning, and long-term engagement so that your students engage deeper, learn more, and feel better about themselves in doing so.

Taking on the Challenge to Motivate Students

To anyone who feels discouraged about opportunities to motivate their students, we understand, and we would like to offer hope. A teacher could feel too overwhelmed by the demands of his or her job to work on promoting students' motivation in addition to everything else. When it seems like all anyone ever expects a teacher to do is improve students' test scores, who has time to think about anything else? And when students come to us with long past histories as mathematics learners, histories often riddled with negative memories of mathematics, how could we possibly influence their motivation and engagement? Below, we would like to share our perspective on these issues.

Motivating students also supports their mathematics learning

When teachers and schools are evaluated, at times with heavy consequences, on whether or not their students achieve highly or have strong gains on achievement test scores, thinking about promoting students' motivation might feel like too much. It might feel like too much to add motivational outcomes onto our other academic content outcomes that we must help our students achieve. It might feel like you have a longer list of content outcomes than you can possibly achieve already! We, the authors, believe that promoting students' motivation should be a major issue in educational policy, but we acknowledge that the current climate of accountability emphasizes students' achievement on state assessments (Harackiewicz and Hulleman 2010). Current federal and state policy focuses on increasing students' achievement, but the policies do not make recommendations for enhancing students' interest, motivation, and engagement in the classroom. Teachers might feel too much pressure in today's political climate to add yet another goal to their instructional practices.

However, considerable empirical evidence suggests that teaching practices that motivate learners also help them learn mathematics. Deborah Stipek and her colleagues (1998) learned that when mathematics teachers emphasize effort over high performance and encourage students' autonomy, students perform better on measures of gains in their conceptual understanding of fractions compared to students whose teachers' instruction did not have these emphases. So, when teachers promote their students' autonomy, aiding them in developing their confidence by helping them see that effort matters and mathematical ability is not fixed, they can not only achieve these motivational outcomes, but also support students' learning. So, we hope that teachers see that this book includes the instructional practices we recommend for supporting students' motivation in mathematics classrooms because these practices will also support their students' learning. We are not trying to add to the list of what teachers should do. Instead, we would like teachers to see how effective mathematics teaching practices can support students' learning development *and* their motivation. The take-away from this discussion should be this: instructional practices that motivate learners' engagement might just be good teaching practices generally.

We can motivate all students

Another reason why teachers might feel overwhelmed by the effort to motivate their students could be their students' age and experience. Students bring baggage with them, accumulated over time from their histories in other mathematics classrooms. Students may appear to think themselves incapable of success at mathematics, and they may express disdain for learning or doing mathematics. But research shows that if teachers use motivational strategies designed to engage students intellectually, they can motivate students more and affect them more positively (Stipek et al. 1998). Further, such strategies will work if the classroom environment emphasizes developing learning goals, effort attributions for success, mutual respect among members, and self-regulation strategies (Meyer and Turner 2006; Turner et al. 2003; Patrick, Ryan, and Kaplan 2007). Choosing tasks that are challenging but retain enough control so that students have a moderately high success probability increases situational interest (Middleton and Spanias 1999). Under the right conditions, we can motivate all students to learn mathematics. It's up to us as teachers to create motivating classrooms and continue creating them.

Looking across the Chapters

We structured this book in two parts: the first set of chapters (2–7) addressed principles of students' motivation, and the following chapters (8–12) discussed instructional strategies that would support teachers' efforts to engage and motivate students intellectually.

Six Principles of Motivation	**Five Instructional Strategies That Motivate Learners**
• Chapter Two: Motivation Is Learned	• Chapter Eight: Judicious Use of Contexts
• Chapter Three: Motivation Is Adaptive	• Chapter Nine: Providing Challenge
• Chapter Four: Motivation Is "in the Moment"	• Chapter Ten: Limiting the Use of Rewards and Other Reinforcers
• Chapter Five: Motivation Creates Long-Term Attitudes	• Chapter Eleven: Exploiting Students' Interests
• Chapter Six: Motivation Is Social	• Chapter Twelve: Building Relationships
• Chapter Seven: Success Matters	

Principles of students' motivation

We wrote about six principles of motivation: motivation is *learned* (chapter 2), motivation is *adaptive* (chapter 3), motivation is *in the moment* (chapter 4), motivation *creates long-term attitudes* (chapter 5), motivation is *social* (chapter 6), and *success matters* (chapter 7). Across these principles, we highlighted that students' engagement—whether or not they appear motivated—is their response to current experiences, guided by what they have learned about engaging in school mathematics from previous experiences. Motivation is learned and adaptive, so students' engagement is a response based on accumulated evidence across numerous *previous* experiences as mathematical learners in and outside classrooms. Yet motivation is in the moment and social, influenced by tasks' design and especially by students' *current* opportunities to engage and build relationships with mathematics, teachers, and peers. Students' social needs can support their intellectual engagement if the teacher structures the learning environment to take advantage of those needs.

Individually, motivation boils down to how students interpret their success—whether they attribute their success to hard work and effort or think their ability to do mathematics is somehow preset or fixed; and whether they see struggle as a normal and, indeed, a necessary part of learning or interpret it as failure. These things will determine how they persist in the face of challenge. These principles help us think about what students bring to the learning situation and the potential effects our instructional practices may have on their current interest and future choices. In this manner, they provide a framework by which we can choose or design tasks that build and sustain interest and promote persistence and efficacy.

Instructional strategies can motivate learners

To support, validate, and inspire the teachers who read this book, we have presented five categories of instructional strategies that research has shown to promote healthy and productive motivation in students. These five categories of strategies are using contexts judiciously (chapter 8), providing challenge to students and scaffolding their learning to build a bridge between where they are motivationally and where we want them to be (chapter 9), judiciously limiting the use of rewards and other reinforcers (chapter 10), exploiting students' interests (chapter 11), and building relationships with mathematics and with one another in the classroom (chapter 12).

These chapters built directly on the principles of students' motivation described previously in the book. If motivation is learned (chapter 2), then instructional strategies can help influence students' motivation, because students learn to be motivated—or not—to a great extent through their experiences in school. Thus, chapters 8–12 all support teachers' thinking about how to help their students learn to become even more motivated. Motivation's adaptive and in-the-moment aspects (chapters 3–4) relate to the strategy of scaffolding students' experiences to support their work on challenging mathematics tasks (chapter 9). After all, if students develop motivation as a response to a situation, then we must create situations that invite and encourage students to engage. Scaffolding is a tailored strategy for designing tasks and adapting them in the moment. Students' current interests and longer-term attitudes (chapters 4–5) can be exploited and influenced by creating more interesting, engaging mathematics classrooms, catching and holding students' interest and fostering intrinsic motivation (chapter 11). Chapter 6 highlights how teachers can steer students' efforts to meet their social needs to support their mathematics learning as well. Chapter 12 complements chapter 6 by focusing on building relationships in the classroom, particularly on how opportunities to work collaboratively can motivate and engage students intellectually as they build relationships with mathematics and one another.

Eyes on the Prize: How Can We Develop Students' Productive Dispositions for Learning and Doing Mathematics?

Although the emphasis on improving mathematics achievement is growing, U.S. students' desire to achieve in mathematics and to choose mathematically sophisticated college programs and occupations is shrinking. In comparison with other countries, far fewer U.S. citizens, proportionally, choose science or engineering career paths than our foreign counterparts do. This trend is due to a widespread motivational epidemic—motivation to avoid mathematics. Teachers and school systems must begin to address the issue of why smart people choose to disengage from mathematical pursuits, and how we can reverse this trend for the betterment of our students and the betterment of our nation.

National-level reports sponsored by the U.S. government, such as the National Research Council's book about mathematical proficiency, *Adding it Up* (Kilpatrick, Swafford, and Findell 2001), and the National Mathematics Advisory Panel's (NMAP) *Strengthening Math Education through Research* (NMAP 2008) report, have encouraged promoting students' motivation to learn. NMAP (2008) described the importance of developing students' self-efficacy and confidence in mathematics. In *Adding it Up*, the NRC wrote about self-efficacy and confidence in mathematics as a subset of a productive disposition toward mathematics. *Productive disposition* is "the inclination to see mathematics as sensible, useful, and worthwhile, coupled with a belief in diligence and one's own efficacy" (Kilpatrick, Swafford, and Findell 2001, p. 116). Most important, the NRC report described productive disposition as one of the five "strands" defining mathematical proficiency, along with procedural fluency, conceptual understanding, adaptive reasoning, and strategic competence.

The instructional strategies we promote in this book can help teachers promote students' productive dispositions toward mathematics. Our discussion of the complexities involved with using contexts in mathematics classrooms (chapter 8) can provide insights for teachers, because problem contexts can both motivate and demotivate students. If we want students to see mathematics as "sensible, useful, and worthwhile," then we want to select mathematical tasks carefully and talk with students purposefully about the tasks so that they can see their value. If we want students to see themselves as capable of doing mathematics, then purposefully scaffolding challenging tasks can help (chapter 9). Limiting extrinsic rewards (chapter 10) and catching and holding students' interest to promote intrinsic motivation (chapter 11) help students see value in doing mathematics. Offering opportunities for collaboration and knowledge building (chapter 12) can help students see that mathematics can make sense and believe that they can make sense of mathematics. In these ways, we intend for this book to give teachers insights into promoting productive dispositions toward mathematics among their students.

Going Forward

Now it's your turn! Although this book ends, the journey to continue learning how to support students' motivation continues. In the spirit of Linking Research and Practice, we hope that teachers who read this book will add to our mathematics education community's knowledge about how to support students' motivation. Perhaps you will try to use some of these instructional strategies, modify them, or construct different strategies that follow from the research principles. If you do, we urge you to consider collecting evidence about what your students learn about mathematics and about their motivation. Write a story exemplifying your experiences. Choose a student or students on which to focus your story. Did the student(s) develop a productive disposition? Did they develop stronger conceptual understanding of mathematics in the lesson? Did they become more interested and engaged? We encourage you to share what you learn in an article for the national community of mathematics teachers, in an NCTM publication such as *Teaching Children Mathematics*, *Mathematics Teaching in the Middle School*, or *Mathematics Teacher*, or to present what you learned at a national, regional, or state conference for mathematics teachers. We have developed a Web site for this book, where teachers can post their own stories and thus continue the conversation (http://www.nctm.org/motivationmatters). Help us learn from you, so that we can close the loop between practice and research.

In the introductory chapter, we asked a question about to what extent we will choose to make changes in our own practices that reflect the best evidence available about motivation's role in students' mathematical learning. Mathematics education is full of uninformed practices. We have plenty of evidence for that. We are asking motivated teachers to take on the challenge of beginning the difficult task of changing what comes easily and naturally and begin to address the challenges of students' motivation head on. We each have choices to make.

References

Harackiewicz, Judith M., and Chris S. Hulleman. "The Importance of Interest: The Role of Achievement Goals and Task Values in Promoting the Development of Interest." *Social and Personality Psychology Compass* 4, no. 1 (February 2010): 42–52.

Kilpatrick, Jeremy, Jane Swafford, and Bradford Findell, eds. *Adding It Up: Helping Children Learn Mathematics*. Washington, D.C.: National Academies Press, 2001.

Meyer, Debra K., and Julianne C. Turner. "Re-Conceptualizing Emotion and Motivation to Learn in Classroom Contexts." *Educational Psychology Review* 18, no. 4 (December 2006): 377–90.

Middleton, James A., and Photini A. Spanias. "Motivation for Achievement in Mathematics: Findings, Generalizations, and Criticisms of the Recent Research." *Journal for Research in Mathematics Education* 30, no. 1 (January 1999): 65–88.

National Mathematics Advisory Panel. "National Mathematics Advisory Panel: Strengthening Math Education through Research." 2008. http://www2.ed.gov/about/bdscomm/list/math-panel/index.html, December 4, 2010

Patrick, Helen, Allison M. Ryan, and Avi Kaplan. "Early Adolescents' Perceptions of the Classroom Social Environment, Motivational Beliefs, and Engagement." *Journal of Educational Psychology* 99, no. 1 (February 2007): 83–98.

Stipek, Deborah, Julie M. Salmon, Karen B. Givvin, Elham Kazemi, Geoffrey Saxe, and Valanne L. MacGyvers. "The Value (and Convergence) of Practices Suggested by Motivation Research and Promoted by Mathematics Education Reformers." *Journal for Research in Mathematics Education* 29, no. 4 (July 1998): 465–88.

Turner, Julianne C., Debra K. Meyer, Carol Midgley, and Helen Patrick. "Teacher Discourse and Sixth Graders' Reported Affect and Achievement Behaviors in Two High-Mastery/High-Performance Mathematics Classrooms." *Elementary School Journal* 103, no. 4 (March 2003): 357–82.